1,000,000 Books

are available to read at

Forgotten Books

www.ForgottenBooks.com

Read online
Download PDF
Purchase in print

ISBN 978-0-282-54935-0
PIBN 10856171

This book is a reproduction of an important historical work. Forgotten Books uses state-of-the-art technology to digitally reconstruct the work, preserving the original format whilst repairing imperfections present in the aged copy. In rare cases, an imperfection in the original, such as a blemish or missing page, may be replicated in our edition. We do, however, repair the vast majority of imperfections successfully; any imperfections that remain are intentionally left to preserve the state of such historical works.

Forgotten Books is a registered trademark of FB &c Ltd.
Copyright © 2018 FB &c Ltd.
FB &c Ltd, Dalton House, 60 Windsor Avenue, London, SW19 2RR.
Company number 08720141. Registered in England and Wales.

For support please visit www.forgottenbooks.com

1 MONTH OF FREE READING

at

www.ForgottenBooks.com

By purchasing this book you are eligible for one month membership to ForgottenBooks.com, giving you unlimited access to our entire collection of over 1,000,000 titles via our web site and mobile apps.

To claim your free month visit:

www.forgottenbooks.com/free856171

* Offer is valid for 45 days from date of purchase. Terms and conditions apply.

English
Français
Deutsche
Italiano
Español
Português

www.forgottenbooks.com

Mythology Photography **Fiction**
Fishing Christianity **Art** Cooking
Essays Buddhism Freemasonry
Medicine **Biology** Music **Ancient Egypt** Evolution Carpentry Physics
Dance Geology **Mathematics** Fitness
Shakespeare **Folklore** Yoga Marketing
Confidence Immortality Biographies
Poetry **Psychology** Witchcraft
Electronics Chemistry History **Law**
Accounting **Philosophy** Anthropology
Alchemy Drama Quantum Mechanics
Atheism Sexual Health **Ancient History**
Entrepreneurship Languages Sport
Paleontology Needlework Islam
Metaphysics Investment Archaeology
Parenting Statistics Criminology
Motivational

Paul 384-581
631-7F0
806-943
988-1152

562-630
441-779
55-1256

Cambridge:

Printed at the University Press.

TO HIS MAJESTY

FREDERIC WILLIAM THE FOURTH,

KING OF PRUSSIA,

THE LIBERAL AND ENLIGHTENED PATRON

OF

LITERATURE, SCIENCE AND ART,

TO WHOM

THE ANTIGONE OF SOPHOCLES

OWES ITS REVIVAL ON THE MODERN STAGE,

THIS WORK

IS MOST RESPECTFULLY DEDICATED.

PREFACE.

IN a recent number of a German periodical[1], there is a paper on "The latest Antigone-Literature," at the head of which appears a list of no fewer than eighteen works,—editions, translations, and essays—referring to this Play, and all, more or less, occasioned by its revival on the Berlin stage. And, perhaps, this list would be more than doubled, if we added to it every book relating to Sophocles which has appeared in Germany during the last twenty years. But although we have followed the example, which the good taste of the King of Prussia has induced the Germans to propose for our imitation, and though the frequenters of English and French theatres in the metropolis have received with applause the somewhat heterogeneous compound of Sophocles and Mendelssohn-Bartholdy, our scholars have done nothing that deserves to be mentioned, either for Sophocles in general, or for the *Antigone* in particular, since the publication of Elmsley's *Scholia Romana* in 1825, and the appearance of Dr. Gaisford's Edition in 1826. In undertaking, therefore, an original Edition of this masterpiece of the Greek Drama, I enjoy one advan-

[1] *Zeitschrift für die Alterthumswissenschaft*, 1846, nr. 78 seqq. p. 617.

tage, of which no German could boast—that I need not fear any disadvantageous comparison with the contemporary labours of my own countrymen.

Neither this Edition, nor the English Version which accompanies it, is the work of yesterday. For many years I have been preparing a critical recension of the seven plays of Sophocles, of which the present publication may be taken as a specimen, and an earnest. Willingly accepting the suggestions of other scholars, where I felt assured that they had discovered the truth, I have also emended the text in many passages where, without their aid, I thought I saw my way to certain or highly probable restorations. Unless the received text is obviously corrupt, no discreet editor would tamper with the traditionary and manuscript readings of a Greek poet. But, on the other hand, I am not one of those who would shrink from conjectural criticism, where it presents itself in a reasonable shape; and there are many cases in which I feel that no manuscript evidence could strengthen my confidence in an emendation proposed by an experienced and sagacious scholar. With regard to the conjectures, which are brought forward in these pages for the first time, it will be a great satisfaction to me if they meet with the approbation of those practised critics, to whose collective judgment every philological labourer submits his handiwork.

The English Version was commenced in the autumn of 1842, at the suggestion of a friend, who is not only eminent as a Translator, but also known as one of the most profound and original writers of the present day. It appeared to him strange that the business of classical translation should be so entirely neglected in this country, and he thought that a literal, but readable, version of Sophocles, would be a great boon to those who are capable of admiring the beauty of these Plays, but have neither leisure nor knowledge sufficient for the careful study of so difficult an author. But though I commenced this version some five years ago, and published a specimen of it in a London periodical in February 1845, other avocations prevented me from completing my work, until the leisure of last summer, and the encouragements of a circle of accomplished gentlemen, with whom I then had the happiness of spending some days in a country-house, furnished at once the opportunity and the inducements which were necessary to bring me back to my long-suspended employment.

As it was a task of no ordinary difficulty, I may be pardoned for making a few observations on the rules which I laid down for myself in thus attempting to transfuse into English a work written by the most profound of poets, for the most ingenious of audiences[2]. O. Müller has justly remarked, in the Preface to his version of the *Eumenides*, that "every Translation, but particularly the imitation of poetical works in another language, is a problem which can never be completely solved; for the Translator, with a hundred conflicting

[2] Müller, *Hist. Lit. Gr.*, 1. pp. 355, 6.

duties, can attain to nothing without relinquishing something else." Now it appeared to me, that if Sophocles were to be translated at all, the work could only be done by some one who had made classical scholarship the business of his life[3]: and that the main object must be to give a full representation of the author's meaning. It remained only to be seen how far a Translator, struggling to effect this object, could comply with the requirements of good taste,—in short, how far the translation could be literal without becoming unreadable. For myself, I make no pretension to the gift of poetry: and if I have succeeded in throwing a little spirit into my faithful copy of the original,—if indeed this Version is free from absolute tameness and languor, I shall have compassed all my own expectations, and shall, perhaps, have done as much as could be reasonably demanded of a professed grammarian and philologer.

With regard to the form of the Translation, it was clearly idle to attempt what the Germans have often effected—to reproduce all the metres of the original.

---

[3] The great difficulties of the plays of Sophocles are due rather to the subtlety of the poet's mind, than to the obscurity of his diction. One might say of Sophocles and Æschylus, what Jean Paul remarks of Göthe and Klopstock (*Levana*, § 150. *Werke*, xxxviii. p. 125): "Klopstock is more frequently easy than Göthe—because difficulties of diction (*Sprachschwierigkeiten*) may be conquered by teaching and industry; but difficulties of conception (*Fassungschwierigkeiten*) can only be mastered by that mental maturity, which is the growth of years."

The English language would not bear such an experiment. Nor could the Translation be made effectively in the conventional rhythm of our English prose. Even Landor would scarcely attempt to write a tragic dialogue in this style. Much of the *Faust* has been most adequately rendered in Mr. Hayward's prose version[4], and Dr. Carlyle's forthcoming translation of the *Inferno* would hardly gain by metrical confinement; but in formal Tragedy, the English ear expects the measured flow of dramatic blank verse; and this style of composition is so easy and unconstrained, that I did not feel myself at liberty to relinquish it. Nor do I think, that, by this concession to the rules of the modern stage, I have unnecessarily expanded the Translation, or omitted any thing—even the force of a compound word—in the original. As there are twelve syllables, at least, in every Greek senarius, and only ten or eleven in the English, which is also hampered by articles, prepositions, and auxiliaries, I could not translate the Greek line for line, except in the *stichomythic* dialogues, where an allowable abruptness, and a freedom from particles of connexion, give our language the advantage. The chorusses are

---

[4] Mr. Hayward, in the Preface to his prose translation of *Faust*, informs us that Mr. Charles Lamb once remarked to Mr. Cary, the translator of Dante, that he had derived more pleasure from the meagre Latin versions of the Greek Tragedians, than from any other versions of them with which he was acquainted. This must be understood as a censure of the professed English translations: no man would take a Latin prose version as his representative of the meaning of a Greek poet, if his own literature furnished him with any tolerable substitute.

PREFACE.

rendered by irregular iambic rhythms, not unlike those which Milton has employed in his *Samson Agonistes*; but I have not arranged them in corresponding strophes. The anapæstic movements, however, are accurately imitated in the version: for this march-cadence is common in our language, as in every other. Without endeavouring to write archaic English, I have not hesitated to introduce words and expressions, which occur in our older dramatic writers, and, throughout, I have preferred a plain, straightforward, and manly expression, to the feeble elegances of modern versification[5].

The notes are not intended to furnish a running commentary on the text. They dwell only on those passages in which I thought that the text was really in want of a fuller exegesis, or where I had an emendation to propose and justify. But the version itself will serve the same purpose as a body of notes written in the usual style, and I think that, with the introductory matter, even the young student will not require any further elucidation of this play.

This mode of publishing a Greek play is supported by many precedents in Germany[6]; and although it is

[5] With regard to the orthography of the Greek names, I may remark that I have always written K, and not C, "making exception for such names as the English reader has been so accustomed to hear with the C, that they may be considered as almost Anglicized." (Grote, *Hist. of Greece*, I. p. 20.)

[6] Besides the well-known translation of the *Eumenides*, by K. O. Müller, I may refer to the *Oresteia* of Franz, the *Gefesselter Prometheus* of Schömann, and to the translations by Böckh and others of this play. Even Aristotle has appeared in a critical edition with an interpaged German version.

probable that this will not be the only specimen of the kind in this country[7], it may be expected, that, proceeding as this work does from a person who has been for many years engaged in the business of tuition, it will have some reference to prospective use in the school or lecture-room. In my own opinion, nothing is wanted by the classical student who has the advantage of listening to the oral expositions of a competent Tutor, except a good text of the author whom he is reading: but if any one proposes to employ this volume as a vehicle of instruction, and asks how far it is suitable for such a purpose, the answer is easy. The few, who are capable of giving original tuition in a play of Sophocles, will care little whether their pupils have more or less assistance from the book before them. The many, who profess to teach Greek without the requisite appliances of learning, ought not to object, if their pupils enjoy, in common with themselves, the results of a careful study of this most difficult author. In any case, the use of a translation need not supersede that grammatical analysis which should be required from every student.

[7] This work will be speedily followed, or even anticipated, by a similar publication of the *Agamemnon*, which has been announced by a young Oxford scholar.

King Edward's School, Bury St. Edmund's,
22nd Feb., 1848.

Cambridge:
Printed at the University Press.

ΣΟΦΟΚΛΕΟΥΣ ΑΝΤΙΓΟΝΗ.

THE ANTIGONE OF SOPHOCLES.

ΤΑ ΤΟΥ ΔΡΑΜΑΤΟΣ ΠΡΟΣΩΠΑ.

ΑΝΤΙΓΟΝΗ.
ΙΣΜΗΝΗ.
ΧΟΡΟΣ ΘΗΒΑΙΩΝ ΓΕΡΟΝΤΩΝ.
ΚΡΕΩΝ.
ΦΥΛΑΞ.
ΑΙΜΩΝ.
ΤΕΙΡΕΣΙΑΣ.
ΑΓΓΕΛΟΣ.
ΕΥΡΥΔΙΚΗ.
ΕΞΑΓΓΕΛΟΣ.

PERSONS REPRESENTED.

ANTIGONE.
ISMENE.
CHORUS OF THEBAN SENATORS.
KREON, KING OF THEBES.
A SENTINEL.
HÆMON, KREON'S SON.
TEIRESIAS.
A MESSENGER.
EURYDIKE, KREON'S WIFE.
AN ATTENDANT.

Guards and Slaves of Kreon; Female Attendants of Eurydike.

SCENE. Before the King's Palace at Thebes.

ΑΝΤΙΓΟΝΗ.

Α. ΠΡΟΛΟΓΟΣ.

ΑΝΤΙΓΟΝΗ.

Ὦ κοινὸν αὐτάδελφον Ἰσμήνης κάρα,
ἆρ' οἶσθ', †ὅτι Ζεὺς τῶν ἀπ' Οἰδίπου κακῶν
ὁποῖον οὐχὶ νῶν ἔτι ζώσαιν τελεῖ;
οὐδὲν γὰρ οὔτ' ἀλγεινὸν, οὔτ᾽ ᵃ ἄτην ἄγον,
οὔτ' αἰσχρὸν, οὔτ' ἄτιμόν ἐσθ', ὁποῖον οὐ
τῶν σῶν τε κἀμῶν οὐκ ὄπωπ' ἐγὼ κακῶν.
καὶ νῦν τί τοῦτ' αὖ φασὶ πανδήμῳ πόλει
κήρυγμα θεῖναι τὸν στρατηγὸν ἀρτίως;
ἔχεις τι, κεἰσήκουσας; ἢ σε λανθάνει
πρὸς τοὺς φίλους στείχοντα τῶν ἐχθρῶν κακά;   10

ΙΣΜΗΝΗ.

ἐμοὶ μὲν οὐδεὶς μῦθος, Ἀντιγόνη, φίλων

ᵃ γρ. ὅ, τι.   ᵇ γρ. ἄτης ἄτερ.

ANTIGONE.

I. PROLOGUE.

Antigone and Ismene enter from the left-hand door in the Proscenium.

ANTIGONE.

Ismene, dear in very sisterhood,
Know'st *thou* that Zeus, for us while yet we live,
Fulfils,—in what sort does he not—the evils
That flow from Œdipus? For there is nothing
That causes pain or tends to mischief—nothing
That inly shames, or outwardly degrades,
Of such sort, that in thine and my misfortunes
I have not seen it manifest. And now
What is this herald's message, which, they say,
Our leader has this very morn put forth
To all the populace who throng the city?
Is't known to thee, and hast thou lent an ear?
Or, by thee all unheeded, does the malice
Of enemies come up against thy friends?

ISMENE.

To me indeed, Antigone, no tale

οὔθ᾽ ἡδὺς, οὔτ᾽ ἀλγεινὸς ἵκετ᾽, ἐξ ὅτου
δυοῖν ἀδελφοῖν ἐστερήθημεν δύο,
μιᾷ θανόντων ἡμέρᾳ διπλῇ χερί·
ἐπεὶ δὲ φροῦδός ἐστιν Ἀργείων στρατὸς 15
ἐν νυκτὶ τῇ νῦν, οὐδὲν οἶδ᾽ ὑπέρτερον
οὔτ᾽ εὐτυχοῦσα μᾶλλον οὔτ᾽ ἀτωμένη.

ΑΝΤΙΓΟΝΗ.

ᾔδη καλῶς, καί σ᾽ ἐκτὸς αὐλείων πυλῶν
τοῦδ᾽ *οὕνεκ᾽ ἐξέπεμπον, ὡς μόνη κλύοις.

ΙΣΜΗΝΗ.

τί δ᾽ ἐστι; δηλοῖς γάρ τι καλχαίνουσ᾽ ἔπος. 20

ΑΝΤΙΓΟΝΗ.

οὐ γὰρ τάφου νῷν τὼ κασιγνήτω Κρέων.
τὸν μὲν προτίσας, τὸν δ᾽ ἀτιμάσας ἔχει;
Ἐτεοκλέα μὲν, ὡς λέγουσι, σὺν δίκῃ,
* προσθεὶς δίκαια, καὶ νόμῳ, κατὰ χθονὸς
ἔκρυψε, τοῖς ἔνερθεν ἔντιμον νεκροῖς· 25
τὸν δ᾽ ἀθλίως θανόντα Πολυνείκους νέκυν
ἀστοῖσί φασιν ἐκκεκηρύχθαι τὸ μὴ
τάφῳ καλύψαι, μηδὲ κωκῦσαί τινα,
ἐᾶν δ᾽ ἄκλαυτον, ἄταφον, οἰωνοῖς γλυκὺν
θησαυρὸν, εἰσορῶσι πρὸς χάριν βορᾶς. 30
τοιαῦτά φασι τὸν ἀγαθὸν Κρέοντα σοὶ
κἀμοὶ, λέγω γὰρ κἀμὲ, κηρύξαντ᾽ ἔχειν,
καὶ δεῦρο νεῖσθαι ταῦτα τοῖσι μὴ εἰδόσιν
σαφῆ προκηρύξοντα· καὶ τὸ πρᾶγμ᾽ ἄγειν
οὐχ ὡς παρ᾽ οὐδέν· ἀλλ᾽ ὃς ἂν τούτων τι δρᾷ, 35
φόνον προκεῖσθαι δημόλευστον ἐν πόλει.

[19] γρ. οὕνεκ᾽. [24] γρ. χρησθεὶς δικαίῳ.

Touching our friends,—be it of joy or sorrow,—
Has come, since we two lost our brethren twain
On the same day by a twin murder slain.
But since the Argive host this night departed,
I have it yet to learn if farther still
Good luck or mischief has been active for me.

ANTIGONE.

I know 'twas so: and therefore did I bring thee
Without the court, that thou alone might'st listen.

ISMENE.

What is't? for sure some tidings stir thee thus.

ANTIGONE.

What! has not Kreon—when our sister-love
Might challenge equal sepulture for both
Of our departed brethren,—one of them
Pre-eminently honoured, and the other
Foully disgraced? Eteokles, they tell me,
The dues of justice with just rites augmenting,
And following all the usages, he buried
Deep in the ground, invested with the honours
Which grace the dead below: but Polyneikes,
Who lies where he so miserably fell,—
They say a proclamation to the people
Forbids that any man should veil his corpse
Within the tomb, or utter wailings for him;
But orders that he lie unwept, unburied,
A welcome store of food laid up for birds
Whenso their greedy eyes desire a banquet.
Such is the proclamation, which, they say,
Good Kreon hath set forth for thee and me—
Aye—e'en for *me*, I tell thee—and to those
Who know it not, they say he cometh here
Himself to make his edict clearly known.
He holds this matter in no small account,
But whoso doeth any one of these things,
His death by public stoning is decreed.

οὕτως ἔχει σοι ταῦτα, καὶ δείξεις τάχα,
εἴτ' εὐγενὴς πέφυκας, εἴτ' ἐσθλῶν κακή.

ΙΣΜΗΝΗ.

τί δ', ὦ ταλαίφρων, εἰ τάδ' ἐν τούτοις, ἐγὼ
λύουσ' ἂν ἢ 'φάπτουσα προσθείμην πλέον;   40

ΑΝΤΙΓΟΝΗ.

εἰ ξυμπονήσεις καὶ ξυνεργάσει, σκόπει.

ΙΣΜΗΝΗ.

ποῖόν τι κινδύνευμα; ποῦ γνώμης ποτ' εἶ;

ΑΝΤΙΓΟΝΗ.

εἰ τὸν νεκρὸν ξὺν τῇδε κουφιεῖς χερί.

ΙΣΜΗΝΗ.

ἦ γὰρ νοεῖς θάπτειν σφ', ἀπόρρητον πόλει;

ΑΝΤΙΓΟΝΗ.

τὸν γοῦν ἐμὸν καὶ τὸν σὸν, ἢν σὺ μὴ θέλῃς,   45
ἀδελφόν. οὐ γὰρ δὴ προδοῦσ' ἁλώσομαι.

ΙΣΜΗΝΗ.

ὦ σχετλία, Κρέοντος ἀντειρηκότος;

ΑΝΤΙΓΟΝΗ.

ἀλλ' οὐδὲν αὐτῷ τῶν ἐμῶν εἴργειν μέτα.

ΙΣΜΗΝΗ.

οἴμοι· φρόνησον, ὦ κασιγνήτη, πατὴρ
ὡς νῷν ἀπεχθὴς δυσκλεής τ' ἀπώλετο,   50
πρὸς αὐτοφώρων ἀμπλακημάτων διπλᾶς
ὄψεις ἀράξας αὐτὸς αὐτουργῷ χερί·
ἔπειτα μήτηρ καὶ γυνή, διπλοῦν ἔπος,
πλεκταῖσιν ἀρτάναισι λωβᾶται βίον·
τρίτον δ' ἀδελφὼ δύο μίαν καθ' ἡμέραν   55

Thou knowest all: and thou wilt show betimes
Whether thou hast an innate nobleness,
Or art, the base-born child of high-born sires.

ISMENE.

What—ah! unhappy—if 'tis so, could *I*
Effect for good by doing or undoing!

ANTIGONE.

Bethink thee—wilt thou share the work and toil!

ISMENE

In what bold deed! tell me, I pray, thy drift.

ANTIGONE.

Wilt aid this hand of mine to lift the corpse!

ISMENE.

And wouldst thou bury whom the state proscribes!

ANTIGONE.

Proscribed or not, my brother and thine too,
Though it mislike thee. *I* will ne'er renounce him.

ISMENE.

O daring maid—when Kreon has forbidden!

ANTIGONE.

He has no right to keep me from my brother.

ISMENE.

Ah me! consider, sister, how detested
And blasted with ill fame our father fell,
When for his self-detected sinfulness
He pierced his eyes with suicidal hand.
And then his mother-wife—a double name—
With twisted nooses made away her life.
Thirdly, our brothers both upon one day

αὐτοκτονοῦντε τὼ ταλαιπώρω, μόρον
κοινὸν κατειργάσαντ' †ἐπαλλήλοιν χεροῖν.
νῦν δ' αὖ μόνα δὴ νὼ λελειμμένα, σκόπει,
ὅσῳ κάκιστ' ὀλούμεθ', εἰ νόμου βίᾳ
ψῆφον τυράννων ἢ κράτη παρέξιμεν.   60
ἀλλ' ἐννοεῖν χρὴ τοῦτο μὲν, γυναῖχ' ὅτι
ἔφυμεν, ὡς πρὸς ἄνδρας οὐ μαχουμένα·
ἔπειτα δ', οὕνεκ' ἀρχόμεσθ' ἐκ κρεισσόνων
καὶ ταῦτ' ἀκούειν κἄτι τῶνδ' ἀλγίονα.
ἐγὼ μὲν οὖν αἰτοῦσα τοὺς ὑπὸ χθονὸς   65
ξύγγνοιαν ἴσχειν, ὡς βιάζομαι τάδε,
τοῖς ἐν τέλει βεβῶσι πείσομαι. τὸ γὰρ
περισσὰ πράσσειν, οὐκ ἔχει νοῦν οὐδένα.

ΑΝΤΙΓΟΝΗ.

οὔτ' ἂν κελεύσαιμ', οὔτ' ἂν, εἰ θέλοις ἔτι
πράσσειν, ἐμοῦ γ' ἂν ἡδέως δρῴης μέτα.   70
ἀλλ' ἴσθ' †ὁποίᾳ σοι δοκεῖ. κεῖνον δ' ἐγὼ
θάψω. καλόν μοι τοῦτο ποιούσῃ θανεῖν.
φίλη μετ' αὐτοῦ κείσομαι, φίλου μέτα,
ὅσια πανουργήσασ'· ἐπεὶ πλείων χρόνος,
ὃν δεῖ μ' ἀρέσκειν τοῖς κάτω, τῶν ἐνθάδε. 75
ἐκεῖ γὰρ ἀεὶ κείσομαι· σοὶ δ' εἰ δοκεῖ,
τὰ τῶν θεῶν ἔντιμ' ἀτιμάσασ' ἔχε.

ΙΣΜΗΝΗ.

ἐγὼ μὲν οὐκ ἄτιμα ποιοῦμαι· τὸ δὲ
βίᾳ πολιτῶν δρᾶν, ἔφυν ἀμήχανος.

ΑΝΤΙΓΟΝΗ.

σὺ μὲν τάδ' ἂν προὔχοι'· ἐγὼ δὲ δὴ τάφον   80

⁵⁹ γρ. ἐπ' ἀλλήλοιν.   ⁷¹ γρ. ὁποῖα σοι.

ANTIGONE.

Slain mutually, wretched pair! have wrought
A kindred death by one another's hands.
Now *we* are left alone: and oh! bethink thee
How much the worst of all *our* fate will be,
If we, the law defying, set at nought
The sovereign will and mandate of our ruler.
But it were well to bear in mind that we
Are women born, and must not fight with men.
And then that overruling power compels us
To bear both these and still more grievous edicts.
I then, beseeching my departed friend
To pardon me, as I have not my will,
Must yield obedience to authority.
For to attempt without the power to do,
Is but a poor significance of wisdom.

ANTIGONE.

No more will I exhort thee: no!—and if
Thou wouldst it now, it would not pleasure me
To have thee as a partner in the deed.
Be what it liketh thee to be, but I
Will bury him; and shall esteem it honour
To die in the attempt: dying for him,
Loving with one who loves me I shall lie,
After a holy deed of sin: the time
Of the world's claims upon me may not mate
With what the grave demands: for there my rest
Will be for everlasting! If it likes thee
Go on degrading all the Gods esteem!

ISMENE.

Nay *I* degrade no rite: but lack the skill
To contravene the edicts of the state.

ANTIGONE.

Then take thee that pretext: but I will go

χώσουσ' ἀδελφῷ φιλτάτῳ πορεύσομαι.

ΙΣΜΗΝΗ.

οἴμοι ταλαίνης, ὡς ὑπερδέδοικά σου.

ΑΝΤΙΓΟΝΗ.

μὴ †'μοῦ προτάρβει· τὸν σὸν ἐξόρθου πότμον.

ΙΣΜΗΝΗ.

ἀλλ' οὖν προμηνύσῃς γε τοῦτο μηδενὶ
τοὔργον· κρυφῇ δὲ κεῦθε· σὺν δ' αὔτως ἐγώ.   85

ΑΝΤΙΓΟΝΗ.

οἴμοι· καταύδα. πολλὸν ἐχθίων ἔσει
σιγῶσ', ἐὰν μὴ πᾶσι κηρύξῃς τάδε.

ΙΣΜΗΝΗ.

θερμὴν ἐπὶ ψυχροῖσι καρδίαν ἔχεις.

ΑΝΤΙΓΟΝΗ.

ἀλλ' οἶδ' ἀρέσκουσ', οἷς μάλισθ' ἁδεῖν με χρή.

ΙΣΜΗΝΗ.

εἰ καὶ δυνήσει γ'· ἀλλ' ἀμηχάνων ἐρᾷς.   90

ΑΝΤΙΓΟΝΗ.

οὐκοῦν, ὅταν δὴ μὴ σθένω, πεπαύσομαι.

ΙΣΜΗΝΗ.

ἀρχὴν δὲ θηρᾶν οὐ πρέπει τἀμήχανα.

ΑΝΤΙΓΟΝΗ.

εἰ ταῦτα λέξεις, ἐχθαρεῖ μὲν ἐξ ἐμοῦ,
†ἐχθρᾷ δὲ τῷ θανόντι προσκείσει δίκῃ.
ἀλλ' ἔα με καὶ τὴν ἐξ ἐμοῦ δυσβουλίαν   95
παθεῖν τὸ δεινὸν τοῦτο. πείσομαι γὰρ οὐ
τοσοῦτον οὐδὲν, ὥστε μὴ οὐ καλῶς θανεῖν.

⁸³ γρ. μή μου.   ⁹⁴ γρ. ἐχθρά.

To heap a funeral mound for my dear brother.

ISMENE.

Ah me! unhappy! how I fear for thee.

ANTIGONE.

Fear not for me: set thine own fortunes right.

ISMENE.

At least to no man tell the deed beforehand,
But keep it hid: and I will hold my peace.

ANTIGONE.

Ha! speak it out to all: by far more hateful
To me will be thy silence than thy blabbing.

ISMENE.

Thy heart is hot upon a chilling business.

ANTIGONE.

I know I please whom most I ought to please.

ISMENE.

Aye: if thou couldst: thy wish transcends thy power.

ANTIGONE.

When that my power has failed, the attempt is o'er.

ISMENE.

But why pursue the impossible at all!

ANTIGONE.

Thus speaking, thou wilt but incur my hatred:
The dead too will regard thee as his foe.
Then suffer me, imprudent as I am,
To meet this menaced evil. Come what will,
It cannot take from me—a noble death!

ΙΣΜΗΝΗ.

ἀλλ᾽, εἰ δοκεῖ σοι, στεῖχε· τοῦτο δ᾽ ἴσθ᾽, ὅτι
ἄνους μὲν ἔρχει, τοῖς φίλοις δ᾽ ὀρθῶς φίλη.

Β. ΠΑΡΟΔΟΣ.

ΧΟΡΟΣ.

Ἀκτὶς ἀελίου, τὸ κάλ-   στροφὴ α΄.   100
λιστον ἑπταπύλῳ φανὲν
Θήβᾳ τῶν προτέρων φάος,
ἐφάνθης ποτ᾽, ὦ χρυσέας
ἁμέρας βλέφαρον,
Διρκαίων ὑπὲρ ῥεέθρων μολοῦσα,   105
τὸν λεύκασπιν †Ἀργέϊον
φῶτα βάντα πανσαγίᾳ,
φυγάδα πρόδρομον ὀξυτέρῳ
κινήσασα χαλινῷ,

ὃν ἐφ᾽ ἁμετέρᾳ γᾷ Πολυνείκης,   σύστημα α΄.   110
ἀρθεὶς νεικέων ἐξ ἀμφιλόγων,
†ἤγειρεν· ὁ δ᾽ εἰς γᾶν, αἰετὸς ὥς,
ὀξέα κλάζων ὑπερέπτα,
λευκῆς χιόνος πτέρυγι στεγανός,
    πολλῶν μεθ᾽ ὅπλων,   115
ξύν θ᾽ ἱπποκόμοις κορίθεσσι.

[106] γρ. Ἀργόθεν.   [112] γρ. ὀξ. κλ. αἰετὸς εἰς γᾶν ὡς ὑ.

ISMENE.

Go, if thou art resolved: and know, I hold thee
Foolish indeed, but still a peerless friend!

(*Ismene returns to the palace: Antigone goes off on the right by the Parascenia. The Chorus immediately enters the orchestra by the lower side entrance on the left.*)

II. PARODOS.

CHORUS.

STROPHE I.

Beam of the sun, the fairest light
That ever shone on Theba, seven-gated!
At length thou comest, eye of golden day,
Careering o'er the fountain-streams of Dirke!
For thou, with bridle still more keenly shaken,
Hast urged to flight before the flying van
The Argive hero of the argent shield.
March as he might in garniture of mail.

(*Anapestic Movement.*)

Whom Polyneikes against our country,
Roused by the nicest of quarrels, had mustered,
And as an eagle terribly shrieking,
With a soaring swoop he alighted.
White as the snow were the pinions that clothed him!
Many his bucklers
And his helmets crested with horse-hair!

ΑΝΤΙΓΟΝΕ. [117—140.

στὰς δ᾽ ὑπὲρ μελάθρων, †φονώ-   ἀντιστ. ά.
σαισιν ἀμφιχανὼν κύκλῳ
λόγχαις ἑπτάπυλον στόμα,
ἔβα, πρίν ποθ᾽ ἁμετέρων   120
αἱμάτων γένυσιν
πλησθῆναί τε, καὶ στεφάνωμα πύργων
πευκάενθ᾽ Ἥφαιστον ἑλεῖν.
τοῖος ἀμφὶ νῶτ᾽ ἐτάθη
πάταγος Ἄρεος, ἀντιπάλῳ   125
δυσχείρωμα δράκοντι.

Ζεὺς γὰρ μεγάλης γλώσσης κόμπους   ἀντισύστ. ά.
ὑπερεχθαίρει· καί σφας ἐσιδὼν
πολλῷ ῥεύματι προσνισσομένους
χρυσοῦ, *καναχῇ θ᾽* ὑπερόπλους,   130
παλτῷ ῥίπτει πυρί, βαλβίδων
  ἐπ᾽ ἄκρων ἤδη
νίκην ὁρμῶντ᾽ ἀλαλάξαι.

ἀντίτυπα δ᾽ ἐπὶ γᾷ πέσε τανταλωθεὶς   στροφὴ β΄.
πυρφόρος, ὃς τότε μαινομένᾳ ξὺν ὁρμᾷ   135
   βακχεύων ἐπέπνει
   ῥιπαῖς ἐχθίστων ἀνέμων.
εἶχε δ᾽ ἄλλᾳ τὰ μὲν,
†ἄλλα δ᾽ ἐπ᾽ ἄλλοις ἐπενώμα στυφελίζων
     μέγας Ἄρης
δεξιόσειρος.   140

117 γρ. φονίαισιν.   130 γρ. καναχῆς ὑπεροπτίας.
138 γρ. τὰ μὲν ἄλλᾳ, τὰ δ᾽ ἐπ᾽.

Antistrophe I.

And having taken his stand above our roofs,
Ravening with spears eager for death
Around the outlets of the seven portals,
Away he went before his jaws were glutted
With Theban blood,
Before the flame of torches
Had caught our circling coronet of towers
Such and so loud the Martial clatter
Which pealed about him as he fled—
No easy task to grapple with it!
The Dragon was his match in war.

(Anapæstic Movement.)

Zeus exceedingly hateth the boastings of
Misproud language: and soon as he saw them,
In a swollen torrent of gold advancing,
And proud in the rattle of armour,
Forth flew his brandisht bolt at the foe, who,
Scaling our ramparts,
Was beginning the pæan of conquest.

Strophe II.

Thrown from our walls against the solid earth,
Torch in hand, he fell,
Who then with frantic impulse raging
Hurtled in angry hurricanes against us.
So went the war with him!
Elsewhere great Ares others
Roughly entreated, on the right
Our tug of battle aiding.

ἑπτὰ λοχαγοὶ γὰρ ἐφ' ἑπτὰ πύλαις   συστημα. β'.
ταχθέντες ἴσοι πρὸς ἴσους, ἔλιπον
Ζηνὶ τροπαίῳ πάγχαλκα τέλη·
πλὴν τοῖν στυγεροῖν, ὣ πατρὸς ἑνὸς
μητρός τε μιᾶς φύντε, καθ' αὑτοῖν   145
δικρατεῖς λόγχας στήσαντ', ἔχετον
κοινοῦ θανάτου μέρος ἄμφω.

ἀλλὰ γὰρ ἁ μεγαλώνυμος ἦλθε Νίκα   ἀντ. β'.
τᾷ πολυαρμάτῳ ἀντιχαρεῖσα Θήβᾳ,
   ἐκ μὲν δὴ πολέμων   150
τῶν νῦν θέσθε λησμοσύναν,
θεῶν δὲ ναοὺς χοροῖς
παννυχίοις πάντας ἐπέλθωμεν· ὁ Θήβας δ' ἐλελίχθων
† Βάκχιος ἄρχοι.

ἀλλ' ὅδε γὰρ δὴ βασιλεὺς χώρας   ἀντισύστ. β'. 155
Κρέων ὁ Μενοικέως [† νέον εἰληχὼς
ἀρχήν,] νεοχμὸς νεαραῖσι θεῶν
ἐπὶ συντυχίαις χωρεῖ, τίνα δὴ
μῆτιν ἐρέσσων, ὅτι σύγκλητον
τήνδε γερόντων προύθετο λέσχην,   160
κοινῷ κηρύγματι πέμψας;

[154] γρ. Βακχεῖσε.   [156] γρ. Κρ. ὁ Μ. νεοχμὸς κ.τ.λ.,

(Anapæstic Movement.)

For seven at seven portals contending,
Chief against chief, each left to his foeman
His armour of bronze as a trophy for Zeus,
Save those two implacable brothers, who
Born of one father and mother, with lances
Equal in victory, foined till they shared
In the fratricide's portion together.

ANTISTROPHE II.

But now that Victory of mighty name
Has come to Theba, rich in cars, with joyous cheer,
Forget the wars that now no longer rage,
And seek we all the temples of the Gods,
With choirs that last the live-long night,
And be the shaker of the Theban land,—
Bacchus,—our dance's leader!

(Anapæstic Movement.)

Lo he approaches—the King of our country,
Kreon, the son of Menœkeus; [the vacant
Throne he ascended e'en now, and] his rule is
New as the fates which the Gods have provided.
What counsel revolving summons he here
This Senate to list to his words,—each elder
By the voice of the herald convening?

(While this movement is singing Kreon enters from the middle door with a long train of attendants, and having taken his seat on the throne, addresses the Chorus.)

Γ. ΕΠΕΙΣΟΔΙΟΝ ΠΡΩΤΟΝ.

ΚΡΕΩΝ.

Ἄνδρες, τὰ μὲν δὴ πόλεος ἀσφαλῶς θεοὶ,
πολλῷ σάλῳ σείσαντες, ὤρθωσαν πάλιν·
ὑμᾶς δ᾽ ἐγὼ πομποῖσιν ἐκ πάντων δίχα
ἔστειλ᾽ ἱκέσθαι· τοῦτο μὲν, τὰ Λαΐου 165
σέβοντας εἰδὼς εὖ θρόνων ἀεὶ κράτη·
τοῦτ᾽ αὖθις, ἡνίκ᾽ Οἰδίπους ὤρθου πόλιν,
κἀπεὶ διώλετ᾽, ἀμφὶ τοὺς κείνων ἔτι
παῖδας μένοντας ἐμπέδοις φρονήμασιν.
ὅτ᾽ οὖν ἐκεῖνοι πρὸς διπλῆς μοίρας μίαν 170
καθ᾽ ἡμέραν ὤλοντο, παίσαντές τε καὶ
πληγέντες αὐτόχειρι σὺν μιάσματι,
ἐγὼ κράτη δὴ πάντα καὶ θρόνους ἔχω
γένους κατ᾽ ἀγχιστεῖα τῶν ὀλωλότων.
ἀμήχανον δὲ παντὸς ἀνδρὸς ἐκμαθεῖν 175
ψυχήν τε καὶ φρόνημα καὶ γνώμην, πρὶν ἂν
ἀρχαῖς τε καὶ νόμοισιν ἐντριβὴς φανῇ.
ἐμοὶ γὰρ, ὅστις πᾶσαν εὐθύνων πόλιν,
μὴ τῶν ἀρίστων ἅπτεται βουλευμάτων,
ἀλλ᾽ ἐκ φόβου του γλῶσσαν † ἐγκλῄσας ἔχει, 180
κάκιστος εἶναι νῦν τε καὶ πάλαι δοκεῖ·
καὶ μείζον᾽ ὅστις ἀντὶ τῆς αὑτοῦ πάτρας
φίλον νομίζει, τοῦτον οὐδαμοῦ λέγω.
ἐγὼ γὰρ, ἴστω Ζεὺς ὁ πάνθ᾽ ὁρῶν ἀεὶ,
οὔτ᾽ ἂν σιωπήσαιμι τὴν ἄτην ὁρῶν 185
στείχουσαν ἀστοῖς ἀντὶ τῆς σωτηρίας,
οὔτ᾽ ἂν φίλον ποτ᾽ ἄνδρα δυσμενῆ χθονὸς
θείμην ἐμαυτῷ, τοῦτο γιγνώσκων, ὅτι

[180] γρ. ἐγκλείσας.

III. FIRST EPISODE.

KREON.

Sirs, for the vessel of the state, the Gods
Had tossed us in a stormy surge, and now
Have righted us again and made us safe.
But you by messengers have I speeded here
To secret council; first, because I knew
How well ye ever held in reverence
The enthroned power of Laius; then again,
While Œdipus maintained the city's weal,
And after he was gone, ye still continued
Good subjects to the children of that house.
Well: now that they by a twin fate have fallen
On one day, each the smiter and the stricken,
Stained with the fratricide's blood-guiltiness,
I all that power, I that throne possess,
On claims of nearest kindred to the dead.
There is no man whose soul and will and meaning
Stand forth as outward things for all to see,
Till he has shown himself by practice versed
In ruling under law and making laws.
As to myself—it is and was of old
My fixed belief, that he is vile indeed
Who when the general state his guidance claims
Dares not adhere to wisest policy,
But keeps his tongue locked up for fear of somewhat.
Him too I reckon nowhere who esteems
A private friend more than his father-land.
For I,—may Zeus who ever seeth all things
Witness my words,—I would not hold my peace,
If, as the price of my peculiar safety,
I saw my citizens unwittingly
Exposed to onslaught from the public mischief;
  Nor would I er count among my friends
My country's enemy: for well I know,

ἥδ' ἐστὶν ἡ σώζουσα, καὶ ταύτης ἔπι
πλέοντες ὀρθῆς τοὺς φίλους ποιούμεθα. 190
τοιοῖσδ' ἐγὼ νόμοισι τήνδ' αὔξω πόλιν,
καὶ νῦν ἀδελφὰ τῶνδε κηρύξας ἔχω
ἀστοῖσι, παίδων τῶν ἀπ' Οἰδίπου πέρι.
Ἐτεοκλέα μὲν, ὃς πόλεως ὑπερμαχῶν
ὄλωλε τῆσδε, πάντ' ἀριστεύσας †δόρει, 195
τάφῳ τε κρύψαι, καὶ τὰ πάντ' ἐφαγνίσαι,
ἃ τοῖς ἀρίστοις ἔρχεται κάτω νεκροῖς.
τὸν δ' αὖ ξύναιμον τοῦδε, Πολυνείκην λέγω,
ὃς γῆν πατρῴαν καὶ θεοὺς τοὺς ἐγγενεῖς,
φυγὰς κατελθὼν, ἠθέλησε μὲν πυρὶ 200
πρῆσαι κατάκρας, ἠθέλησε δ' αἵματος
κοινοῦ πάσασθαι, τοὺς δὲ δουλώσας ἄγειν,
τοῦτον πόλει τῇδ' †ἐκκεκήρυκται τάφῳ
μήτε κτερίζειν, μήτε κωκῦσαί τινα,
ἐᾶν δ' ἄθαπτον καὶ πρὸς οἰωνῶν δέμας 205
καὶ πρὸς κυνῶν ἐδεστὸν αἰκισθέντ' ἰδεῖν.
τοιόνδ' ἐμὸν φρόνημα· κοὔποτ' ἔκ γ' ἐμοῦ
τιμὴν προέξουσ' οἱ κακοὶ τῶν ἐνδίκων.
ἀλλ' ὅστις εὔνους τῇδε τῇ πόλει, θανὼν
καὶ ζῶν ὁμοίως ἐξ ἐμοῦ τιμήσεται. 210

ΧΟΡΟΣ.

σοὶ ταῦτ' ἀρέσκει, παῖ Μενοικέως Κρέον,
τὸν τῇδε δύσνουν, καὶ τὸν εὐμενῆ πόλει.
νόμῳ δὲ χρῆσθαι *πανταχοῦ †πάρεστί σοι,
καὶ τῶν θανόντων, χὠπόσοι ζῶμεν, πέρι.

¹⁹⁵ γρ. δορί.   ²⁰³ γρ. ἐκκεκηρύχθαι.
²¹³ γρ. παντί πού τ' ἔνεστι.

She is the bark that brings us safe to port;
Sailing in her unswayed by sidelong gales
We make the only friends we ought to make.
By laws like these I seek this city's welfare.
And now the herald's voice by my command,
In words akin to these, has told the people
My will about the sons of Œdipus.
For Eteokles, who as this city's champion
Bore off the meed of prowess with his spear
And fell for us,—not burial alone,
But every after-ordinance which soothes
The parted souls of the heroic dead.
Now for the other brother—Polyneikes—
Who, as a runagate returning home,
Wished in the flames to burn to nothingness
His father-land and tutelary gods,
Who wished to glut himself with kindred blood,
Or lead away the living as his bondmen,—
For him the herald's voice forbids this city
To pay or funeral rites or lamentations,
But sternly orders that his body lie
Unsepulchred and devoured by birds and dogs—
A most unsightly spectacle to view.
Such is my will.—
And if it rests with me, the base shall never
Forestall the rightful honours of the righteous.
But whoso loves this city, both in death
And life shall be alike esteemed by me.

CHORUS.

We hear thy will, Kreon, Menœkeus' son,
Upon this city's foeman and her friend.
It rests with thee to give the law full play,
As for the dead, so for us all who live.

ΚΡΕΩΝ.
ὡς ἂν σκοποὶ νῦν ἦτε τῶν εἰρημένων. 215

ΧΟΡΟΣ.
νεωτέρῳ τῳ τοῦτο βαστάζειν πρόθες.

ΚΡΕΩΝ.
ἀλλ' εἴσ' ἕτοιμοι τοῦ νεκροῦ γ' ἐπίσκοποι.

ΧΟΡΟΣ.
τί δῆτ' ἂν ἄλλο τοῦτ' ἐπεντέλλοις ἔτι;

ΚΡΕΩΝ.
τὸ μὴ 'πιχωρεῖν τοῖς ἀπιστοῦσιν τάδε.

ΧΟΡΟΣ.
οὐκ ἔστιν οὕτω μῶρος, ὃς θανεῖν ἐρᾷ. 220

ΚΡΕΩΝ.
καὶ μὴν ὁ μισθός γ' οὗτος. ἀλλ' ὑπ' ἐλπίδων
ἄνδρας τὸ κέρδος πολλάκις διώλεσεν.

ΦΥΛΑΞ.
ἄναξ, ἐρῶ μὲν οὐχ ὅπως τάχους ὕπο
δύσπνους ἱκάνω κοῦφον ἐξάρας πόδα.
πολλὰς γὰρ ἔσχον φροντίδων ἐπιστάσεις, 225
ὁδοῖς κυκλῶν ἐμαυτὸν εἰς ἀναστροφήν.
ψυχὴ γὰρ ηὔδα πολλά μοι μυθουμένη·
τάλας, τί χωρεῖς, οἷ μολὼν δώσεις δίκην;
τλήμων, μενεῖς αὖ; κεἰ τάδ' εἴσεται Κρέων
ἄλλου παρ' ἀνδρός, πῶς σὺ δῆτ' οὐκ ἀλγυνεῖ;— 230

ISMENE.

Go, if thou art resolved: and know, I hold thee
Foolish indeed, but still a peerless friend!

*(Ismene returns to the palace: Antigone goes off on the right
by the Parascenia. The Chorus immediately enters the orchestra by the lower side entrance on the left.)*

II. PARODOS.

CHORUS.

Strophe I.

Beam of the sun, the fairest light
That ever shone on Theba, seven-gated!
At length thou comest, eye of golden day,
Careering o'er the fountain-streams of Dirke!
For thou, with bridle still more keenly shaken,
Hast urged to flight before the flying van
The Argive hero of the argent shield.
March as he might in garniture of mail.

(Anapæstic Movement.)

Whom Polyneikes against our country,
Roused by the nicest of quarrels, had mustered.
And as an eagle terribly shrieking,
With a soaring swoop he alighted.
White as the snow were the pinions that clothed him!
Many his bucklers
And his helmets crested with horse-hair!

στὰς δ᾽ ὑπὲρ μελάθρων, †φονώ-   ╷ωῖς ἀντιστ. ά.
σαισιν ἀμφιχανὼν κύκλῳ
λόγχαις ἑπτάπυλον στόμα,
ἔβα, πρίν ποθ᾽ ἁμετέρων   120
αἱμάτων γένυσιν
πλησθῆναί τε, καὶ στεφάνωμα πύργων
πευκάενθ᾽ Ἥφαιστον ἑλεῖν.
τοῖος ἀμφὶ νῶτ᾽ ἐτάθη
πάταγος Ἄρεος, ἀντιπάλῳ   125
δυσχείρωμα δράκοντι.

Ζεὺς γὰρ μεγάλης γλώσσης κόμπους   ἀντισύστ. ά.
ὑπερεχθαίρει· καί σφας ἐσιδὼν
πολλῷ ῥεύματι προσνισσομένους
χρυσοῦ, * καναχῇ θ᾽ * ὑπερόπλους,   130
παλτῷ ῥιπτεῖ πυρί, βαλβίδων
ἐπ᾽ ἄκρων ἤδη
νίκην ὁρμῶντ᾽ ἀλαλάξαι.

ἀντίτυπα δ᾽ ἐπὶ γᾷ πέσε τανταλωθεὶς   στροφὴ β´.
πυρφόρος, ὃς τότε μαινομένᾳ ξὺν ὁρμᾷ   135
  βακχεύων ἐπέπνει
  ῥιπαῖς ἐχθίστων ἀνέμων.
  εἶχε δ᾽ ἄλλᾳ τὰ μέν,
  †ἄλλα δ᾽ ἐπ᾽ ἄλλοις ἐπενώμα στυφελίζων
    μέγας Ἄρης
  δεξιόσειρος.   140

[117] γρ. φονίαισιν.   [120] γρ. καναχῆς ὑπεροπτίας.
[138] γρ. τὰ μὲν ἄλλᾳ, τὰ δ᾽ ἐπ᾽.

then wilt thou escape the penalty?" While thus my mind
revolved, the speed I made was tardy in its swiftness: and
so a short road is made long. Well; at last coming hither
to thee carried the day; and though thou mayest think my
words naught, I yet will speak. For here come I, with
griping hold fast clinging to the hope, that I can but suffer
what my fate demands.

KREON.

What grounds hast thou for this despondency?

SENTINEL.

I fain would tell thee first about myself.
The deed I neither did nor saw the doer:
Nor were it just that I should come to mischief.

KREON.

Whate'er the matter is, thou fencest well,
And mak'st a hedge all round thee. And 'tis clear
'Tis something disagreeable to hear.

SENTINEL.

True: threats of danger needs must give us pause.

KREON.

Well: speak at once, and take thyself away.

SENTINEL.

At once I tell thee. Some one has just now
Entombed the body and is gone; that is,
He has sprinkled thirsty dust over the corpse
And done what else religious fear requires.

KREON.

How sayest thou?—
What man is he who dared to do this deed?

SENTINEL.

I know not, I: for there was neither blow
Of any mattock, nor the earth thrown up

καὶ χέρσος, ἀῤῥὼξ οὐδ' ἐπημαξευμένη
τροχοῖσιν, ἀλλ' ἄσημος οὑργάτης τις ἦν.
ὅπως δ' ὁ πρῶτος ἡμὶν ἡμεροσκόπος
δείκνυσι, πᾶσι θαῦμα δυσχερὲς παρῆν.
ὁ μὲν γὰρ ἠφάνιστο, τυμβήρης μὲν οὔ, 255
λεπτὴ δ', ἅγος φεύγοντος ὥς, ἐπῆν κόνις.
σημεῖα δ' οὔτε θηρὸς, οὔτε του κυνῶν
ἐλθόντος, οὐ σπάσαντος ἐξεφαίνετο.
λόγοι δ' ἐν ἀλλήλοισιν ἐῤῥόθουν κακοί,
φύλαξ ἐλέγχων φύλακα· κἂν ἐγίγνετο 260
πληγὴ τελευτῶσ', οὐδ' ὁ κωλύσων παρῆν.
εἷς γάρ τις ἦν ἕκαστος οὑξειργασμένος,
κοὐδεὶς ἐναργὴς, ἀλλ' ἔφευγε μὴ εἰδέναι.
ἦμεν δ' ἕτοιμοι καὶ μύδρους αἴρειν χεροῖν,
καὶ πῦρ διέρπειν, καὶ θεοὺς ὁρκωμοτεῖν, 265
τὸ μήτε δρᾶσαι, μήτε τῳ ξυνειδέναι
τὸ πρᾶγμα βουλεύσαντι, μήτ' εἰργασμένῳ.
τέλος δ', ὅτ' οὐδὲν ἦν ἐρευνῶσιν πλέον,
λέγει τις εἷς, ὃς πάντας ἐς πέδον κάρα
νεῦσαι φόβῳ προὔτρεψεν. οὐ γὰρ εἴχομεν 270
οὔτ' ἀντιφωνεῖν, οὔθ' ὅπως δρῶντες καλῶς
πράξαιμεν. ἦν δ' ὁ μῦθος, ὡς ἀνοιστέον
σοὶ τοὔργον εἴη τοῦτο, κοὐχὶ κρυπτέον.
καὶ ταῦτ' ἐνίκα, κἀμὲ τὸν δυσδαίμονα
πάλος καθαιρεῖ τοῦτο τἀγαθὸν λαβεῖν. 275
πάρειμι δ' ἄκων οὐχ ἑκοῦσιν, οἶδ' ὅτι.
στέργει γὰρ οὐδεὶς ἄγγελον κακῶν ἐπῶν.

ΧΟΡΟΣ.

ἄναξ, ἐμοί τοι, μή τι καὶ θεήλατον
τοὔργον τόδ', ἡ ξύννοια βουλεύει πάλαι.

²⁷⁸ γρ. τὸ μὴ.

By shovelling: but the ground was hard and dry:
Unbroken and untracked by rut of wheels;
And he who worked had left no trace behind him.
When the first day-watch pointed to the deed,
On all fell wonder mixed with pain. For he
Was out of sight—not closed within a tomb,
But lightly over-heapt with sprinkled dust,
As when some passer-by will shun the curse.
Nor were there outward signs that beast or dog
Had come and torn him. Thereupon among us
The bandied threat sped up and down; each guard
Accused his fellow; and at last it seemed
That blows would come; nor was the make-peace by.
For each man stood indicted of the deed,
And no man was convicted, but the plea
Was ignorance of the facts. And ready were we
The glowing steel to handle, and to walk
Through fire, or swear us by the Gods that we
Had neither done the deed nor had consented
To either him who planned or him who did it.
But when with all our probes we got no farther,
There spoke out some one, and his words were such
That to the ground we bowed our heads in fear.
For we had neither skill to say him nay,
Nor knew we doing what we should do well.
His counsel was—to tell the whole to thee,
And not to mask it from thee. This prevailed,
And then the lot condemns me, hapless wight,
To get this piece of luck. So here I come,
Unwilling to the unwilling well I wot :
For no one loves the bearer of bad tidings.

CHORUS.

To me, O King, the thought is present ever—
This was some dispensation from the Gods.

ΚΡΕΩΝ.

παῦσαι, πρὶν ὀργῆς †καί με μεστῶσαι, λέγων, 280
μὴ 'φευρεθῇς ἄνους τε καὶ γέρων ἅμα.
λέγεις γὰρ οὐκ ἀνεκτά, δαίμονας λέγων
πρόνοιαν ἴσχειν τοῦδε τοῦ νεκροῦ πέρι.
πότερον ὑπερτιμῶντες ὡς εὐεργέτην
ἔκρυπτον αὐτόν, ὅστις ἀμφικίονας 285
ναοὺς πυρώσων ἦλθε κἀναθήματα,
καὶ γῆν ἐκείνων καὶ νόμους διασκεδῶν;
ἢ τοὺς κακοὺς τιμῶντας εἰσορᾷς θεούς;
οὐκ ἔστιν. ἀλλὰ ταῦτα καὶ πάλαι πόλεως
ἄνδρες μόλις φέροντες ἐρρόθουν ἐμοί, 290
κρυφῇ κάρα σείοντες· οὐδ' ὑπὸ ζυγῷ
λόφον δικαίως εἶχον, ὡς στέργειν ἐμέ.
ἐκ τῶνδε τούτους ἐξεπίσταμαι καλῶς
παρηγμένους μισθοῖσιν εἰργάσθαι τάδε.
οὐδὲν γὰρ ἀνθρώποισιν, οἷον ἄργυρος,
κακὸν νόμισμ' ἔβλαστε. τοῦτο καὶ πόλεις
πορθεῖ, τόδ' ἄνδρας ἐξανίστησιν δόμων·
τόδ' ἐκδιδάσκει καὶ παραλλάσσει φρένας
χρηστὰς πρὸς αἰσχρὰ πράγμαθ' ἵστασθαι βροτῶν·
πανουργίας δ' ἔδειξεν ἀνθρώποις ἔχειν, 300
καὶ παντὸς ἔργου δυσσέβειαν εἰδέναι.
ὅσοι δὲ μισθαρνοῦντες ἤνυσαν τάδε,
χρόνῳ ποτ' ἐξέπραξαν ὡς δοῦναι δίκην.
ἀλλ' εἴπερ ἴσχει Ζεὺς ἔτ' ἐξ ἐμοῦ σέβας,
εὖ τοῦτ' ἐπίστασ', ὅρκιος δέ σοι λέγω, 305

γρ. κἀμέ.

KREON.

Hold, ere your words fill me with very rage,
Nor prove yourself foolish at once and old.
Not to be borne the words thou say'st in saying
That Gods keep watchful heed for this vile corpse.
What! was it then because his benefactions
Had won their high esteem—was it for this
They sought to bury *him* who came to burn
Their pillar-girded temples and their treasures,—
To scatter to the winds their land and laws!
Or is it thy experience that the Gods
Honour the base? No!—That was not the cause;
But these enactments from the first misliking,
Some of our townsmen murmured against *me*,
Shaking their heads in silence, and they kept not
Their necks in equal poise beneath the yoke
So as to meet my favour. Well I know
These with their bribes have won the sentinels
To perpetrate this deed. For there is nothing,
Of all the coinage current in the world,
So base as silver. This it is, nought else,
That sacks the city; this it is, nought else,
That parts the goodman from his hearth and home;
This too unteaches and perverts the minds
Of upright mortals, till they take their post
Upon the side of ignominious actions;
This points the way of knavery to mankind,
And finds a school for every deed of sin.
Yet they whom pelf has prompted to this work
At length have all secured their punishment.
Nay more, if Zeus upholds my sovran awe,
Be well assured, and with an oath I say it,

εἰ μὴ τὸν αὐτόχειρα τοῦδε τοῦ τάφου
εὑρόντες ἐκφανεῖτ' ἐς ὀφθαλμοὺς ἐμούς,
οὐχ ὑμῖν Ἅιδης μοῦνος ἀρκέσει, πρὶν ἂν
ζῶντες κρεμαστοὶ τήνδε δηλώσηθ' ὕβριν,
ἵν' εἰδότες τὸ κέρδος ἔνθεν οἰστέον, 310
τὸ λοιπὸν ἁρπάζητε, καὶ μάθηθ', ὅτι
οὐκ ἐξ ἅπαντος δεῖ τὸ κερδαίνειν φιλεῖν.
ἐκ τῶν γὰρ αἰσχρῶν λημμάτων τοὺς πλείονας
ἀτωμένους ἴδοις ἂν ἢ σεσωσμένους.

ΦΥΛΑΞ.
εἰπεῖν τι δώσεις, ἢ στραφεὶς οὕτως ἴω; 315

ΚΡΕΩΝ.
οὐκ οἶσθα καὶ νῦν ὡς ἀνιαρῶς λέγεις;

ΦΥΛΑΞ.
ἐν τοῖσιν ὠσὶν, ἢ 'πὶ τῇ ψυχῇ δάκνει;

ΚΡΕΩΝ.
τί δὲ ῥυθμίζεις τὴν ἐμὴν λύπην ὅπου;

ΦΥΛΑΞ.
ὁ δρῶν σ' ἀνιᾷ τὰς φρένας, τὰ δ' ὦτ' ἐγώ.

ΚΡΕΩΝ.
οἴμ', ὡς †ἅλημα δῆλον ἐκπεφυκὸς εἶ. 320

ΦΥΛΑΞ.
οὔκουν τό †γ' ἔργον τοῦτο ποιήσας ποτέ.

ΚΡΕΩΝ.
καὶ ταῦτ' ἐπ' ἀργύρῳ γε τὴν ψυχὴν προδούς.

ΦΥΛΑΞ.
φεῦ·
ἦ δεινὸν ᾧ δοκεῖ γε καὶ ψευδῆ δοκεῖν.

γρ. λάλημα.   γρ. τόδ'.

Unless ye find and openly produce
Before my eyes the man whose very hands
Performed these obsequies, your death alone
Shall not suffice, until, hung up alive,
Ye have denounced the insolent offender.
To the end that, knowing whence to get your gains,
Ye may pursue your filching, till ye learn
That love of pelf must somewhere find its limit;
For by degrading lucre thou mayest see
More men get mischief than security.

SENTINEL.

Wilt let me speak, or must I go at once?

KREON.

Know'st not that even now thy words offend?

SENTINEL.

Where is the pinch? i' th' ears or in the soul?

KREON.

Why mark the boundary line of my displeasure?

SENTINEL.

The doer plagues thy heart; I, but thine ears.

KREON.

Oh! it is clear thou art a coxcomb born.

SENTINEL.

It may be so; but not who did this deed.

KREON.

Thou didst it, man, selling thy soul for silver.

SENTINEL.

Alas!
'Tis sad when one thinks good to think a lie.

ΚΡΕΩΝ.

κόμψενε νῦν τὴν δόξαν· εἰ δὲ ταῦτα μὴ
φανεῖτέ μοι τοὺς δρῶντας, ἐξερεῖθ', ὅτι   325
τὰ †δειλὰ κέρδη πημονὰς ἐργάζεται.

ΦΥΛΑΞ.

ἀλλ' εὑρεθείη μὲν μάλιστ'· ἐὰν δέ τοι
ληφθῇ τε καὶ μὴ, τοῦτο γὰρ τύχη κρινεῖ,
οὐκ ἔσθ' ὅπως ὄψει σὺ δεῦρ' ἐλθόντα με.
καὶ νῦν γὰρ ἐκτὸς ἐλπίδος γνώμης τ' ἐμῆς   330
σωθείς, ὀφείλω τοῖς θεοῖς πολλὴν χάριν.

Δ. ΣΤΑΣΙΜΟΝ ΠΡΩΤΟΝ.

ΧΟΡΟΣ.

Πολλὰ τὰ δεινά, κοὐδὲν ἀν-   στροφὴ ά.
θρώπου δεινότερον πέλει.
τοῦτο καὶ πολιοῦ πέραν
πόντου χειμερίῳ νότῳ   335
χωρεῖ, περιβρυχίοισιν
περῶν ἐπ' οἴδμασιν,
θεῶν τε τὰν ὑπερτάταν, Γᾶν
ἄφθιτον, ἀκαμάταν ἀποτρύεται
ἰλλομένων ἀρότρων ἔτος εἰς ἔτος,   340
ἱππείῳ γένει πολεύων.

†κουφονόων τε φῦλον ὀρ-   ἀντιστ. ά.
νίθων ἀμφιβαλὼν ἄγει,

³²⁶ γρ. δεινά.   ³⁴² γρ. κουφονέων.

KREON.

Prate as thou wilt on *thinking*, but unless
Ye point me out the doers, ye shall say
That sneaking profits only purchase pain.

SENTINEL.

Nay, by all means I would the man were known:
Be he caught or not, for luck will settle this,
Thou wilt not see *me* coming here again.
E'en now preserved beyond my hope and thought,
I owe a debt of gratitude to heaven.

IV. FIRST STASIMON.

CHORUS.

STROPHE I.

Many the things that mighty be,
And nought is mightier than—Man.
For he can cross the foaming ocean,
What time the stormy South is blowing,
Steering amid the mantling waves that roar around him.
—And for his uses he wearieth
Earth, the highest Deity,
The immortal, the untiring one,
As year by year the ploughs are drawn
Up and down the furrow'd field,
To and fro his harness'd teams—
The seed of horses—driving.

ANTISTROPHE I.

Man, full of ingenuity,
Entraps in folds of woven meshes
And leads away the tribe
Of flighty-purpos'd birds,

καὶ θηρῶν ἀγρίων ἔθνη,
πόντου τ' εἰναλίαν φύσιν   345
σπείραισι δικτυοκλώστοις,
περιφραδὴς ἀνήρ·
κρατεῖ δὲ μηχαναῖς ἀγραύλου
θηρὸς ὀρεσσιβάτα, λασιαύχενί θ'
ἵππον †ὀχμάζεται ἀμφὶ λόφον† ζυγῶν   350
οὔρειόν τ' ἀδμῆτα ταῦρον.

καὶ φθέγμα καὶ ἠνεμόεν φρό-   στροφὴ β'.
νημα καὶ ἀστυνόμους ὀρ-
γὰς ἐδιδάξατο καὶ δυσαύλων
πάγων †ὑπαίθρεια καὶ   355
δύσομβρα φεύγειν βέλη.
παντοπόρος,
ἄπορος ἐπ' οὐδὲν ἔρχεται
τὸ μέλλον· Ἅιδα μόνον
φεῦξιν οὐκ ἐπάξεται·   360
νόσων δ' ἀμηχάνων φυγὰς
ξυμπέφρασται.

σοφόν τι τὸ μηχανόεν τέχ-   ἀντιστ. β'.
νας ὑπὲρ ἐλπίδ' ἔχων, ποτὲ
μὲν κακὸν, ἄλλοτ' ἐπ' ἐσθλὸν ἕρπει· 365
νόμους †γεραίρων χθονὸς
θεῶν τ' ἔνορκον δίκαν,
ὑψίπολις·

[350] γρ. ἄξεται ἀμφίλοφον ζυγόν.   (355) γρ. αἴθρια.
[356] γρ. παρείρων.

And the kindreds of wild beasts,
And the ocean brood, whose home is in the waters,
With wiles he tames
The mountain-beast that roams the moor:
And fastens, yoking him about the neck,
The long-maned steed and stubborn mountain-bull.

STROPHE II.

Language, and lofty thought,
And dispositions meet for order'd cities,
These he hath taught himself;—and how to shun
The shafts of comfortless winter,—
Both those which smite when the sky is clear,
And those which fall in showers;—
With plans for all things,
Planless in nothing, meets he the future!
Of death alone the avoidance
No foreign aid will bring.
But from disease, that sports with skill,
He hath gotten him means of fleeing.

ANTISTROPHE II.

Wise in his craft of art
Beyond the bounds of expectation,
The while to good he goes, the while to evil.
Honouring his country's laws and heaven's oath-
bound right.
High is he in the state!

ἄπολις ὅτῳ τὸ μὴ καλὸν
ξύνεστι· τόλμας χάριν 370
μήτ' ἐμοὶ παρέστιος
γένοιτο, μήτ' ἴσον φρονῶν,
ὃς τάδ' ἔρδει.

ἐς δαιμόνιον τέρας ἀμφινοῶ (σύστημα).
τόδε. πῶς εἰδὼς ἀντιλογήσω 375
τήνδ' οὐκ εἶναι παῖδ' Ἀντιγόνην;
ὦ δύστηνος,
καὶ δυστήνου πατρὸς Οἰδιπόδα,
τί ποτ'; οὐ δή που σέ γ' ἀπιστοῦσαν
τοῖς βασιλείοις †ἀπάγουσι νόμοις, 380
καὶ ἐν ἀφροσύνῃ καθελόντες;

Ε. ΕΠΕΙΣΟΔΙΟΝ ΔΕΥΤΕΡΟΝ.

ΦΥΛΑΞ.

Ἥδ' ἔστ' ἐκείνη τοὔργον ἡ 'ξειργασμένη.
τήνδ' εἵλομεν θάπτουσαν. ἀλλὰ ποῦ Κρέων;

ΧΟΡΟΣ.

ὅδ' ἐκ δόμων ἄψορρος εἰς δέον περᾷ.

ΚΡΕΩΝ.

τί δ' ἔστι; ποίᾳ ξύμμετρος προὔβην τύχῃ; 385

ΦΥΛΑΞ.

ἄναξ, βροτοῖσιν οὐδέν ἐστ' ἀπώμοτον.

---
380 γρ. ἄγουσιν.

But cityless is he with whom inherent baseness dwells;
When boldness dares so much,
No seat by me at festive hearth,
No seat by me in sect or party,
For him that sinneth!

(Sentinel re-enters with Antigone, guarded.)

CHORUS.

(Anapæstic Movement.)

Gazing with doubt and wonder I look on this
Strangest of sights! how dare I belie my
Knowledge that this is the maid Antigone!
Hapless princess!
Child of a hapless sire, Œdipodes!
Tell us—ah surely they are not bringing thee
Hither, defiant of royal commandments,
In the act of foolishness taken!

V. SECOND EPISODE.

SENTINEL.

'Tis she who did the deed. We took her paying
The funeral obsequies. But where is Kreon!

CHORUS.

See, in good time, he cometh forth again.

(Enter Kreon.)

KREON.

What hap holds sortance with my coming forth?

SENTINEL.

My liege, a man should never swear he will not;

ψεύδει γὰρ ἡ 'πίνοια τὴν γνώμην· ἐπεὶ
σχολῇ ποθ' ἥξειν δεῦρ' ἂν ἐξηύχουν ἐγώ,
ταῖς σαῖς ἀπειλαῖς, αἷς ἐχειμάσθην τότε.
ἀλλ', ἡ γὰρ ἐκτὸς καὶ παρ' ἐλπίδας χαρὰ   390
ἔοικεν ἄλλῃ μῆκος οὐδὲν ἡδονῇ,
ἥκω, δι' ὅρκων καίπερ ὢν ἀπώμοτος,
κόρην ἄγων τήνδ', ἣ καθευρέθη τάφον
κοσμοῦσα. κλῆρος ἐνθάδ' οὐκ ἐπάλλετο,
ἀλλ' ἔστ' ἐμὸν θοὔρμαιον, οὐκ ἄλλου, τόδε.   395
καὶ νῦν, ἄναξ, τήνδ' αὐτός, ὡς θέλεις, λαβών,
καὶ κρῖνε κἀξέλεγχ'· ἐγὼ δ' ἐλεύθερος
δίκαιός εἰμι τῶνδ' ἀπηλλάχθαι κακῶν.

ΚΡΕΩΝ.

ἄγεις δὲ τήνδε τῷ τρόπῳ πόθεν λαβών;

ΦΥΛΑΞ.

αὕτη τὸν ἄνδρ' ἔθαπτε. πάντ' ἐπίστασαι.   400

ΚΡΕΩΝ.

ἦ καὶ ξυνίης καὶ λέγεις ὀρθῶς ἃ φῄς;

ΦΥΛΑΞ.

ταύτην γ' †ἰδὼν θάπτουσαν ὃν σὺ τὸν νεκρὸν
ἀπεῖπας. ἆρ' ἔνδηλα καὶ σαφῆ λέγω;

ΚΡΕΩΝ.

καὶ πῶς ὁρᾶται, κἀπίληπτος †ᾑρέθη;

ΦΥΛΑΞ.

τοιοῦτον ἦν τὸ πρᾶγμ'. ὅπως γὰρ ἥκομεν,   405
πρὸς σοῦ τὰ δείν' ἐκεῖν' ἐπηπειλημένοι,
πᾶσαν κόνιν σήραντες, ἣ κατεῖχε τὸν

₄₀₂ γρ. ἰδόν.   ₄₀₄ γρ. εὑρέθη.

For second thoughts belie the intention. Thus,
When that thy storm of threats had greeted me,
I boldly said my coming here again
Would, if I came at all, be long and slow.
But still in spite of oaths behold me here—
For joy, which hopes surprises and transcends,
Is like no other pleasure in extent—
Bringing this maid, who was detected paying
The funeral honours: here no lot was drawn,
But this is mine, none other's lucky find.
And now, my liege, just take her as it likes thee,
And test and question: right it is that I
Should be well quit and free from all these troubles.

KREON.

Whence and how taken bringest thou this damsel?

SENTINEL.

She tried to bury *him*—thou knowest all.

KREON.

Dost understand and speak'st thy words discreetly?

SENTINEL.

Yes, for I saw her burying the corpse
By thee denounced. Are my words plain and clear?

KREON.

How was she seen and taken in the fact?

SENTINEL.

The circumstance was thus. When we returned,
Urged by such fearful menaces from thee,
We swept clean off the dust which covered him,

νέκυν, μυδῶν τε σῶμα γυμνώσαντες εὖ,
καθήμεθ᾽ ἄκρων ἐκ πάγων ὑπήνεμοι,
ὀσμὴν ἀπ᾽ αὐτοῦ μὴ βάλοι, πεφευγότες. 410
ἐγερτὶ κινῶν ἄνδρ᾽ ἀνὴρ ἐπιρρόθοις
κακοῖσιν, εἴ τις τοῦδ᾽ ἀφειδήσοι πόνου.
χρόνον τάδ᾽ ἦν τοσοῦτον, ἔς τ᾽ ἐν αἰθέρι
μέσῳ κατέστη λαμπρὸς ἡλίου κύκλος,
καὶ καῦμ᾽ ἔθαλπε· καὶ τότ᾽ ἐξαίφνης χθονὸς 415
τυφὼς ἀείρας σκηπτὸν, οὐράνιον ἄχος,
πίμπλησι πεδίον, πᾶσαν αἰκίζων φόβην
ὕλης πεδιάδος· ἐν δ᾽ ἐμεστώθη μέγας
αἰθήρ· μύσαντες δ᾽ εἴχομεν θείαν νόσον.
καὶ τοῦδ᾽ ἀπαλλαγέντος ἐν χρόνῳ μακρῷ, 420
ἡ παῖς ὁρᾶται, κἀνακωκύει πικρᾶς
ὄρνιθος ὀξὺν φθόγγον, ὡς ὅταν κενῆς
εὐνῆς νεοσσῶν ὀρφανὸν βλέψῃ λέχος·
οὕτω δὲ χαὔτη, ψιλὸν ὡς ὁρᾷ νέκυν,
γόοισιν ἐξῴμωξεν, ἐκ δ᾽ ἀρὰς κακὰς 425
ἠρᾶτο τοῖσι τοὔργον ἐξειργασμένοις.
καὶ χερσὶν εὐθὺς διψίαν φέρει κόνιν,
ἔκ τ᾽ εὐκροτήτου χαλκέας ἄρδην πρόχου
χοαῖσι τρισπόνδοισι τὸν νέκυν στέφει.
χἠμεῖς ἰδόντες ἱέμεσθα, σὺν δέ νιν 430
θηρώμεθ᾽ εὐθὺς οὐδὲν ἐκπεπληγμένην·
καὶ τάς τε πρόσθεν τάς τε νῦν ἠλέγχομεν
πράξεις· ἄπαρνος δ᾽ οὐδενὸς καθίστατο
†ἅμ᾽ ἡδέως ἔμοιγε κἀλγεινῶς ἅμα.
τὸ μὲν γὰρ αὐτὸν ἐκ κακῶν πεφευγέναι, 435
ἥδιστον· ἐς κακὸν δὲ τοὺς φίλους ἄγειν,

434 γρ. ἀλλ᾽.

And baring thoroughly the clammy corpse,
We sat so far beneath the hill-top that
The wind blew o'er our heads, lest peradventure
Some evil odour from the corse should reach us,
And each man stirred his 'fellow, rousing him
With bandied threats, if any, carelessly,
This work neglected. So it was until
The sun's refulgent orb stood now midway
In the clear sky, and the heat began to burn.
Then suddenly a rushing mighty wind
Raised from the ground a circling cloud of dust,
A heaven-sent trouble! and it filled the plain,
Marring with ugly rack the tress-like foliage
Of all the olive-groves that fringed the meadow;
And e'en the lofty sky was choked with it.
With eyes set fast, we bore this god-sent plague;
And when at length it cleared away, this damsel
Was straightway seen. In loud and treble tones
She lifted up her voice, like some sad bird
Which finds her young torn from her emptied nest.
So she, when she beheld the corpse uncovered,
With groans bewailed herself, and bitter curses
She called down upon those who did the deed.
Without delay in both her hands she bears
The thirsty dust, and raising in the air
The well-wrought pitcher made of hammered bronze,
She poured around the corpse the threefold streams.
Soon as we saw this deed we rushed upon her,
And all together brought the game to bay.
Not terrified was she; and when we charged her
With both the former and the present deeds,
She nought disowned, so as to gladden me
And grieve me too. For though most sweet it is
Oneself to escape from trouble, yet to bring

ἀλγεινόν. ἀλλὰ πάντα ταῦθ' ἥσσω λαβεῖν
ἐμοὶ πέφυκε τῆς ἐμῆς σωτηρίας.

ΚΡΕΩΝ.

σὲ δή, σὲ τὴν νεύουσαν ἐς πέδον κάρα,
φῂς ἢ καταρνεῖ μὴ δεδρακέναι τάδε; 440

ΑΝΤΙΓΟΝΗ.

καὶ φημὶ δρᾶσαι, κοὐκ ἀπαρνοῦμαι τὸ μή.

ΚΡΕΩΝ.

σὺ μὲν κομίζοις ἂν σεαυτόν, ᾗ θέλεις,
ἔξω βαρείας αἰτίας ἐλεύθερον.
σὺ δ' εἰπέ μοι, μὴ μῆκος, ἀλλὰ σύντομα,
ᾔδης τὰ κηρυχθέντα, μὴ πράσσειν τάδε; 445

ΑΝΤΙΓΟΝΗ.

ᾔδη. τί δ' οὐκ ἔμελλον; ἐμφανῆ γὰρ ἦν.

ΚΡΕΩΝ.

καὶ δῆτ' ἐτόλμας τούσδ' ὑπερβαίνειν νόμους;

ΑΝΤΙΓΟΝΗ.

οὐ γάρ τί μοι Ζεὺς ἦν ὁ κηρύξας τάδε,
οὐδ' ἡ ξύνοικος τῶν κάτω θεῶν Δίκη,
οἳ τούσδ' ἐν ἀνθρώποισιν ὥρισαν νόμους. 450
οὐδὲ σθένειν τοσοῦτον ᾠόμην τὰ σὰ
κηρύγμαθ', ὥστ' ἄγραπτα κἀσφαλῆ θεῶν
νόμιμα δύνασθαι θνητὸν ὄνθ' ὑπερδραμεῖν.
οὐ γάρ τι νῦν τε κἀχθές, ἀλλ' ἀεί ποτε
ζῇ ταῦτα, κοὐδεὶς οἶδεν ἐξ ὅτου 'φάνη. 455
τούτων ἐγὼ οὐκ ἔμελλον, ἀνδρὸς οὐδενὸς
φρόνημα δείσασ', ἐν θεοῖσι τὴν δίκην

ANTIGONE.

A friend into misfortune is most sad.
But these and such like thoughts, as 'tis my nature,
I set aside my safety to ensure.

KREON.

Ho! thou that sinkest to the ground thine eyes,
Sayest thou or dost deny this deed was thine.

ANTIGONE.

I say I did it: I deny it not.

KREON

Now, sirrah, take thee wheresoe'er thou wilt,
Free from this heavy charge.   (*Exit Sentinel.*)
                          But tell me, thou,
And not at large, but briefly, didst thou know
The proclamation which forbade this deed?

ANTIGONE.

I knew it—wherefore not? twas plain enough.

KREON.

And durst thou natheless overstep these laws?

ANTIGONE.

It was not Zeus who heralded these words,
Nor Justice, help-meet of the Gods below.
'Twas they who ratified those other laws,
And set their record in the human heart.
Nor did I deem thy heraldings so mighty,
That thou, a mortal man, could'st trample on
The unwritten and unchanging laws of heaven.
They are not of to-day or yesterday;
But ever live, and no one knows their birth-tide.
Thus, for the dread of any human anger,
To be not minded to annul, and so
Then, the punishment which heaven exacts.

δώσειν. θανουμένη γὰρ ἐξῄδη, τί δ' οὔ;
κεἰ μὴ σὺ προὐκήρυξας. εἰ δὲ τοῦ χρόνου
πρόσθεν θανοῦμαι, κέρδος αὔτ' ἐγὼ λέγω. 460
ὅστις γὰρ ἐν πολλοῖσιν, ὡς ἐγώ, κακοῖς
ζῇ, πῶς ὅδ' οὐχὶ κατθανὼν κέρδος φέρει;
οὕτως ἔμοιγε τοῦδε τοῦ μόρου τυχεῖν
παρ' οὐδὲν ἄλγος· ἀλλ' ἄν, εἰ τὸν ἐξ ἐμῆς
μητρὸς θανόντ' ἄθαπτον ἠνσχόμην νέκυν, 465
κείνοις ἂν ἤλγουν· τοῖσδε δ' οὐκ ἀλγύνομαι.
σοὶ δ' εἰ δοκῶ νῦν μῶρα δρῶσα τυγχάνειν,
σχεδόν τι μώρῳ μωρίαν ὀφλισκάνω.

ΧΟΡΟΣ.

δηλοῖ τὸ γέννημ' ὠμὸν ἐξ ὠμοῦ πατρὸς
τῆς παιδός· εἴκειν δ' οὐκ ἐπίσταται κακοῖς. 470

ΚΡΕΩΝ.

ἀλλ' ἴσθι τοι τὰ σκλήρ' ἄγαν φρονήματα
πίπτειν μάλιστα· καὶ τὸν ἐγκρατέστατον
σίδηρον ὀπτὸν ἐκ πυρὸς περισκελῆ
θραυσθέντα καὶ ῥαγέντα πλεῖστ' ἂν εἰσίδοις.
σμικρῷ χαλινῷ δ' οἶδα τοὺς θυμουμένους 475
ἵππους καταρτυθέντας. οὐ γὰρ ἐκπέλει
φρονεῖν μέγ' ὅστις δοῦλός ἐστι τῶν πέλας.
αὕτη δ' ὑβρίζειν μὲν τότ' ἐξηπίστατο,
νόμους ὑπερβαίνουσα τοὺς προκειμένους·
ὕβρις δ', ἐπεὶ δέδρακεν, ἥδε δευτέρα, 480
τούτοις ἐπαυχεῖν, καὶ δεδρακυῖαν γελᾶν.
ἦ νῦν ἐγὼ μὲν οὐκ ἀνήρ, αὕτη δ' ἀνήρ,

ANTIGONE.   47

I know—how should I not? that I must die,
Without thy proclamations to foredoom it.
And if my time is shortened, this to me
Is gain indeed. For whoso lives, as I live,
Beset with many sorrows, how does he
Not win by dying? Hence, to me at least,
Thus to have met with death is not a grief,
Which I can count or reckon. Had I suffered
My mother's dear dead child to lie unburied,
Then grief would vex my heart; but now I grieve not.
For thee—if this my deed seems foolishness,
The fool has caught the foolish in her folly.

CHORUS.

How the stern father speaks in his stern child!
She knows not, she, to bow beneath the storm.

KREON.

Be well assured the stubborn temper still
Is bent the soonest, and the hardest iron,
When forged to brittleness, is oftenest seen
To crack and splinter. So I know that steeds
Of a high mettle yield to a small bit.
For whosoever owns a master's will,
Him the proud stomach ill beseems. This damsel
First learned the knack of insolent offence,
When she transgressed the promulgated laws.
That done, her second insolence was this—
To boast her evil deed and revel in it.
Then, marry, I'm no *man*, but she is one,

εἰ ταῦτ' ἀνατὶ τῇδε κείσεται κράτη.
ἀλλ' εἴτ' ἀδελφῆς, εἴθ' ὁμαιμονεστέρας
τοῦ παντὸς ἡμῖν Ζηνὸς Ἑρκείου κυρεῖ, 485
αὐτή τε χἠ ξύναιμος οὐκ ἀλύξετον
μόρου κακίστου. καὶ γὰρ οὖν κείνην ἴσον
ἐπαιτιῶμαι τοῦδε βουλεῦσαι τάφου.
καί νιν καλεῖτ'. ἔσω γὰρ εἶδον ἀρτίως
λυσσῶσαν αὐτήν, οὐδ' ἐπήβολον φρενῶν. 490
φιλεῖ δ' ὁ θυμὸς πρόσθεν ᾑρῆσθαι κλοπεὺς
τῶν μηδὲν ὀρθῶς ἐν σκότῳ τεχνωμένων.
μισῶ γε μέντοι χὤταν ἐν κακοῖσί τις
ἁλοὺς ἔπειτα τοῦτο καλλύνειν θέλῃ.

ΑΝΤΙΓΟΝΗ.

θέλεις τι μεῖζον ἢ κατακτεῖναί μ' ἑλών; 495

ΚΡΕΩΝ.

ἐγὼ μὲν οὐδέν· τοῦτ' ἔχων, ἅπαντ' ἔχω.

ΑΝΤΙΓΟΝΗ.

τί δῆτα μέλλεις; ὡς ἐμοὶ τῶν σῶν λόγων
ἀρεστὸν οὐδέν, μηδ' ἀρεσθείη ποτέ·
οὕτω δὲ καὶ σοὶ τἄμ' ἀφανδάνοντ' ἔφυ.
καίτοι πόθεν κλέος γ' ἂν εὐκλεέστερον 500
κατέσχον, ἢ τὸν αὐτάδελφον ἐν τάφῳ
τιθεῖσα; τούτοις τοῦτο πᾶσιν ἀνδάνειν
λέγοιτ' ἄν, εἰ μὴ γλῶσσαν †ἐγκλῄοι φόβος·
ἀλλ' ἡ τυραννὶς πολλά τ' ἄλλ' εὐδαιμονεῖ,
κἄξεστιν αὐτῇ δρᾶν, λέγειν θ', ἃ βούλεται. 505

γρ. ἐγκλείσοι.

If she unscathed shall flout my sovranty.
But be she sister's child, or born of one
Of nearer kindred to my blood than all
Who worship Zeus at our domestic altar,
She and her sister shall not fend away
A death most dire. For her, in equal sort,
I charge with framing plans for this interment.
And summon her. I saw her even now
Within the palace raving, and unable
To rule her thoughts. And so it is—the mind
Is first detected in its knavery,
When dark devices aim at wickedness.
Howbeit, to me it is no less abhorrent,
When, caught in criminality, the culprit
Seeks with fine words to beautify his deed.

ANTIGONE.

Wouldst thou aught more than thus to take and slay me!

KREON.

Nought else—this done, my every wish is sated.

ANTIGONE.

Why loiter then? the words which thou hast spoken
Displease me, all, and ne'er may such words please me!
And it is meet that thou shouldst mislike mine.
And yet from whence might I have earned a glory
More glorious than by placing in the tomb
My own dear brother? Every man of these
Would say he liked the deed, did not his fear
Bar up his utterance: but absolute power,
With many other happy privi'eges,
May speak and do whate'er the wish suggests.

ΚΡΕΩΝ.
σὺ τοῦτο μούνη τῶνδε Καδμείων ὁρᾷς.

ΑΝΤΙΓΟΝΗ.
ὁρῶσι χοὖτοι, σοὶ δ᾽ ὑπίλλουσι στόμα.

ΚΡΕΩΝ.
σὺ δ᾽ οὐκ ἐπαιδεῖ, τῶνδε χωρὶς εἰ φρονεῖς;

ΑΝΤΙΓΟΝΗ.
οὐδὲν γὰρ αἰσχρὸν τοὺς ὁμοσπλάγχνους σέβειν.

ΚΡΕΩΝ.
οὔκουν ὅμαιμος χὠ καταντίον θανών;   510

ΑΝΤΙΓΟΝΗ.
ὅμαιμος ἐκ μιᾶς τε, καὶ ταὐτοῦ πατρός.

ΚΡΕΩΝ
πῶς δῆτ᾽ ἐκείνῃ δυσσεβῆ τιμᾷς χάριν;

ΑΝΤΙΓΟΝΗ.
οὐ μαρτυρήσει *ταῦτα χὠ κατὰ χθονός.

ΚΡΕΩΝ.
εἴ τοί σφε τιμᾷς ἐξ ἴσου τῷ δυσσεβεῖ.

ΑΝΤΙΓΟΝΗ.
οὐ γάρ τι δοῦλος, ἀλλ᾽ ἀδελφὸς ὤλετο.   515

ΚΡΕΩΝ.
πορθῶν γε τήνδε γῆν· ὁ δ᾽ ἀντιστὰς ὕπερ.

ΑΝΤΙΓΟΝΗ.
ὅμως ὁ γ᾽ Ἅιδης τοὺς νόμους ἴσους ποθεῖ.

ΚΡΕΩΝ.
ἀλλ᾽ οὐχ ὁ χρηστὸς τῷ κακῷ λαχεῖν ἴσος.

*513 γρ. ταῦθ᾽ ὁ κατθανὼν νέκυς.

ANTIGONE.

KREON.

Of all Kadmeans thou alone seest this.

ANTIGONE.

These see it too, but thou hast made them mum.

KREON.

Art not ashamed to stand apart from these?

ANTIGONE.

To reverence kith and kin is nothing shameful.

KREON.

Was not he, too, who died for us, thy kin?

ANTIGONE.

He was my kin by sire and mother both.

KREON.

Then why this duty, impious to him?

ANTIGONE.

The fallen foe will not attest thy words.

KREON.

Yes—if the impious shares thy equal love.

ANTIGONE.

It was no slave that fell—it was my brother.

KREON.

Seeking thy country's hurt—but *he* fought for us.

ANTIGONE.

The laws which death exacts are equal laws.

KREON.

Not for the good and bad in equal measure.

ΑΝΤΙΓΟΝΗ.

τίς οἶδεν, εἰ †κάτωθεν εὐαγῆ τάδε;

ΚΡΕΩΝ.

οὔτοι ποθ' οὑχθρὸς, οὐδ' ὅταν θάνῃ, φίλος.   520

ΑΝΤΙΓΟΝΗ.

οὔτοι συνέχθειν, ἀλλὰ συμφιλεῖν ἔφυν.

ΚΡΕΩΝ.

κάτω νυν ἐλθοῦσ', εἰ φιλητέον, φίλει
κείνους· ἐμοῦ δὲ ζῶντος οὐκ ἄρξει γυνή.

ΧΟΡΟΣ.

καὶ μὴν πρὸ πυλῶν ἥδ' Ἰσμήνη   (σύστημα.)
φιλάδελφα κάτω δάκρυ' εἰβομένη,   525
νεφέλη δ' ὀφρύων ὕπερ αἱματόεν
ῥέθος αἰσχύνει,
τέγγουσ' εὐῶπα παρειάν.

ΚΡΕΩΝ.

σὺ δ', ἣ κατ' οἴκους, ὡς ἔχιδν', ὑφειμένη
λήθουσά μ' ἐξέπινες, οὐδ' ἐμάνθανον   530
τρέφων δύ' ἄτα, κἀπαναστάσεις θρόνων,
φέρ', εἰπὲ δή μοι, καὶ σὺ τοῦδε τοῦ τάφου
φήσεις μετασχεῖν, ἢ 'ξομεῖ τὸ μὴ εἰδέναι;

ΙΣΜΗΝΗ.

δέδρακα τοὔργον, εἴπερ ἥδ' ὁμορροθεῖ,
καὶ ξυμμετίσχω καὶ φέρω τῆς αἰτίας.   535

ΑΝΤΙΓΟΝΗ.

ἀλλ' οὐκ ἐάσει τοῦτό γ' ἡ δίκη σ', ἐπεὶ
οὔτ' ἠθέλησας, οὔτ' ἐγὼ 'κοινωσάμην.

[519] γρ. κάτω 'στίν.

ANTIGONE.

Who knows, if strifes like these still live below!

KREON.

— The foe is ne'er a friend—not e'en in death.

ANTIGONE.

My heart is love's co-mate, not hatred's partner.

KREON.

Down then, and love them if they must be loved:
But while I live, no woman shall hold sway.

(Anapæstic Movement.)

CHORUS.

Lo! from the gates Ismene approaches,
Shedding the tears of sisterly sorrow.
And the cloud o'er the brow the bloom of the cheek with
Blushes has mantled,
Her beautiful features bedewing.

KREON.

Thou that within the palace snake-like gliding
Didst suck my blood,—nor knew I that I nurtured
Two fiends for the subversion of my throne—
Come, tell me now, wilt thou too claim a share
In this exploit, or swear thou knowest nothing!

ISMENE.

I did the deed, if she says aye to that,
And claim and bear a share in all the blame.

ANTIGONE.

Justice forbid thee that! thou didst not will it,
Nor did I give thee art or part in it.

ΙΣΜΗΝΗ.

ἀλλ' ἐν κακοῖς τοῖς σοῖσιν οὐκ αἰσχύνομαι
ξύμπλουν ἐμαυτὴν τοῦ πάθους ποιουμένη.

ΑΝΤΙΓΟΝΗ.

ὧν τοὔργον, Ἅιδης χοἰ κάτω ξυνίστορες·   540
λόγοις δ' ἐγὼ φιλοῦσαν οὐ στέργω φίλην.

ΙΣΜΗΝΗ.

μή τοι, κασιγνήτη, μ' ἀτιμάσῃς τὸ μὴ οὐ
θανεῖν τε σὺν σοί, τὸν θανόντα θ' ἁγνίσαι.

ΑΝΤΙΓΟΝΗ.

μή μοι θάνῃς σὺ κοινά, μηδ' ἃ μὴ 'θιγες
ποιοῦ σεαυτῆς. ἀρκέσω θνῄσκουσ' ἐγώ.   545

ΙΣΜΗΝΗ

καὶ τίς βίος μοι, σοῦ λελειμμένῃ, φίλος;

ΑΝΤΙΓΟΝΗ

Κρέοντ' ἐρώτα. τοῦδε γὰρ σὺ κηδεμών.

ΙΣΜΗΝΗ.

τί ταῦτ' ἀνιᾷς μ', οὐδὲν ὠφελουμένη;

ΑΝΤΙΓΟΝΗ.

ἀλγοῦσα μὲν δῆτ', εἰ γέλωτ' ἐν σοὶ γελῶ.

ΙΣΜΗΝΗ.

τί δῆτ' ἂν ἀλλὰ νῦν σ' ἔτ' ὠφελοῖμ' ἐγώ;   550

ΑΝΤΙΓΟΝΗ.

σῶσον σεαυτήν. οὐ φθονῶ σ' ὑπεκφυγεῖν.

ΙΣΜΗΝΗ.

οἴμοι τάλαινα, κἀμπλάκω τοῦ σοῦ μόρου;

ΑΝΤΙΓΟΝΗ.

σὺ μὲν γὰρ εἵλου ζῆν, ἐγὼ δὲ κατθανεῖν.

ISMENE.

Yet, in thy troubles, I am not ashamed
To mount the sinking vessel of thy fortunes.

ANTIGONE.

Death and the dead know well whose was the deed.
I scout the friend whose friendship is but words.

ISMENE.

Nay, sister, shame me not, but let me die
With thee, and with thee reverence the dead.

ANTIGONE.

Die not with me, nor claim a share in deeds
That were not thine—my death will be enough.

ISMENE.

What life is dear to me when thou art gone!

ANTIGONE.

Ask Kreon—all thy care is set on him.

ISMENE.

How canst thou utter taunts which nought avail thee!

ANTIGONE.

I laugh in sorrow, if I laugh at thee.

ISMENE.

Tell me, how I can serve thee even now!

ANTIGONE.

Preserve thyself—I grudge not thy escape.

ISMENE.

Ah! woe is me—and may I not die with thee!

ANTIGONE.

No! for thy choice was life, but mine was death.

ΙΣΜΗΝΗ.
ἀλλ' οὐκ ἐπ' ἀρρήτοις γε τοῖς ἐμοῖς λόγοις.

ΑΝΤΙΓΟΝΗ.
καλῶς σὺ μὲν τοῖς, τοῖς δ' ἐγὼ 'δόκουν φρονεῖν.   555

ΙΣΜΗΝΗ.
καὶ μὴν ἴση νῷν ἐστὶν ἡ 'ξαμαρτία.

ΑΝΤΙΓΟΝΗ.
θάρσει. σὺ μὲν ζῇς· ἡ δ' ἐμὴ ψυχὴ πάλαι
τέθνηκεν, ὥστε τοῖς θανοῦσιν ὠφελεῖν.

ΚΡΕΩΝ.
τὼ παῖδε φημὶ τώδε, τὴν μὲν ἀρτίως
ἄνουν πεφάνθαι, τὴν δ' ἀφ' οὗ τὰ πρῶτ' ἔφυ.   560

ΙΣΜΗΝΗ.
οὐ γάρ ποτ', ὦναξ, οὐδ' ὃς ἂν †βλάστῃ μένει
νοῦς τοῖς κακῶς πράσσουσιν, ἀλλ' ἐξίσταται.

ΚΡΕΩΝ.
σοὶ γοῦν, ὅθ' εἵλου ξὺν κακοῖς πράσσειν κακά.

ΙΣΜΗΝΗ.
τί γὰρ μόνῃ μοι τῆσδ' ἄτερ βιώσιμον;

ΚΡΕΩΝ.
ἀλλ' ΗΔΕ μέντοι μὴ λέγ', οὐ γὰρ ἔστ' ἔτι.   565

ΙΣΜΗΝΗ.
ἀλλὰ κτενεῖς νυμφεῖα τοῦ σαυτοῦ τέκνου;

ΚΡΕΩΝ
ἀρώσιμοι γὰρ χἀτέρων εἰσὶν γύαι.

ΙΣΜΗΝΗ.
οὐχ ὥς γ' ἐκείνῳ τῇδέ τ' ἦν ἡρμοσμένα;

⁵⁶¹ γρ. βλαστῇ.

ISMENE.

Not where my secret words remained unspoken.

ANTIGONE.

Some will applaud thy wisdom—others mine.

ISMENE.

Nay, but our absolute error was the same.

ANTIGONE.

So be it. Thou still livest; but my soul
Is dead the while, e'en since I served the dead.

KREON.

Of these two maids, it seems that one just now
Has lost the wits the other never had.

ISMENE.

Yes, sire, when sorrow comes, what sense there was
Abides no longer there, but flees away.

KREON.

True, when thou sought'st to suffer with the guilty.

ISMENE.

For what is life to me deprived of her?

KREON.

Speak not of *her;* for she exists no longer.

ISMENE.

What! wilt thou slay thine own son's bridal hopes?

KREON.

The glebes of other women may be ploughed.

ISMENE.

Where else the troth which he has plighted her?

ΚΡΕΩΝ.

κακὰς ἐγὼ γυναῖκας υἱέσιν στυγῶ.

ΑΝΤΙΓΟΝΗ.

ὦ φίλταθ' Αἷμων, ὥς σ' ἀτιμάζει πατήρ.   570

ΚΡΕΩΝ.

ἄγαν γε λυπεῖς, καὶ σὺ, καὶ τὸ σὸν λέχος.

ΧΟΡΟΣ.

ἦ γὰρ στερήσεις τῆσδε τὸν σαυτοῦ γόνον;

ΚΡΕΩΝ.

Ἅιδης ὁ παύσων τούσδε τοὺς γάμους ἔφυ.

ΧΟΡΟΣ.

δεδογμέν', ὡς ἔοικε, τήνδε κατθανεῖν.

ΚΡΕΩΝ.

καὶ σοί γε κἀμοί. μὴ τριβὰς ἔτ'· ἀλλὰ νιν   575
κομίζετ' εἴσω, δμῶες· ἐκ δὲ τοῦδε χρὴ
γυναῖκας εἶναι τάσδε μηδ' ἀνειμένας.
φεύγουσι γάρ τοι χοἰ θρασεῖς, ὅταν πέλας
ἤδη τὸν Ἅιδην εἰσορῶσι τοῦ βίου.

ϛ. ΣΤΑΣΙΜΟΝ ΔΕΥΤΕΡΟΝ.

ΧΟΡΟΣ.

ΕΥΔΑΙΜΟΝΕΣ, οἷσι κακῶν ἄγευστος αἰών.   στρ. α'.   580
ὡς γὰρ ἂν σεισθῇ θεόθεν δόμος, ἄτας
οὐδὲν ἐλλείπει, γενεᾶς ἐπὶ πλῆθος ἕρπον·
ὅμοιον ὥστε †ποντίαις
οἶδμα δυσπνόοις ὅταν

γρ. ποντίας ἁλὸς.

KREON.

No worthless woman shall espouse my son.

ANTIGONE.

Dear Hæmon, how thy father disallows thee!

KREON.

Enough, enough of thee and of thy marriage.

CHORUS.

And wilt thou tear thy child from his betrothed!

KREON.

The grave is destined to forbid these banns.

CHORUS.

So then thou thinkest to ensue her death!

KREON.

I think to do e'en as thou think'st I will.
No more delay, but take them in, ye slaves.
From henceforth it were fitting that these maidens
Should be as women are, and not at large.
For e'en the boldest fly when they behold
The grave too near a neighbour to their life.

VI. SECOND STASIMON.

CHORUS.

Strophe 1.

Blessed are they whose race has 'scaped
  The first taste of disaster!
  For those, whose house from heaven
  Has once received a shock,
Down to the very fulness of their race
Shall nothing lack of mischief.
Just so, when Thracian blasts are blowing

Θρήσσησιν ἔρεβος ὕφαλον ἐπιδράμῃ πνοαῖς, κυλίνδει 585
   βυσσόθεν κελαινὰν
   θῖνα καὶ δυσάνεμον,
στόνῳ βρέμουσι δ' ἀντιπλῆγες ἀκταί.

   ἀρχαῖα τὰ Λαβδακιδᾶν οἴκων ὁρῶμαι   ἀντιστ. ά.
   πήματα †φθιτῶν ἐπὶ πήμασι πίπτοντ'· 590
   οὐδ' ἀπαλλάσσει γενεὰν γένος, ἀλλ' ἐρείπει
      θεῶν τις, οὐδ' ἔχει λύσιν.
      νῦν γὰρ ἐσχάτας ὑπὲρ
ῥίζας ὃ τέτατο φάος ἐν Οἰδίπου δόμοις, κατ' αὖ νιν
      φοινία θεῶν τῶν 595
      νερτέρων ἀμᾷ κόνις,
λόγου τ' ἄνοια, καὶ φρενῶν Ἐρινύς.

   τεάν, Ζεῦ, δύνασιν τίς ἀνδρῶν   στρ. β'.
   ὑπερβασίᾳ κατάσχοι,
τὰν οὔθ' ὕπνος αἱρεῖ ποθ' ὁ *παγκρατὴς οὔτ' 600
   ἀκάματοι *θέοντες
μῆνες· ἀγήρῳ δὲ χρόνῳ δυνάστας κατέχεις Ὀλύμπου
   μαρμαρόεσσαν αἴγλαν.
   τό τ' ἔπειτα, καὶ τὸ μέλλον,
   καὶ τὸ πρὶν ἐπαρκέσει 605
   νόμος ὅδ' *[ἀνδρὸς αἶσαν·]
"θνατῶν βιότῳ πάμπολις *εἶσιν ἄτα."

      ⁵⁹⁰ γρ. φθιμένων.   ⁶⁰⁴ λείπει ὁ.
      ⁶⁰⁰ γρ. παντογήρως.   ⁶⁰¹ γρ. θεῶν.
      ⁶⁰⁶ γρ. οὐδὲν ἕρπει.   ⁶⁰⁷ γρ. ἐκτὸς ἄτας.

Strong from the sea-ward,
The undulations rushing o'er
The ~kness submarine,
Roll downwards, wave on wave, until they stir
From lowest depths
The gloom-encompass'd, storm-defying shingle:
Loud roar the breakers on the counter-cliffs!

ANTISTROPHE II

From old beginnings spring the ills
Of the Labdakid race,
Which now descending I behold
On ills heapt up before for those
Who moulder in the grave. The sire
Quits not his children.
Some God still works their ruin,
And none unties the knot of fate!
For now what light had beamed
O'er the last root
Within the house of Œdipus, again
The deathful dust of Gods that reign below
Is levell'd o'er it,
By foolish speech and frantic indignation.

STROPHE II.

Thy power, O Zeus, what sin of men can touch!
That power, which neither sleep, all-conquering, can
    master,
Nor months unwearied in their ceaseless race.
But thou—a potentate through time which grows not
    old—
Rulest the glittering splendours of Olympus.
For the present and the future and the past,
This law will meetly tell man's destiny:
" In all the life of mortals
" Mischief in every state her franchise claims."

ἁ γὰρ δὴ πολύπλαγκτος ἐλπὶς   ἀντ. β'.
πολλοῖς μὲν ὄνασις ἀνδρῶν,
πολλοῖς δ' ἀπάτα κουφονόων ἐρώτων·   610
εἰδότι δ' οὐδὲν ἕρπει,
πρὶν πυρὶ θερμῷ πόδα τις προσαύσῃ. σοφίᾳ γὰρ ἔκ του
κλεινὸν ἔπος πέφανται·
"Τὸ κακὸν δοκεῖν ποτ' ἐσθλὸν
τῷδ' ἔμμεν, ὅτῳ φρένας   615
θεὸς ἄγει πρὸς ἄταν·
πράσσει δ' ὀλιγοστὸν χρόνον ἐκτὸς *ἄλγους."

ὅδε μὴν Αἵμων, παίδων τῶν σῶν   (σύστημα)
νέατον γέννημ'· ἆρ' ἀχνύμενος
τάλιδος ἥκει μόρον Ἀντιγόνης,   620
ἀπάτας λεχέων ὑπεραλγῶν;

Z. ΕΠΕΙΣΟΔΙΟΝ ΤΡΙΤΟΝ.

ΚΡΕΩΝ.

Τάχ' εἰσόμεσθα μάντεων ὑπέρτερον.
ὦ παῖ, τελείαν ψῆφον ἆρα μὴ κλύων
τῆς μελλονύμφου, πατρὶ λυσσαίνων πάρει;
ἢ σοὶ μὲν ἡμεῖς πανταχῇ δρῶντες φίλοι;   625

ΑΙΜΩΝ.

πάτερ, σός εἰμι· καὶ σύ μοι γνώμας ἔχων
χρηστὰς ἀπορθοῖς, αἷς ἔγωγ' ἐφέψομαι.
ἐμοὶ γὰρ οὐδεὶς ἀξίως ἔσται γάμος
μείζων φέρεσθαι, σοῦ καλῶς ἡγουμένου.

[617] γρ. ἄτας.   [620] γρ. τῆς μελλογάμου τάλιδος.

Antistrophe ii.

In truth to many men, hope, though deceiving many,
Turns to advantage; yet to many more
'Tis but the mockery of love's flighty purpose.
Nothing knows he, to whom this disappointment cometh,
Until his foot hath touched the glowing flame.
Wisely by some one is this strain set forth:
" Evil seems ever good to him whose mind
" God leadeth on to mischief.
" Short is the time which sees him free from anguish."

(Anapæstic Movement.)

Lo to thee, Hæmon,—of all thy children
Alone he survives: and cometh he vexed
By the destined fate of his bride Antigone,
For the loss of his nuptials grieving!

VII. THIRD EPISODE.

KREON.

Soon shall we know better than seers could tell us.
Thou com'st not, boy, incensed against thy father,
On tidings of the doom of thy betrothed one!
Howso we act, thou, if thou only, lov'st us!

HÆMON.

Father, I am thine only: and if thou
Resolvest wisely, thou provid'st for me
An even rule of life which I will follow.
For, as right reason dictates, never shall
A wife bear in my eyes a higher price
Than thou, while wisdom marks thy guidance of me.

ΚΡΕΩΝ.

οὕτω γὰρ, ὦ παῖ, χρὴ διὰ στέρνων ἔχειν, 630
γνώμης πατρῴας πάντ' ὄπισθεν ἑστάναι.
τούτου γὰρ *εἵνεκ' ἄνδρες εὔχονται γονὰς
κατηκόους φύσαντες ἐν δόμοις ἔχειν,
ὡς καὶ τὸν ἐχθρὸν ἀνταμύνωνται κακοῖς,
καὶ τὸν φίλον τιμῶσιν ἐξ ἴσου πατρί. 635
ὅστις δ' ἀνωφέλητα φιτύει τέκνα,
τί τόνδ' ἂν εἴποις ἄλλο πλὴν αὑτῷ †πέδας
φῦσαι, πολὺν δὲ τοῖσιν ἐχθροῖσιν γέλων;
μή νύν ποτ', ὦ παῖ, τὰς φρένας †πρὸς ἡδονῆς,
γυναικὸς *εἵνεκ', ἐκβάλῃς, εἰδὼς ὅτι 640
ψυχρὸν παραγκάλισμα τοῦτο γίγνεται,
γυνὴ κακὴ ξύνευνος ἐν δόμοις. τί γὰρ
γένοιτ' ἂν ἕλκος μεῖζον ἢ φίλος κακός;
ἀλλὰ πτύσας ὡσεί τε δυσμενῆ, μέθες
τὴν παῖδ' ἐν Ἅιδου τήνδε νυμφεύειν τινί. 645
ἐπεὶ γὰρ αὐτὴν εἷλον ἐμφανῶς ἐγὼ
πόλεως ἀπιστήσασαν ἐκ πάσης μόνην,
ψευδῆ γ' ἐμαυτὸν οὐ καταστήσω πόλει,
ἀλλὰ κτενῶ. πρὸς ταῦτ' ἐφυμνείτω Δία
Ξύναιμον. εἰ γὰρ δὴ †τά γ' ἐγγενῆ φύσει 650
ἄκοσμα θρέψω, κάρτα τοὺς ἔξω γένους.
ἐν τοῖς γὰρ οἰκείοισιν ὅστις ἔστ' ἀνὴρ
χρηστός, φανεῖται κἀν πόλει δίκαιος ὤν.
ὅστις δ' ὑπερβὰς ἢ νόμους βιάζεται,
ἢ τοὐπιτάσσειν τοῖς †κρατύνουσιν νοεῖ, 655
οὐκ ἔστ' ἐπαίνου τοῦτον ἐξ ἐμοῦ τυχεῖν.

---

⁶³² γρ. οὕνεκ'.   ⁶³⁷ γρ. πόνους.
⁶³⁹ γρ. γ' ὑφ'.   ⁶⁴⁰ γρ. οὕνεκ'.
⁶⁵⁰ γρ. τά τ'.   ⁶⁵⁵ γρ. κρατοῦσιν ἐννοεῖ.

KREON.

Such thoughts, my son, should rule thy bosom ever:
A son in all his acts should yield the lead
To what his sire resolves. It is for this
That men beseech the Gods to give the children,
Whom they beget and keep at home, a spirit
Of dutiful obedience, that so
They may requite with ill their father's foe,
And honour whom their father loves to honour.
But when a man's own children help him not,
What shall we say he has begotten but
Clogs for himself and laughter for his foes?
Then be it far from thee, my son, for lust
And for a woman's love, to make a shipwreck
Of all thy understanding, knowing that
Cold mocks the warmth of thy embraces when
A vile companion of thy bed holds sway
Within thy house and home. For who could probe
A wound more festering than a faithless friend?
Then spurn this maid, and cast her off as one
Whose heart is hostile to thee, so that she
May seek some spouse within the realm of Hades.
For now that I have caught her openly
Alone of all the city disobedient,
I will not place myself before the state
As one whose words are naught: but she shall die.
Then let her weary with repeated prayers
Zeus, who protects the ties of blood relations.
For if I rear obedient to no rule
Those who are born within my family,
How shall I govern those without the pale?
For whoso in his household acts discreetly,
In public also will approve himself
A righteous man. But whoso wantonly
Or strains the laws or sets about dictating
To those who rule, it is not possible
That such a one should ever earn my praise.

SOPH. ANTIG. F

ἀλλ' ὃν πόλις στήσειε, τοῦδε χρὴ κλύειν,
καὶ σμικρὰ, καὶ δίκαια, καὶ τἀναντία.]
καὶ τοῦτον ἂν τὸν ἄνδρα θαρσοίην ἐγὼ
καλῶς μὲν ἄρχειν, εὖ δ' ἂν ἄρχεσθαι θέλειν·   660
δορός τ' ἂν ἐν χειμῶνι προστεταγμένον
μένειν δίκαιον κἀγαθὸν παραστάτην.
ἀναρχίας δὲ μεῖζον οὐκ ἔστιν κακόν.
αὕτη πόλεις τ' ὄλλυσιν, ἥδ' ἀναστάτους
οἴκους τίθησιν, ἥδε σὺν μάχῃ δορὸς   665
τροπὰς καταρρήγνυσι· τῶν δ' ὀρθουμένων
σώζει τὰ πολλὰ σώμαθ' ἡ πειθαρχία.
οὕτως ἀμυντέ᾽ ἐστὶ τοῖς κοσμουμένοις,
κοὔτοι γυναικὸς οὐδαμῶς ἡσσητέα.
κρεῖσσον γὰρ, εἴπερ δεῖ, πρὸς ἀνδρὸς ἐκπεσεῖν   670
κοὐκ ἂν γυναικῶν ἥσσονες καλοίμεθ' ἄν.

ΧΟΡΟΣ.

ἡμῖν μὲν, εἰ μὴ τῷ χρόνῳ κεκλέμμεθα,
λέγειν φρονούντως ὧν λέγεις δοκεῖς πέρι.

ΑΙΜΩΝ.

πάτερ, θεοὶ φύουσιν ἀνθρώποις φρένας,
πάντων, ὅσ' ἐστὶ, κτημάτων ὑπέρτατον.   675
ἐγὼ δ' ὅπως σὺ μὴ λέγεις ὀρθῶς τάδε,
οὔτ' ἂν δυναίμην, μήτ' ἐπισταίμην λέγειν·
γένοιτο μέντἂν χἀτέρῳ καλῶς ἔχον.
σοῦ δ' οὖν πέφυκα πάντα προσκοπεῖν, ὅσα
λέγει τις, ἢ πράσσει τις, ἢ ψέγειν ἔχει.   680

No! when a city constitutes a chief,
It well befitteth all men to obey
His great or small, just or unjust, behests.
And I should confidently trust that he,
Whose law is such, would from fixed habitude
Both wisely rule and loyally obey.
He too, when posted in the battled line,
Amid the storm of fight, would keep his ground,
Brave and unswerving by his comrade's side.
There is no greater ill than disobedience.
'Tis this which ruins cities: this it is
Which works the downfall of the noble house.
And when, in battle, spear is locked with spear,
'Tis this again which breaks and routs the phalanx.
But when men keep the line, their discipline
For the most part ensures their safety. Thus,
It is our duty still to aid the laws,
And power must ne'er be yielded to a woman.
For if we must succumb, 'twere better far
To crouch before a man; and thus at least
No one could taunt us with a woman's rule.

CHORUS.

To us at least, unless old age misleads us,
Thou seemest to say wisely all thou say'st.

HAEMON.

The Gods, my father, nourish in the soul
The growth of wisdom, best of all possessions.
But I should lack the power, and may I ne'er
Be skilled to tax with error these thy words.
Howbeit that task might well beseem another.
And, as thy son, it is my natural office
To watch, on thy behalf, the sayings, doings,
And grievances of every citizen.

τὸ γὰρ σὸν ὄμμα δεινὸν ἀνδρὶ δημότῃ,
λόγοις τοιούτοις, οἷς σὺ μὴ τέρψει κλύων·
ἐμοὶ δ' ἀκούειν ἔσθ' ὑπὸ σκότου τάδε,
τὴν παῖδα ταύτην οἷ' ὀδύρεται πόλις,
πασῶν γυναικῶν ὡς ἀναξιωτάτη   685
κάκιστ' ἀπ' ἔργων εὐκλεεστάτων φθίνει·
ἥτις τὸν αὑτῆς αὐτάδελφον ἐν φοναῖς
πεπτῶτ' ἄθαπτον, μήθ' ὑπ' ὠμηστῶν κυνῶν
εἴασ' ὀλέσθαι, μήθ' ὑπ' οἰωνῶν τινος·
οὐχ ἥδε χρυσῆς ἀξία τιμῆς λαχεῖν;   690
τοιάδ' ἐρεμνὴ σῖγ' ἐπέρχεται φάτις.
ἐμοὶ δέ, σοῦ πράσσοντος εὐτυχῶς, πάτερ,
οὐκ ἔστιν οὐδὲν κτῆμα τιμιώτερον.
τί γὰρ πατρὸς θάλλοντος εὐκλείας τέκνοις
ἄγαλμα μεῖζον, ἢ τί πρὸς παίδων πατρί;   695
μή νυν ἓν ἦθος μοῦνον ἐν σαυτῷ φόρει,
ὡς φὴς σύ, κοὐδὲν ἄλλο, τοῦτ' ὀρθῶς ἔχειν.
ὅστις γὰρ αὐτὸς ἢ φρονεῖν μόνος δοκεῖ,
ἢ γλῶσσαν, ἣν οὐκ ἄλλος, ἢ ψυχὴν ἔχειν,
οὗτοι διαπτυχθέντες, ὤφθησαν κενοί.   700
ἀλλ' ἄνδρα κεἴ τις ᾖ σοφός, τὸ μανθάνειν
πόλλ', αἰσχρὸν οὐδέν, καὶ τὸ μὴ τείνειν ἄγαν.
ὁρᾷς παρὰ ῥείθροισι χειμάρροις ὅσα
δένδρων ὑπείκει, κλῶνας ὡς ἐκσώζεται·
τὰ δ' ἀντιτείνοντ' αὐτόπρεμν' ἀπόλλυται.   705
αὔτως δὲ ναὸς ὅστις ἐγκρατῆ πόδα
τείνας, ὑπείκει μηδέν, ὑπτίοις κάτω
στρέψας τὸ λοιπὸν σέλμασιν ναυτίλλεται.
ἀλλ' εἶκε θυμοῦ καὶ μετάστασιν δίδου.
γνώμῃ γὰρ εἴ τις κἀπ' ἐμοῦ νεωτέρου   710

Thine eye might well deter the common burgess
From speeches which would grate upon thine ear.
But *I* can hear the covert lamentations
Wherewith the city grieveth for this maiden—
How of all women most unworthy she
Meets basest death for deeds most glorious.
" For *she*," say they, " who, when her very brother
Had fallen in bloodshed and unburied lay,
Would not permit him to be rent and torn
By carrion-eating dogs and greedy birds—
Doth *she* not merit golden recompense ?"
Such the dark rumour that in silence spreads.
But, O my father, thy prosperity
In worth transcends all other goods beside.
For where can children find a greater shoon
Of glory than their father's high estate!
Or where a father, than his children's bliss!
Then cleave not solely to this principle—
Thy words, no other man's, are free from error.
For whoso thinks that he alone is wise,
That his discourse and reason are unmatched,
He, when unwrapt, displays his emptiness.
But that a man, how wise soe'er, should learn
In many things and slack his stubborn will,
This is no derogation. When the streams
Are swollen by mountain-torrents, thou hast seen
That all the trees which bend them to the flood
Preserve their branches from the angry current,
While those which stem it perish root and branch.
So too the pilot, when he keeps the sheet
Taught and ne'er slacks it, overturns his bark,
And sails, what else he sails, with thwarts reversed.
Then stoop from anger and ensue a change
Of will and purpose: for, if grounded maxims

πρόσεστι, φήμ' ἔγωγε πρεσβεύειν πολύ,
φῦναι τὸν ἄνδρα πάντ' ἐπιστήμης πλέων·
εἰ δ' οὖν, φιλεῖ γὰρ τοῦτο μὴ ταύτῃ ῥέπειν,
καὶ τῶν λεγόντων εὖ καλὸν τὸ μανθάνειν.

ΧΟΡΟΣ.
ἄναξ, σέ τ' εἰκὸς, εἴ τι καίριον λέγει, 715
μαθεῖν, σέ τ' αὖ τοῦδ'· εὖ γὰρ εἴρηται διπλῇ.

ΚΡΕΩΝ.
οἱ τηλικοίδε καὶ διδαξόμεσθα δὴ
φρονεῖν πρὸς ἀνδρὸς τηλικοῦδε τὴν φύσιν;

ΑΙΜΩΝ.
μηδὲν τὸ μὴ δίκαιον· εἰ δ' ἐγὼ νέος,
οὐ τὸν χρόνον χρὴ μᾶλλον ἢ τἄργα σκοπεῖν. 720

ΚΡΕΩΝ.
ἔργον γάρ ἐστι τοὺς ἀκοσμοῦντας σέβειν;

ΑΙΜΩΝ.
οὐδ' ἂν κελεύσαιμ' εὐσεβεῖν εἰς τοὺς κακούς.

ΚΡΕΩΝ.
οὐχ ἥδε γὰρ τοιᾷδ' ἐπείληπται νόσῳ;

ΑΙΜΩΝ.
οὔ φησι Θήβας τῆσδ' ὁμόπτολις λεώς.

ΚΡΕΩΝ.
πόλις γὰρ ἡμῖν ἁμὲ χρὴ τάσσειν ἐρεῖ; 725

ΑΙΜΩΝ.
ὁρᾷς τόδ' ὡς εἴρηκας ὡς ἄγαν νέος;

ΚΡΕΩΝ.
ἄλλῳ γὰρ ἢ 'μοὶ χρὴ *'πὶ τῆσδ' ἄρχειν χθονός;

⁷²⁷ γρ. χρή γε.

May find their utterance e'en in me your son,
I dare be bold to say 'tis better far
That understanding should be born in man:
But if this may not be:—and, to say sooth,
The common scale inclines not thus,—'tis well
To learn from any one who reasons soundly.

CHORUS.
Sire, thou shouldst learn where he has hit the mark:
Thou too from him: for both have spoken well.

KREON.
And shall we, in our riper age, receive
Lessons in prudence from his youthful mind!

HÆMON.
In nought but what is just. If I am young,
'Tis meet to scan my purpose, not my years.

KREON.
Is't this—to pay respect to the unruly!

HÆMON.
Not to the base, though 'twere to please the Gods.

KREON.
And is not she caught in this malady!

HÆMON.
The folk who throng this city answer, *No!*

KREON.
What! does the city's pleasure guide my mandates!

HÆMON.
Seest thou what childish words thou utterest!

KREON.
Why, who but I should in this country rule!

ΑΙΜΩΝ.
πόλις γὰρ οὐκ ἔσθ', ἥτις ἀνδρός ἐσθ' ἑνός.

ΚΡΕΩΝ.
οὐ τοῦ κρατοῦντος ἡ πόλις νομίζεται;

ΑΙΜΩΝ.
καλῶς ἐρήμης γ' ἂν σὺ γῆς ἄρχοις μόνος.   730

ΚΡΕΩΝ.
ὅδ', ὡς ἔοικε, τῇ γυναικὶ συμμαχεῖ.

ΑΙΜΩΝ.
εἴπερ γυνὴ σύ· σοῦ γὰρ οὖν προκήδομαι.

ΚΡΕΩΝ.
ὦ παγκάκιστε, διὰ δίκης ἰὼν πατρί.

ΑΙΜΩΝ.
οὐ γὰρ δίκαιά σ' ἐξαμαρτάνονθ' ὁρῶ.

ΚΡΕΩΝ.
ἁμαρτάνω γὰρ τὰς ἐμὰς ἀρχὰς σέβων;   735

ΑΙΜΩΝ.
οὐ γὰρ σέβεις, τιμάς γε τὰς θεῶν πατῶν.

ΚΡΕΩΝ.
ὦ μιαρὸν ἦθος, καὶ γυναικὸς ὕστερον.

ΑΙΜΩΝ.
†οὔταν ἕλοις ἥσσω με τῶν αἰσχρῶν ποτε.

ΚΡΕΩΝ.
ὁ γοῦν λόγος σοι πᾶς ὑπὲρ κείνης ὅδε.

ΑΙΜΩΝ.
καὶ σοῦ γε κἀμοῦ καὶ θεῶν τῶν νερτέρων.   740

ΚΡΕΩΝ.
ταύτην ποτ' οὐκ ἔσθ' ὡς ἔτι ζῶσαν γαμεῖς.

[738] γρ. οὐκ ἄν.

ANTIGONE. 73

HÆMON.
That is no city which belongs to one.

KREON.
Is not the city called of him who governs?

HÆMON.
Well wouldst thou rule alone an empty land!

KREON.
Here we have one who fights a woman's battle.

HÆMON.
If thou art woman—for I sue for *thee*.

KREON.
Vile boy, to take thy father's suit in hand.

HÆMON.
Yes, for thy errors are unsuitable.

KREON.
And suits it not mine office to respect?

HÆMON.
When that thou spurnst the Gods thou nought respectest.

KREON.
O paltry character—a woman's slave!

HÆMON.
Slave to dishonour thou shalt never find me.

KREON.
Thy whole discourse but advocates her cause.

HÆMON.
And thine and mine, and of the Gods below.

KREON.
Living this maid shall never be thy bride.

ΑΝΤΙΓΟΝΗ.

ΑΙΜΩΝ.
ἥδ᾽ οὖν θανεῖται, καὶ θανοῦσ᾽ ὀλεῖ τινα.

ΚΡΕΩΝ.
ἦ κἀπαπειλῶν ὧδ᾽ ἐπεξέρχει θρασύς;

ΑΙΜΩΝ.
τίς δ᾽ ἔστ᾽ ἀπειλὴ πρὸς κενὰς γνώμας λέγειν;

ΚΡΕΩΝ.
κλαίων φρενώσεις, ὢν φρενῶν αὐτὸς κενός.   745

ΑΙΜΩΝ.
εἰ μὴ πατὴρ ἦσθ᾽, εἶπον ἄν σ᾽ οὐκ εὖ φρονεῖν.

ΚΡΕΩΝ.
γυναικὸς ὢν δούλευμα, μὴ κώτιλλέ με.

ΑΙΜΩΝ.
βούλει λέγειν τι, καὶ λέγων μηδὲν κλύειν;

ΚΡΕΩΝ.
ἄληθες; ἀλλ᾽ οὐ, τόνδ᾽ Ὄλυμπον, ἴσθ᾽ ὅτι
χαίρων ἐπὶ ψόγοισι δεννάσεις ἐμέ.   750
ἄγετε τὸ μῖσος, ὡς κατ᾽ ὄμματ᾽ αὐτίκα
παρόντι θνήσκῃ πλησία τῷ νυμφίῳ.

ΑΙΜΩΝ.
οὐ δῆτ᾽ ἔμοιγε, τοῦτο μὴ δόξῃς ποτὲ,
οὔθ᾽ ἥδ᾽ ὀλεῖται πλησία, σύ τ᾽ οὐδαμὰ
τοὐμὸν προσόψει κρᾶτ᾽ ἐν ὀφθαλμοῖς ὁρῶν,   755
ὡς τοῖς θέλουσι τῶν φίλων μαίνῃ ξυνών.

ΧΟΡΟΣ.
ἀνήρ, ἄναξ, βέβηκεν ἐξ ὀργῆς ταχύς·
νοῦς δ᾽ ἐστὶ τηλικοῦτος ἀλγήσας βαρύς.

ANTIGONE.

HÆMON.
Dies she, her death shall work the death of some one.

KREON.
And dares thy boldness vent itself in threats!

HÆMON.
What threats, to speak against an empty meaning!

KREON.
Unschooled thyself, beware of schooling me.

HÆMON.
Wert not my father, I had call'd thee simple.

KREON.
Away with thy small wit, thou woman's serf!

HÆMON.
Wouldst speak, and speaking never hear an answer!

KREON.
And is it so indeed! Nay, by Olympus,
Thou shalt not thus unscathed vituperate.
Bring forth the hateful minx, that, on the spot,
Before his very eyes she meet her doom,
And die, her 'fianced bridegroom standing by her.

HÆMON.
She dies not in my presence—never think it—
And thou shalt never see my face again
With real vision. If it liketh any
Among thy friends—let them thy madness share.

Exit Hæmon.

CHORUS.
The prince, my liege, is gone in anger hasty—
Deep is the pain that pangs the youthful mind.

ΚΡΕΩΝ.

δράτω, φρονείτω μεῖζον, ἢ κατ' ἄνδρ', ἰών·
τὰ δ' οὖν κόρα τάδ' οὐκ ἀπαλλάξει μόρου.   760

ΧΟΡΟΣ.

ἄμφω γὰρ αὐτὰ καὶ κατακτεῖναι νοεῖς;

ΚΡΕΩΝ.

οὐ τήν γε μὴ θιγοῦσαν. εὖ γὰρ οὖν λέγεις.

ΧΟΡΟΣ.

μόρῳ δὲ ποίῳ καί σφε βουλεύει κτανεῖν;

ΚΡΕΩΝ.

ἄγων ἔρημος ἔνθ' ἂν ᾖ βροτῶν στίβος,
κρύψω πετρώδει ζῶσαν ἐν κατώρυχι,   765
φορβῆς τοσοῦτον, ὡς ἄγος μόνον, προθείς,
ὅπως μίασμα πᾶσ' ὑπεκφύγῃ πόλις.
κἀκεῖ τὸν Ἅιδην, ὃν μόνον σέβει θεῶν,
αἰτουμένη που, τεύξεται τὸ μὴ θανεῖν,
ἢ γνώσεται γοῦν ἀλλὰ τηνικαῦθ', ὅτι   770
πόνος περισσός ἐστι τὰν Ἅιδου σέβειν.

Η. ΣΤΑΣΙΜΟΝ ΤΡΙΤΟΝ.

ΧΟΡΟΣ.

Ἔρως ἀνίκατε μάχαν,   στροφή.
Ἔρως, ὃς ἐν κτήμασι πίπτεις, ὃς ἐν μαλακαῖς παρει-
  αῖς νεάνιδος ἐννυχεύεις·
φοιτᾷς δ' ὑπερπόντιος, ἔν τ' ἀγρονόμοις αὐλαῖς· 775
καί σ' οὔτ' ἀθανάτων φύξιμος οὐδείς,
οὔθ' ἁμερίων ἐπ' ἀνθρώπων· ὁ δ' ἔχων, μέμηνεν.

KREON.

Be then his thoughts and actions more than mortal.
He shall not quit from death these maidens two.

CHORUS.

And hast thou doomed them both to instant death!

KREON.

Not her who touched him not.—Thou sayest well.

CHORUS.

And for the other, what the mode of death!

KREON.

Where mortal feet have never stopt I'll take her,
And there entomb her in a rocky chamber,
Alive, with so much food before her set
As may suffice to expiate the curse,
That so the general city 'scape pollution.
And there, beseeching Hades, whom alone
Of all the Gods she worships, let her gain,
If gain she can, a license not to die:
Or, come what will, she then at least will learn
'Tis wasted toil to reverence the dead.

VIII. THIRD STASIMON.

CHORUS.

Strophe.

Love! in the fight invincible:
Love! whose attacks at once enslave:
Who on the young maid's delicate cheeks thy nightly
    vigils keepest:
Who roamest o'er the main and mid the rustic cots!
None can escape thee,—neither Gods immortal,
Nor men whose lives are fleeting as the day:
He raves whom thou possessest.

σὺ καὶ δικαίων ἀδίκους   ἀντιστ.
φρένας παρασπᾷς ἐπὶ λώβᾳ· σὺ καὶ τόδε νεῖκος ἀν-
    δρῶν ξύναιμον ἔχεις ταράξας·   780
νικᾷ δ᾽ ἐναργὴς βλεφάρων ἵμερος εὐλέκτρου
νύμφας, τῶν μεγάλων *παιδὶ πάρεδρος
θεσμῶν· ἄμαχος γὰρ ἐμπαίζει θεὸς Ἀφροδίτα.

νῦν δ᾽ ἤδη ᾽γὼ καὐτὸς θεσμῶν   σύστημα.
ἔξω φέρομαι τάδ᾽ ὁρῶν, ἴσχειν δ᾽   785
οὐκ ἔτι πηγὰς δύναμαι δακρύων,
τὸν παγκοίταν ὅθ᾽ ὁρῶ θάλαμον
τήνδ᾽ Ἀντιγόνην ἀνύτουσαν.

Θ. ΕΠΕΙΣΟΔΙΟΝ ΤΕΤΑΡΤΟΝ ΚΑΙ ΚΟΜΜΟΣ ΠΡΩΤΟΣ.

ΑΝΤΙΓΟΝΗ.

ὉΡΑΤ᾽ ἔμ᾽, ὦ γᾶς πατρίας πολῖται,   στρ. α´.
    τὰν νεάταν ὁδὸν   790
στείχουσαν, νέατον δὲ φέγγος
    λεύσσουσαν ἀελίου, κού ποτ᾽ αὖθις· ἀλλά μ᾽ ὁ παγ-
        κοίτας
    Ἅιδας ζῶσαν ἄγει
    τὰν Ἀχέροντος
    ἀκτάν, οὔθ᾽ ὑμεναίων   795
ἔγκληρον, οὔτ᾽ †ἐπινύμφειός† πω μέ τις ὕμνος
ὕμνησεν, ἀλλ᾽ Ἀχέροντι νυμφεύσω.

782 γρ. μεγ. πάρεδρος ἐν ἀρχαῖς.   796 γρ. ἐπινυμφίδιος.

ANTISTROPHE.

Thou too the upright mind to wrong pervertest,
Till mischief comes.
Thou too hast stirred this strife of kindred men.
Love, that was learnèd in the lustrous eyes
Of her whose bridal bed he coveted,
A son constrains,
Benching for him, with equal voice,
Beside the holiest laws: for there resistless
The goddess Aphrodite holds her revels.

(Antigone is led forth by the guards.)

(Anapæstic Movement.)

I, even I, from the bondage of laws am
Carried away, as this spectacle greets me!
Fountains of tears no longer I check when I
See Antigone bound for the chamber where
All men are destined to slumber.

IX. FOURTH EPISODE AND FIRST KOMMOS.

ANTIGONE.

See me, ye citizens of my father-land,
Treading the last of paths,—the latest sun-light
Beholding now, and ne'er again. But Hades,
Who lays all men to rest, leads *me* still living
To the banks of Acheron;
The Hymenæal strain denied me,
Nor hath any bridal hymn
Hymned me as yet; but Acheron will wed me.

ΧΟΡΟΣ.

οὐκοῦν κλεινὴ καὶ ἔπαινον ἔχουσ'
ἐς τόδ' ἀπέρχει κεῦθος νεκύων,
οὔτε φθινάσιν πληγεῖσα νόσοις,   800
οὔτε ξιφέων ἐπίχειρα λαχοῦσ'·
ἀλλ' αὐτόνομος, ζῶσα, μόνη δὴ
θνατῶν, Ἀίδαν καταβήσει.

ΑΝΤΙΓΟΝΗ.

ἤκουσα δὴ λυγροτάταν ὀλέσθαι   ἀντιστ. α'.
   τὰν Φρυγίαν ξέναν   805
Ταντάλου, Σιπύλῳ πρὸς ἄκρῳ·
   τὰν, κισσὸς ὡς ἀτενὴς, πετραία βλάστα δάμασεν·
καί νιν
†ὄμβροι τακομέναν,
ὡς φάτις ἀνδρῶν,
χιών τ' οὐδαμὰ λείπει,   810
τέγγει †δ' ὑπ' ὀφρύσι παγκλαύτοις δειράδας· ᾇ με
δαίμων ὁμοιοτάταν κατευνάζει.

ΧΟΡΟΣ.

ἀλλὰ θεός τοι καὶ θεογεννής·
ἡμεῖς δὲ βροτοὶ καὶ θνητογενεῖς·
καί τοι φθιμένῳ τοῖς ἰσοθέοις   815
ἔγκληρα λαχεῖν μέγ' ἀκοῦσαι.

ΑΝΤΙΓΟΝΗ.

οἴμοι γελῶμαι. τί με, πρὸς θεῶν πατρῴων,   στρ. β'.
οὐκ †οὐλομέναν ὑβρίζεις,
   ἀλλ' ἐπίφαντον;

---
[800] γρ. ὄμβρῳ.   [811] γρ. τέγγει θ'.
[814, 815] γρ. μέγ' ἀκοῦσαι τοῖς ἰσοθ. ἔγκληρα λαχεῖν.
[818] γρ. ὀλομέναν.

CHORUS.

Nay, but renowned and freighted with praises,
To the dark recess of the dead thou departest.
Wasting disease has not smitten thy form,
Nor the meed of the sword thy portion has been.
Self-controlled and alive thou wilt go,
Thou only of mortals, to Hades!

ANTIGONE.

Erewhile I heard how piteously perished
That Phrygian dame, who came to rule among us,
The child of Tantalus,
Whom, clinging to her as the ivy clings,
A sprouting rock controlled,
And as she wastes away, the legend tells us,
She lacks nor rain nor snow,
But still, beneath her ever-weeping brows,
Bedeweth she her bosom:
Likest to her, fate leads me to my rest!

CHORUS.

A Goddess was she, and Gods were her fathers:
We are but mortals, and mortal our sires:
Bethink thee how great for a perishing soul,
To challenge the fame of the Godlike!

ANTIGONE.

Ah! I am laughed to scorn! why by my father's Gods
Dost so deride me ere my death,
While yet the sun beholds me?

SOPH. ANT.   G

ΑΝΤΙΓΟΝΗ.

ὦ πόλις, ὦ πόλεως 820
πολυκτήμονες ἄνδρες·
ἰὼ Διρκαῖαι κρῆναι, Θήβας τ'
εὐαρμάτου ἄλσος, ἔμπας
ξυμμάρτυρας ὔμμ' ἐπικτῶμαι,
οἵα φίλων ἄκλαυτος, οἵοις νόμοις 825
πρὸς †ἔρμα τυμβόχωστον ἔρχομαι τάφου ποταινίου,
  ἰὼ δύστανος,
οὔτ' ἐν †τοῖσιν ἔτ', οὔτε τοῖσιν
μέτοικος, οὐ ζῶσιν, οὐ θανοῦσιν,

ΧΟΡΟΣ.

προβᾶσ' ἐπ' ἔσχατον θράσους, 830
ὑψηλὸν ἐς Δίκας βάθρον
προσέπεσες, ὦ τέκνον, πολύ.
πατρῷον δ' *ἐκτελεῖς τιν' ἆθλον.

ΑΝΤΙΓΟΝΗ.

ἔψαυσας ἀλγεινοτάτας ἐμοὶ μερίμνας, ἀντιστ. β'.
πατρὸς τριπόλιστον †οἶτον, 835
  τοῦ τε πρόπαντος
  ἁμετέρου πότμου
κλεινοῖς Λαβδακίδαισιν.
  ἰὼ ματρῷαι λέκτρων ἆται,
κοιμήματά τ' αὐτογέννητ' 840
ἀμῷ πατρὶ δυσμόρου ματρός,
οἵων ἐγώ ποθ' ἁ ταλαίφρων ἔφυν·
πρὸς οὕς ἀραῖος, ἄγαμος, ἅδ' ἐγὼ μέτοικος ἔρχομαι.

―――

823 γρ. ἔρμα.   828 γρ. βροτοῖσιν οὔτ' ἐν νεκροῖσι.
831 γρ. ἐκτείνεις.   843 γρ. οἶκτον.

City, and citizens of high estate,
Ah! and ye streams of Dirke, and thou grove
Of Thebe car-renowned,
You at least I gain
For me as fellow-witnesses,
How by my friends unwept, by laws how cruel,
I go to the tomb-heapt mound of a strange sepulture.
Ah woe is me!
Neither with these nor those a settler I;
The living deny and the dead disown me.

CHORUS

To the height of boldness soaring
On Dirke's lofty throne, my child,
Full rudely hast thou stumbled.
— 'Tis some ancestral task thou art fulfilling.

ANTIGONE.

Most painful are the thoughts which thou hast harped—
My father's thrice-renownéd tale of sorrow,
Which touches too the lot of all of us—
The famed Labdakidæ.
Woe! woe! the curse of the maternal bed—
The incestuous nuptials of my ill-starred mother,
With her own son my father!
Ah! what a match was that
To which I owe my birth, unhappy me!
To them, under the curse, unblest by marriage,
I go an emigrant from life to death!

ἰὼ δυσπότμων
κασίγνητε γάμων κυρήσας,   845
θανὼν ἔτ' οὖσαν κατήναρές με.

ΧΟΡΟΣ.

σέβειν μὲν, εὐσέβειά τις·
κράτος δ', ὅτῳ κράτος μέλει,
παραβατὸν οὐδαμῇ πέλει.
σὲ δ' αὐτόγνωτος ὤλεσ' ὀργά.   850

ΑΝΤΙΓΟΝΗ.

ἄκλαυτος, ἄφιλος, ἀνυμέναιος,   ἐπῳδός·
*ἁ ταλαίφρων ἄγομαι
τάνδ' ἑτοίμαν ὁδύν.
οὐκ ἔτι μοι τόδε λαμπάδος †ἱερὸν ὄμμα
θέμις ὁρᾶν ταλαίνᾳ·   855
τὸν δ' ἐμὸν πότμον ἀδάκρυτον
οὐδεὶς φίλων στενίζει.

ΚΡΕΩΝ.

Ἆρ' ἴστ', ἀοιδὰς καὶ γόους πρὸ τοῦ θανεῖν
ὡς οὐδ' ἂν εἷς παύσαιτ' ἄν, εἰ χρείη λέγειν;
οὐκ ἄξεθ' ὡς τάχιστα, καὶ κατηρεφεῖ   860
τύμβῳ περιπτύξαντες, ὡς εἴρηκ' ἐγὼ,
ἄφετε μόνην ἔρημον, εἴτε †χρῇ θανεῖν,
εἴτ' ἐν τοιαύτῃ ζῶσα τυμβεύειν στέγῃ·
ἡμεῖς γὰρ ἁγνοὶ τοὐπὶ τήνδε τὴν κόρην·
μετοικίας δ' οὖν τῆς ἄνω στερήσεται.   865

⸺ λείπ. ἁ.   ⸺ γρ. ἱερὸν.   ⸺ γρ. χρή.

Ah! brother mine,
Thy marriage too has brought no good—
Dying, thou hast destroyed me living still.

CHORUS.

All reverence good reverence is:
But might, when might is rightly held,
May on no plea be overstept;
Thy self-willed temper hath destroyed thee!

ANTIGONE.

Unwept, unfriended, and unwedded, I,
A weary-hearted maid,
Am led along this road of imminent death.
No longer may I see
This luminary's sacred eye, unhappy!
All unbemoaned by friends,
My fate calls forth no tear!

KREON.

(Advancing from the Palace.)

Know ye that no man e'er would make an end
If it might serve his purpose to defer
With groans and dirges the approach of death!
Away with her at once, and close her round
With the o'erarching tomb, as I commanded.
There leave her to herself, whether she wills
To die or live entombed in such a house:
We wash our hands of her, and take no sin
Whate'er befals; but of a settlement
In upper air we doom her alienate.

(Retires again.)

ΑΝΤΙΓΟΝΗ.

ὦ τύμβος, ὦ νυμφεῖον, ὦ κατασκαφὴς
οἴκησις ἀείφρουρος, οἷ πορεύομαι
πρὸς τοὺς ἐμαυτῆς, ὧν ἀριθμὸν ἐν νεκροῖς
πλεῖστον δέδεκται Περσέφασσ' ὀλωλότων·
ὧν λοισθία 'γὼ καὶ κάκιστα δὴ μακρῷ   870
κάτειμι, πρίν μοι μοῖραν ἐξήκειν βίου.
ἐλθοῦσα μέντοι, κάρτ' ἐν ἐλπίσιν τρέφω
φίλη μὲν ἥξειν πατρί, προσφιλὴς δὲ σοί,
μῆτερ, φίλη δὲ σοί, κασίγνητον κάρα·
ἐπεὶ θανόντας αὐτόχειρ ὑμᾶς ἐγὼ   875
ἔλουσα, κἀκόσμησα, κἀπιτυμβίους
χοὰς ἔδωκα· νῦν δέ, Πολύνεικες, τὸ σὸν
δέμας περιστέλλουσα, τοιάδ' ἄρνυμαι.
καίτοι σ' ἐγὼ 'τίμησα τοῖς φρονοῦσιν εὖ.
οὐ γάρ ποτ' οὔτ' ἄν, εἰ τέκνων μήτηρ ἔφυν,   880
οὔτ' εἰ πόσις μοι κατθανὼν ἐτήκετο,
βίᾳ πολιτῶν τόνδ' ἂν ᾐρόμην πόνον.
τίνος νόμου δὴ ταῦτα πρὸς χάριν λέγω;
πόσις μὲν ἄν μοι, κατθανόντος, ἄλλος ἦν,
καὶ παῖς ἀπ' ἄλλου φωτός, εἰ τοῦδ' ἤμπλακον,   885
μητρὸς δ' ἐν Ἅιδου καὶ πατρὸς κεκευθότοιν,
οὐκ ἔστ' ἀδελφὸς ὅστις ἂν βλάστοι ποτέ.
τοιῷδε μέντοι σ' ἐκπροτιμήσασ' ἐγὼ
νόμῳ, Κρέοντι ταῦτ' ἔδοξ' ἁμαρτάνειν,
καὶ δεινὰ τολμᾶν, ὦ κασίγνητον κάρα.   890
καὶ νῦν ἄγει με διὰ χερῶν οὕτω λαβών,

ANTIGONE.

O tomb, O bridal chamber, O thou dwelling,
Dug in the solid rock, and ever guarded!
Whither I go to join my kindred dead.
Dead are they—few remain—and Persephassa
Has taken them to herself. And I the last,
And far most miserably, shall now desce[nd]
Before my term of life has reached th[e]
Allotted me by fate. Yet, going th[ither]
I cherish it among my fondest hopes
I shall be welcomed with my father['s],
With thy affection, mother, and thy
O brother mine; because, when that
With mine own hands I bathed and
And poured around your sepulchres
Due to the tomb: but now, O Po[lynices]
Such is my meed for honouring th[ee].
Yet did I well to honour thee, if
Who judge aright will judge the d[eed].
Or had I lost the children I had
Or had my husband pined away in
Would I have taken up this toil,
The public will. And wherefore say I this?
What rule of right is *there?*—My husband dead,
Another husband might have filled his place.
And if I lost my child, another mate
Might have begotten me another son.
But now that Hades veils from mortal eyes
Father and mother both, there is no root
From which a brother's life could bloom again.
Guided by such a rule, I thought it meet
To seek thy honour, and neglect all else:
But Kreon deems it sin and dire transgression,
O brother mine! And now he leads me forth
By force of hand, unbedded and unwedded,

ἄλεκτρον, ἀνυμέναιον, οὔτε του γάμου
μέρος λαχοῦσαν, οὔτε παιδείου τροφῆς·
ἀλλ' ὧδ' ἔρημος πρὸς φίλων ἡ δύσμορος,
ζῶσ' εἰς θανόντων ἔρχομαι κατασκαφάς. 895
ποίαν παρεξελθοῦσα δαιμόνων δίκην;
τί χρή με τὴν δύστηνον ἐς θεοὺς ἔτι
βλέπειν; τίν' αὐδᾶν ξυμμάχων; ἐπεί γε δὴ
τὴν δυσσέβειαν εὐσεβοῦσ' ἐκτησάμην.
ἀλλ', εἰ μὲν οὖν τάδ' ἐστὶν ἐν θεοῖς καλά, 900
παθόντες ἂν ξυγγνοῖμεν ἡμαρτηκότες·
εἰ δ' οἵδ' ἁμαρτάνουσι, μὴ πλείω κακὰ
πάθοιεν, ἢ καὶ δρῶσιν ἐκδίκως ἐμέ.

ΧΟΡΟΣ.

ἔτι τῶν αὐτῶν ἀνέμων †αὗται
ψυχῆς ῥιπαὶ τήνδε γ' ἔχουσιν. 905

ΚΡΕΩΝ.

τοιγὰρ τούτων τοῖσιν ἄγουσιν
βραδυτῆτος ὕπερ κλαύμαθ' ὑπάρξει.

ΑΝΤΙΓΟΝΗ.

οἴμοι, θανάτου τοῦτ' ἐγγυτάτω
τοὔπος ἀφῖκται.

ΧΟΡΟΣ.

θαρσεῖν οὐδὲν παραμυθοῦμαι 910
μὴ οὐ τάδε ταύτῃ κατακυροῦσθαι.

ΑΝΤΙΓΟΝΗ.

ὦ γῆς Θήβης ἄστυ πατρῷον,
καὶ θεοὶ προγενεῖς,

— γρ. αὐταί.

The promised nuptial tie denied to me,
And the sweet care of children. Ill-starred maid!
Thus reft of friends I go, while yet alive,
Down to the cavernous chambers of the dead!
In what sort have I wronged the laws of heaven?
Ah! why, unhappy, must I still regard
The Gods—what aid invoke? when now I earn
The name of impious by my piety.
Then be it so—if heaven approves these deeds,
My punishment shall prove to me my guilt;
But if the sin is theirs, may they not suffer
More sorrow than they wrongly wreak on me!

(Kreon comes forward again.)

(Anapæstic Movement.)

CHORUS.

Blowing still from the self-same quarter the
Storm of the soul this maiden possesseth.

KREON.

For this, and for loitering thus by the way,
With weeping and wailing these guards shall atone.

ANTIGONE.

Ah me! this announcement has come to mine ears,
The near neighbour of death!

(KREON) CHORUS.

No comfort I give for the confident hope
That this sentence will lack its fulfilment.

ANTIGONE.

Land of my fathers! city of Thebe!
Gods of my lineage!

ἄγομαι δή, κοὐκ ἔτι μέλλω.
λεύσσετε, Θήβης †τὴν κοιρανιδῶν   {ϛ⳽} 915
μούνην λοιπήν,
οἷα πρὸς οἵων ἀνδρῶν πάσχω,
τὴν εὐσεβίαν σεβίσασα.

I. ΣΤΑΣΙΜΟΝ ΤΕΤΑΡΤΟΝ.

ΧΟΡΟΣ.

Ἔτλα καὶ Δανάας οὐράνιον φῶς   στρ. α΄.
ἀλλάξαι δέμας ἐν χαλκοδέτοις αὐλαῖς·   920
  κρυπτομένα δ᾽ ἐν τυμβήρει θαλάμῳ κατεζεύχθη.
καίτοι †καὶ γενεᾷ τίμιος, ὦ παῖ, παῖ,
  καὶ Ζηνὸς ταμιεύεσκε γονὰς χρυσορύτους.
ἀλλ᾽ ἁ μοιριδία τις δύνασις δεινά·
οὔτ᾽ ἄν νιν †ὄλβος, οὔτ᾽ Ἄρης,   925
οὐ πύργος, οὐχ ἁλίκτυποι κελαιναὶ
ναῦς ἐκφύγοιεν.

ζεύχθη δ᾽ †ὀξύχολος παῖς ὁ Δρύαντος,   ἀντ. α΄.
Ἠδωνῶν βασιλεύς, κερτομίοις ὀργαῖς,
  ἐκ Διονύσου πετρώδει κατάφαρκτος ἐν δεσμῷ.   930
οὕτω τᾶς μανίας δεινὸν ἀποστάζει
  ἀνθηρόν τε μένος κεῖνος· ἐπέγνω †δὲ *δύαις
ψαύων τὸν θεὸν ἐν κερτομίοις γλώσσαις.
παύεσκε μὲν γὰρ ἐνθέους
γυναῖκας, εὔιόν τε πῦρ, φιλαύλους τ᾽   935

⁹¹⁵ γρ. οἱ κοιρανίδαι τὴν βασιλίδα.   ⁹²⁸ λείπ. καί.
⁹²⁵ γρ. ὄμβρος.   ⁹²⁸ γρ. ὀξυχόλων.   ⁹³² γρ. μανίαις.

They seize me—no longer I tarry!
See me, the only surviving branch of the
Princes of Thebe,
See what a doom, and from whom, is upon me,
Because I the holy have hallowed!

(*Antigone is led away.*)

X. FOURTH STASIMON.

CHORUS.

STROPHE I.

E'en Danae's form endured to lose
In brass-clampt halls the light of heaven.
Concealed and pent was she in tomb-like chamber;
And yet, my child, my child,
From lineage high she came,
And husbanded the seed of Zeus,
Flowing in golden streams.
The power of destiny is mighty still!
Nor wealth nor war,
Nor tower on land, nor the black ships, sea-stricken,
Can escape it.

ANTISTROPHE I.

He too, so keen in wrath, the son of Dryas,
Edonia's King, received the yoke,
Thanks to his taunting mood.
By Dionysus closed around with rocky bonds.
So mighty and so vigorous the strength
Of madness which distilled from *him*.
But sorrow taught him
It was a God his jeering tongue had mocked.
For he sought to let and hinder
The dames possessed by God,
And the Bacchanalian torches;

ἠρέθιζε Μούσας.

παρὰ δὲ κυανέων πελαγέων διδύμας ἁλὸς,   στρ. β'.
ἀκταὶ Βοσπόριαι, ἰδ' ὁ Θρηκῶν †[ἄξενος]
Σαλμυδησσός, ἵν' *ἄγχιστος Ἄρης
    δισσοῖσι Φινείδαις   940
    εἶδεν ἀρατὸν ἕλκος,
τυφλωθὲν ἐξ ἀγρίας δάμαρτος,
ἀλαὸν ἀλαστόροισιν ὀμμάτων κύκλοις ἀραχθὲν,
    ἐγχέων *ἄτερθε,
    χείρεσσι καὶ κερκίδων ἀκμαῖσι·   945

κατὰ δὲ τακόμενοι μέλεοι μελέαν πάθαν   ἀντιστ. β'.
κλαῖον ματρὸς, ἔχοντες ἀνύμφευτον γονάν·
ἁ δὲ σπέρμα μὲν ἀρχαιογόνων
    †αὔδασ' Ἐρεχθειδᾶν,
    τηλεπόροις δ' ἐν ἄντροις   950
τράφη θυέλλῃσιν ἐν πατρῴαις
Βορεὰς ἄμιππος ὀρθόποδος ὑπὲρ πάγου θεῶν παῖς·
ἀλλὰ κἀπ' ἐκείνᾳ
    Μοῖραι μακραίωνες ἔσχον, ὦ παῖ.

ΙΑ. ΕΠΕΙΣΟΔΙΟΝ ΠΕΜΠΤΟΝ.

ΤΕΙΡΕΣΙΑΣ.

ΘΗΒΗΣ ἄνακτες, ἥκομεν κοινὴν ὁδὸν   955

938 λείπ. ἄξενος.   939 γρ. ἀγχίπυλις.
944 γρ. ἐγχ. ὑφ' αἱματηραῖς.   949 αὔτασ'.

And much provoked the Muses of the flute.

STROPHE II.

By the Cyanean shoals, where two seas meet,
Are the Bosporian cliffs, and Salmydesus,
Where Thracians dwell, unkind to voyagers.
There Mars, the neighbour, saw the accursed wound,
Inflicted, blindness-bringing,
On the two sons of Phineus,
By his savage wife;
A wound sight-leasing to the ghostly eye-balls,
Stabbed without spears
By violent hands and with the shuttle's point.

ANTISTROPHE II.

Wasting away their mother's piteous sufferings,
Full piteously they bewailed,
Sprung as they were from one
In marriage most unblest.
But she, by line maternal, challenged her share
In the old honours of the Erechtheidæ.
And, Boreas-daughter, she was reared amid paternal
    gales,
In the deep-grottoed caverns:
Swift as the steed she clomb the precipices—
Child of the deities was she,
But yet the everlasting Fates
O'ertook e'en her, my child.

(Teiresias enters led by a boy.)

XI. FIFTH EPISODE.

TEIRESIAS.

Nobles of Thebes, behold us here consorted,

δύ' ἐξ ἑνὸς βλέποντε. τοῖς τυφλοῖσι γὰρ
αὕτη κέλευθος ἐκ προηγητοῦ πέλει.

ΚΡΕΩΝ.
τί δ' ἔστιν, ὦ γεραιὲ Τειρεσία, νέον;

ΤΕΙΡΕΣΙΑΣ.
ἐγὼ διδάξω· καὶ σὺ τῷ μάντει πιθοῦ.

ΚΡΕΩΝ.
οὔκουν πάρος γε σῆς ἀπεστάτουν φρενός.   960

ΤΕΙΡΕΣΙΑΣ.
τοιγὰρ δι' ὀρθῆς τήνδε ναυκληρεῖς πόλιν.

ΚΡΕΩΝ.
ἔχω πεπονθὼς μαρτυρεῖν ὀνήσιμα.

ΤΕΙΡΕΣΙΑΣ.
φρόνει βεβὼς αὖ νῦν ἐπὶ ξυροῦ τύχης.

ΚΡΕΩΝ.
τί δ' ἔστιν; ὡς ἐγὼ τὸ σὸν φρίσσω στόμα.

ΤΕΙΡΕΣΙΑΣ.
γνώσει, τέχνης σημεῖα τῆς ἐμῆς κλύων.   965
εἰς γὰρ παλαιὸν θᾶκον ὀρνιθοσκόπον
ἵζων, ἵν' ἦν μοι παντὸς οἰωνοῦ λιμήν,
ἀγνῶτ' ἀκούω φθόγγον ὀρνίθων, κακῷ
κλάζοντας οἴστρῳ καὶ βεβαρβαρωμένῳ,
καὶ σπῶντας ἐν χηλαῖσιν ἀλλήλους φοναῖς   970
ἔγνων· πτερῶν γὰρ ῥοῖβδος οὐκ ἄσημος ἦν.
εὐθὺς δὲ δείσας, ἐμπύρων ἐγευόμην
βωμοῖσι παμφλέκτοισιν· ἐκ δὲ θυμάτων

ANTIGONE.

Yokefellows of the road, and one for both
Doth spy the way: for thus it is, the blind
Must stay at home, unless his guide go with him.

KREON.

O old Teiresias, say, what hath befallen?

TEIRESIAS

That shalt thou learn: do thou the seer obey.

KREON.

Never as yet have I thy counsel scorned.

TEIRESIAS.

Therefore thou steer'st the state unswerved by storms.

KREON

I own the profit that I owe to thee.

TEIRESIAS.

Once more thou standest on the edge of fate.

KREON.

What is't? I shudder as I hear thy words.

TEIRESIAS.

The tokens of my art will tell thee. Listen!
I sat upon mine old augurial throne,
Where was my haven for each fowl of the air,
And lo! I hear an unknown voice of birds,
Clamouring with fierce and inarticulate rage,
And clawing one another to the death.
Thus much I knew: for their wings' whizzing sound
Told a plain tale. And forthwith in my fear
I sent to try the ignispicious signs
Amid the blaze of the enkindled altars.
There from the victim no clear flame arose,

ΑΝΤΙΓΟΝΗ.

Ἥφαιστος οὐκ ἔλαμπεν, ἀλλ' ἐπὶ σποδῷ
μυδῶσα κηκὶς μηρίων ἐτήκετο, 975
κἄτυφε, κἀνέπτυε· καὶ μετάρσιοι
χολαὶ διεσπείροντο, καὶ καταρρυεῖς
μηροὶ καλυπτῆς ἐξέκειντο πιμελῆς.
τοιαῦτα παιδὸς τοῦδ' ἐμάνθανον πάρα,
φθίνοντ' ἀσήμων ὀργίων μαντεύματα. 980
ἐμοὶ γὰρ οὗτος ἡγεμών, ἄλλοις δ' ἐγώ.
καὶ ταῦτα τῆς σῆς ἐκ φρενὸς νοσεῖ πόλις.
βωμοὶ γὰρ ἡμῖν ἐσχάραι τε παντελεῖς
πλήρεις ὑπ' οἰωνῶν τε καὶ κυνῶν βορᾶς
τοῦ δυσμόρου πεπτῶτος Οἰδίπου γόνου. 985
κᾆτ' οὐ δέχονται θυστάδας λιτὰς ἔτι
θεοὶ παρ' ἡμῶν, οὐδὲ μηρίων φλόγα,
οὐδ' ὄρνις εὐσήμους ἀπορραιβδεῖ βοάς,
ἀνδροφθόρου βεβρῶτες αἵματος λίπος.
ταῦτ' οὖν, τέκνον, φρόνησον. ἀνθρώποισι γὰρ 990
τοῖς πᾶσι κοινόν ἐστι τοὐξαμαρτάνειν·
ἐπεὶ δ' ἁμάρτῃ, κεῖνος οὐκ ἔτ' ἔστ' ἀνὴρ
ἄβουλος οὐδ' ἄνολβος, ὅστις ἐς κακὸν
πεσὼν ἀκεῖται, μηδ' ἀκίνητος πέλει.
αὐθαδία τοι σκαιότητ' ὀφλισκάνει. 995
ἀλλ' εἶκε τῷ θανόντι, μηδ' ὀλωλότα
κέντει. τίς ἀλκὴ τὸν θανόντ' ἐπικτανεῖν;
εὖ σοι φρονήσας εὖ λέγω· τὸ μαθάνειν δ'
ἥδιστον εὖ λέγοντος, εἰ κέρδος λέγοι.

ΚΡΕΩΝ.

ὦ πρέσβυ, πάντες, ὥστε τοξόται σκοποῦ, 1000
τοξεύετ' ἀνδρὸς τοῦδε, κοὐδὲ μαντικῆς

But in the ashes liquefying grease
From off the bones did ooze and smoke and sputter.
High in the air the vesicles were scattered:
And from the solid fat, which covered them,
The thighs fell out, and lay all bare below.
Such baffled signs of omens indistinct
This boy made known to me. For, as to others
I serve as guide, he serves as guide to me.
Thy will has brought this sickness on the state.
Our altars, high and low, of every sort,
Have taken infection from the birds and dogs
Which feed upon the son of Œdipus,
Fallen by such a dismal-fatal end.
Therefore the Gods no longer take our proffers
Of sacrificial prayers and thigh-bone flames;
Nor do the birds with flapping wings give out
Sounds of good omen, for they all have eaten
The fattening blood of man in battle slain.
Then take these things to heart, my son: for error
Is as the universal lot of man:
But whensoe'er he errs, that man no longer
Is witless or unblest, who, having fallen
Into misfortune, seeks to mend his ways
And is not obstinate: the stiffneckt temper
Must oft plead guilty to the charge of folly.
Then yield thee to the dead, nor further stab
The fallen foe: what bravery is this,
To kill the dead again? With good intentions
I give thee now good counsel, and to learn
Is sweetest when good counsel counsels gain.

KREON.

Old man, ye all, like bowmen at the butts,
Are aiming at me: e'en with prophet's lore

ἄπρακτος ὑμῖν εἰμί, τῶν *ὑπ', ἀργύρου,
ἐξημπόλημαι κἀκπεφόρτισμαι πάλαι.
κερδαίνετ', ἐμπολᾶτε τὸν πρὸς Σάρδεων
ἤλεκτρον, εἰ βούλεσθε, καὶ τὸν Ἰνδικὸν 1005
χρυσόν· τάφῳ· δ' ἐκεῖνον οὐχὶ κρύψετε,
οὐδ' εἰ θέλουσ' οἱ Ζηνὸς αἰετοὶ βορὰν
φέρειν νιν ἁρπάζοντες ἐς Διὸς θρόνους,
οὐδ' ὣς μίασμα τοῦτο μὴ τρέσας ἐγὼ
θάπτειν παρήσω κεῖνον. εὖ γὰρ οἶδ' ὅτι 1010
θεοὺς μιαίνειν οὔτις ἀνθρώπων σθένει.
πίπτουσι δ', ὦ γεραιὲ Τειρεσία, βροτῶν
χοἱ πολλὰ δεινοὶ πτώματ' αἰσχρ', ὅταν λόγους
αἰσχροὺς καλῶς λέγωσι τοῦ κέρδους χάριν.

ΤΕΙΡΕΣΙΑΣ.

φεῦ· 1015
ἆρ' οἶδεν ἀνθρώπων τις, ἆρα φράζεται—

ΚΡΕΩΝ.

τί χρῆμα; ποῖον τοῦτο πάγκοινον λέγεις.

ΤΕΙΡΕΣΙΑΣ.

ὅσῳ κράτιστον κτημάτων εὐβουλία;

ΚΡΕΩΝ.

ὅσῳπερ, οἶμαι, μὴ φρονεῖν πλείστη βλάβη.

ΤΕΙΡΕΣΙΑΣ.

ταύτης σὺ μέντοι τῆς νόσου πλήρης ἔφυς. 1020

ΚΡΕΩΝ.

οὐ βούλομαι τὸν μάντιν ἀντειπεῖν κακῶς.

[1002] γρ. τῶν δ' ὑπαὶ γένους.

I am bartered for by you, by whom, for silver,
This long while have I been both bought and sold.
Well! make your gains: earn, as ye will, by traffick
The Lydian amber-gold and Indian gold:
But natheless ye shall never bury *him;*—
Not though Jove's eagles take him as their food,
And bear him to the God's supernal throne,
Not by the dread of this pollution moved
Will I give him to burial: for I know
'Tis not in man to foul heaven's purity.
But, old Teiresias, e'en the ablest mortals
Fall shamefully, when, for the sake of gain,
They utter shameful speeches speciously.

TEIRESIAS.

Oh!
What man is there that knows? who that considers—

KREON.

In what? thou askest comprehensive questions.

TEIRESIAS.

How far the best of goods good counsel is?

KREON.

As far as folly is the greatest loss.

TEIRESIAS.

Well, thou at least hast caught that grievous ailment.

KREON.

I will not bandy insults with a prophet.

ΤΕΙΡΕΣΙΑΣ.
καὶ μὴν λέγεις, ψευδῆ με θεσπίζειν λέγων.

ΚΡΕΩΝ.
τὸ μαντικὸν γὰρ πᾶν φιλάργυρον γένος.

ΤΕΙΡΕΣΙΑΣ.
τὸ δ᾽ ἐκ τυράννων, αἰσχροκέρδειαν φιλεῖ.

ΚΡΕΩΝ.
ἆρ᾽ οἶσθα ταγοὺς ὄντας, ἂν λέγῃς, λέγων;   1025

ΤΕΙΡΕΣΙΑΣ.
οἶδ᾽· ἐξ ἐμοῦ γὰρ τήνδ᾽ ἔχεις σώσας πόλιν.

ΚΡΕΩΝ.
σοφὸς σὺ μάντις, ἀλλὰ τἀδικεῖν φιλῶν.

ΤΕΙΡΕΣΙΑΣ.
ὄρσεις με τἀκίνητα διὰ φρενῶν φράσαι;

ΚΡΕΩΝ.
κίνει, μόνον δὲ μὴ ᾽πὶ κέρδεσιν λέγων.

ΤΕΙΡΕΣΙΑΣ.
οὕτω γὰρ ἤδη καὶ δοκῶ, τὸ σὸν μέρος;   1030

ΚΡΕΩΝ.
ὡς μὴ ᾽μπολήσων ἴσθι τὴν ἐμὴν φρένα.

ΤΕΙΡΕΣΙΑΣ.
ἀλλ᾽ εὖ γέ τοι κάτισθι μὴ πολλοὺς ἔτι
τροχοὺς ἁμιλλητῆρας Ἡλίου τελῶν,
ἐν οἷσι τῶν σῶν αὐτὸς ἐκ σπλάγχνων ἕνα
νέκυν νεκρῶν ἀμοιβὸν ἀντιδοὺς ἔσει·   1035
ἀνθ᾽ ὧν ἔχεις μὲν τῶν ἄνω βαλὼν κάτω,

TEIRESIAS.

Nay but thou dost, belying my predictions.

KREON.

The race of seers is wholly given to pelf.

TEIRESIAS.

The tyrant-race is given to filthy lucre.

KREON.

Know'st thou it is thy King thou greetest thus?

TEIRESIAS.

Thou rul'st the state my aid preserved for thee.

KREON.

A wise seer art thou, but unrighteous ever.

TEIRESIAS.

Must I awake the secrets of my soul?

KREON.

Awake them: only speak no more for gain.

TEIRESIAS.

And thinkest thou I am seeking gain from *thee?*

KREON.

Know this—thou shalt not traffick in my will.

TEIRESIAS.

And know thou this—the next few revolutions
Of the sun's wheels in rival circles rolling
Scarce shalt thou compass, ere thou hast exchanged,
Dead for the dead a recompense, a child
In whom thy heart's blood flows; because that thou
Hast cast below one who should be above,

ψυχὴν τ' ἀτίμως ἐν τάφῳ *μετοικίσας·
ἔχεις δὲ τῶν κάτωθεν ἐνθάδ' αὖ θεῶν
ἄμοιρον, ἀκτέριστον, ἀνόσιον νέκυν.
ὧν οὔτε σοι μέτεστιν οὔτε τοῖς ἄνω   1040
θεοῖσιν, ἀλλ' ἐκ σοῦ βιάζονται τάδε.
τούτων σε λωβητῆρες ὑστεροφθόροι
λοχῶσιν Ἅιδου καὶ θεῶν Ἐριννύες,
ἐν τοῖσιν αὐτοῖς τοῖσδε ληφθῆναι κακοῖς.
καὶ ταῦτ' ἄθρησον εἰ κατηργυρωμένος   1045
λέγω. φανεῖ γὰρ οὐ μακροῦ χρόνου τριβὴ
ἀνδρῶν, γυναικῶν, σοῖς δόμοις κωκύματα.
ἐχθραὶ δὲ πᾶσαι ξυνταράσσονται πόλεις,
ὅσων σπαράγματ' ἢ κύνες †καθήγισαν,
ἢ θῆρες, ἤ τις πτηνὸς οἰωνὸς, φέρων   1050
ἀνόσιον ὀσμὴν ἑστιοῦχον ἐς πόλιν.
τοιαῦτά σου, λυπεῖς γὰρ, ὥστε τοξότης
ἀφῆκα θυμῷ καρδίας τοξεύματα
βέβαια, τῶν σὺ θάλπος οὐχ ὑπεκδραμεῖ.
ὦ παῖ, σὺ δ' ἡμᾶς ἄπαγε πρὸς δόμους, ἵνα   1055
τὸν θυμὸν οὗτος ἐς νεωτέρους ἀφῇ,
καὶ γνῷ τρέφειν τὴν γλῶσσαν ἡσυχωτέραν,
τὸν νοῦν τ' ἀμείνω τῶν φρενῶν, ἢ νῦν φέρει.

ΧΟΡΟΣ.

ἀνὴρ, ἄναξ, βέβηκε δεινὰ θεσπίσας.
ἐπιστάμεσθα δ', ἐξ ὅτου λευκὴν ἐγὼ   1060
τήνδ' ἐκ μελαίνης ἀμφιβάλλομαι τρίχα,
μή πώ ποτ' αὐτὸν ψεῦδος ἐς πόλιν λακεῖν.

ΚΡΕΩΝ.

ἔγνωκα καὐτὸς, καὶ ταράσσομαι φρένας.

¹⁰³⁷ γρ. κατῴκισας.   ¹⁰⁴⁹ γρ. καθήγισαν.

And, stript of franchise in the land of life,
Hast sent a soul to settle in the grave,
And, on the other part, detainest here,
From Gods infernal excommunicate,
An unentombed and unaneled corpse.
Thou hast not art or part in him, nor have
The Gods above, but thou constrainest them.
Therefore, with dreadful thoughts of future mischief,
The avenging Sprites of Hades and of Heaven
Lay wait to take thee in the self-same evils.
Look to it now, if I say this for silver.
For, yet a little while, and thou shalt hear
The wails of men and women in thy palace;
And all the states are stirred in rage together,
Whose mangled citizens have found a tomb
In hungry maw of dogs and beasts of prey,
Or where some winged fowl of the air has borne
Unholy odours to their hearth and home.
Such arrows in mine anger, for thou gall'st me,
I, as an archer, shoot against thy heart,
Well-aimed, and thou wilt not escape their sting.
Boy, lead me home again that he may vent
His rage on younger men, and learn to keep
His tongue more quiet, and to train his mind
To wiser thoughts than those which guide him now.

(*Teiresias retires.*)

CHORUS.

Sire, he is gone, after dread prophecies.
And since the hoary hairs which crown my head
Were raven locks, I never know him speak
Falsely in what concerns the common weal.

KREON.

I know it too: my mind is ill at ease.

τό τ' εἰκάθειν γὰρ δεινόν· ἀντιστάντι δὲ
ἄτῃ πατάξαι θυμὸν, ἐν δεινῷ πάρα.   1065

ΧΟΡΟΣ.
εὐβουλίας δεῖ, παῖ Μενοικέως, Κρέον.

ΚΡΕΩΝ.
τί δῆτα χρὴ δρᾶν; φράζε· πείσομαι δ' ἐγώ.

ΧΟΡΟΣ.
ἐλθὼν, κόρην μὲν ἐκ κατώρυχος στέγης
ἄνες· κτίσον δὲ τῷ προκειμένῳ τάφον.

ΚΡΕΩΝ.
καὶ ταῦτ' ἐπαινεῖς, καὶ δοκεῖς παρεικάθειν;   1070

ΧΟΡΟΣ.
ὅσον γ', ἄναξ, τάχιστα. συντέμνουσι γὰρ
θεῶν ποδώκεις τοὺς κακόφρονας βλάβαι.

ΚΡΕΩΝ.
οἴμοι. μόλις μὲν, καρδίας δ' ἐξίσταμαι
τὸ δρᾶν· ἀνάγκῃ δ' οὐχὶ δυσμαχητέον.

ΧΟΡΟΣ.
δρᾶ νυν τάδ' ἐλθὼν, μηδ' ἐπ' ἄλλοισιν τρέπε.   1075

ΚΡΕΩΝ.
ὧδ' ὡς ἔχω στείχοιμ' ἄν· ἴτ' ἴτ', ὀπάονες,
οἵ τ' ὄντες, οἵ τ' ἀπόντες, ἀξίνας χεροῖν
ὁρμᾶσθ' ἑλόντες εἰς ἐπόψιον τόπον.
ἐγὼ δ', ἐπειδὴ δόξα τῇδ' ἐπεστράφη,
αὐτός τ' ἔδησα, καὶ παρὼν ἐκλύσομαι.   1080

For if to yield is painful, opposition,
Where mischief smites our wrath, is painful too.

CHORUS.

Advise thee well, Kreon, Menœkeus' son.

KREON.

What must I do? Speak; I will heed thy words.

CHORUS.

Go, free the damsel from the cavern'd chamber,
And make a tomb for the neglected corse.

KREON.

Is this thy counsel, and must I give way?

CHORUS.

At once, O King! The hind'rances of heaven
Swiftly, by cross-ways, overtake our folly.

KREON.

Ah me!
'Tis hard, but still my heart must yield to do it;
For he who fights with fate must fight in vain.

CHORUS.

Then go and do it. Leave it not to others.

KREON.

Forth from this spot I go: up, up, my servants,
Present and absent, hasten, axe in hand,
To the high downs which rise before our eyes.
And I, since that my mind has ta'en this turn,
Myself will free her whom I bound myself.

δέδοικα γὰρ μὴ τοὺς καθεστῶτας νόμους
ἄριστον ᾖ σώζοντα τὸν βίον τελεῖν. *Stop*

IB. ΟΡΧΗΣΤΙΚΟΝ.

ΧΟΡΟΣ.

Πολυώνυμε, Καδμείας νύμφας ἄγαλμα,   στροφὴ α΄.
καὶ Διὸς βαρυβρεμέτα
γένος, κλυτὰν ὃς ἀμφέπεις   1085
Ἰταλίαν, μέδεις δὲ
παγκοίνοις Ἐλευσινίας
Δηοῦς ἐν κόλποις,
Βακχεῦ Βακχᾶν
†ματρόπολιν Θήβαν   1090
..τῶν, παρ' ὑγρῶν
Ἰσμηνοῦ †ῥείθρων ἀγρίου τ'
ἐπὶ σπορᾷ δράκοντος·

σὲ δ' ὑπὲρ †διλόφοιο πέτρης στέροψ
    ὄπωπε   ἀντιστ. α΄.
λιγνύς, ἔνθα Κωρύκιαι   1095
Νύμφαι †στίχουσι Βακχίδες,
Κασταλίας δὲ νᾶμα·
καί σε Νυσαίων ὀρέων.
κισσήρεις ὄχθαι,
χλωρά τ' ἀκτὰ   1100
πολυστάφυλος πέμπει,
ἀμβρότων ἐπέων
εὐαζόντων, Θηβαίας
ἐπισκοποῦντ' ἀγυιάς·

¹⁰⁸⁹ γρ. ὦ Βακχεῦ.   ¹⁰⁹⁰ γρ. μητρόπολιν.   ¹⁰⁸¹ γρ. ναίων.
¹⁰⁹² γρ. ῥείθρων.   ¹⁰⁹⁴ γρ. διλόφου.   ¹⁰⁹⁶ γρ. στείχουσι.

For now I greatly fear 'tis best to pass
Through life observant of the established laws.

(Hastens off the stage, followed by his guards.)

XII. TRAGIC DANCING SONG.

CHORUS.

STROPHE I.

Thou of the many names,
Whom Kadmus' daughter loves with a mother's pride,
Whom Jove the awful thunderer begot;
Guardian of far-famed Italy, and King
In dales of Eleusinian Deo, votary-thronged,
Baccheus, the Bacchante's mother-city,
Thebe inhabiting,
By the Ismenus' over-flowing streams,
Where the grim dragon's teeth were sown.

ANTISTROPHE I.

Thee o'er the double-crested rock
The illumined smoke beholds,
Whither ascend Korycian nymphs in Bacchanalian chorus:
Thee too beholds Kastalia's fount: and thee
The ivy-mantled slopes of Nysa's hills,
And that green headland, where thick clusters hang,
Send, when religious voices hymn thy name,
A visitant to our Thebæan streets.

τὰν †ἔκπαγλα τιμᾷς   στροφὴ β'.   1105
ὑπὲρ †πασᾶν πόλεων
ματρὶ σὺν κεραυνίᾳ·
καὶ νῦν, ὡς βιαίας
ἔχεται πάνδημος †ἁμὰ πόλις ἐπὶ νόσου,
μολεῖν καθαρσίῳ ποδὶ Παρνησίαν   1110
ὑπὲρ κλιτὺν
ἢ στονόεντα πορθμόν.

ἰὼ πῦρ πνεόντων   ἀντιστροφὴ β'.
χόραγ' ἄστρων, νυχίων
φθεγμάτων ἐπίσκοπε,   1115
παῖ †Ζηνὸς γένεθλον,
†προφάνηθ' ὦ Ναξίαις σαῖς ἅμα περιπόλοις
†Θυίαισιν, αἵ σε μαινόμεναι πάννυχοι
χορεύουσι
τὸν ταμίαν Ἴακχον.   1120

ΙΓ. ΕΞΟΔΟΣ.

ΑΓΓΕΛΟΣ.

ΚΑΔΜΟΥ πάροικοι καὶ δόμων Ἀμφίονος,
οὐκ ἔσθ' ὁποῖον στάντ' ἂν ἀνθρώπου βίον
οὔτ' αἰνέσαιμ' ἂν, οὔτε μεμψαίμην ποτέ.
Τύχη γὰρ ὀρθοῖ καὶ Τύχη καταρρέπει
τὸν εὐτυχοῦντα, τόν τε δυστυχοῦντ', ἀεί·   1125
καὶ μάντις οὐδεὶς τῶν καθεστώτων βροτοῖς.

[1105] ᵃ γρ. ἐκ πασᾶν τιμᾶς ὑπερτάταν.   [1109] λείπ. ἁμά.
[1114] γρ. καὶ νυχίων.   [1116] γρ. Διός.   [1117] λείπει ὦ.
[1118] γρ. θυιάσιν.

Strophe II.

Her of all cities chief thou honourest,
Thou and thy mother, lightning-blasted!
And now that all the city-folk are vexed
With violent distemper, come to us
With cleansing foot, o'er the Parnasian height,
Or 'cross the roaring strait.

Antistrophe II.

What ho! choir-leader of fire-breathing stars,
That listenest still to nightly acclamations,
Begotten child of Zeus, appear before us,
With all thy Naxian revel-rout around thee,
Who with mad choirs from sun-down to sun-rise
Honour thee, giver of all good, Iacchus!

XIII. THE EXODUS.

*Enter a messenger: then Eurydike: lastly Kreon,
and to him one of the slaves of his household.*

MESSENGER.

(Enters on the right by the Parascenia, as from the country.)

O YE who dwell as neighbours by the palace
Of Kadmus and Amphion, howso stands
The life of any man, I ne'er would venture
To speak of it with only praise or blame.
For be our present fortune good or bad,
Our fortune's scale is ever on the turn,
And prophets ne'er predict stability.

Κρέων γὰρ ἦν ζηλωτὸς, ὡς ἐμοὶ, ποτὲ,
σώσας μὲν ἐχθρῶν τήνδε Καδμείαν χθόνα,
λαβών τε χώρας παντελῆ μοναρχίαν
εὔθυνε, θάλλων εὐγενεῖ τέκνων σπορᾷ· 1130
καὶ νῦν ἀφεῖται πάντα. τὰς γὰρ ἡδονὰς
ὅταν προδῶσιν ἄνδρες, οὐ τίθημ' ἐγὼ
ζῆν τοῦτον, ἀλλ' ἔμψυχον ἡγοῦμαι νεκρόν.
πλούτει τε γὰρ κατ' οἶκον, εἰ βούλει, μέγα,
καὶ ζῆ τύραννον σχῆμ' ἔχων· ἐὰν δ' ἀπῇ 1135
τούτων τὸ χαίρειν, τἄλλ' ἐγὼ καπνοῦ σκιᾶς
οὐκ ἂν πριαίμην ἀνδρὶ πρὸς τὴν ἡδονήν.

ΧΟΡΟΣ.
τί δ' αὖ τόδ' ἄχθος βασιλέων ἥκεις φέρων;

ΑΓΓΕΛΟΣ.
τεθνᾶσιν· οἱ δὲ ζῶντες αἴτιοι θανεῖν.

ΧΟΡΟΣ.
καὶ τίς φονεύει; τίς δ' ὁ κείμενος; λέγε. 1140

ΑΓΓΕΛΟΣ.
Αἵμων ὄλωλεν, αὐτόχειρ δ' αἱμάσσεται.

ΧΟΡΟΣ.
πότερα πατρῴας, ἢ πρὸς οἰκείας χερός;

ΑΓΓΕΛΟΣ.
αὐτὸς πρὸς αὑτοῦ, πατρὶ μηνίσας φόνου.

ΧΟΡΟΣ.
ὦ μάντι, τοὔπος ὡς ἄρ' ὀρθὸν ἤνυσας.

ΑΓΓΕΛΟΣ.
ὡς ὧδ' ἐχόντων, τἄλλα βουλεύειν πάρα. 1145

Thus Kreon's lot erewhile provoked my envy,
When that he saved this country from its foes,
And ruled in absolute sovranty the land
Of Kadmus, blest with noble progeny.
Now—all is gone. For him I reckon but
An animate corpse, and not a living man,
Whose life's delights are cast away. Thy house,
I grant thee, may be richly stored with wealth;
And thou may'st live in royal pomp: but if
Joy is not there the while, and I must lose
All happiness thereby, I would not give
Smoke's shadow as the price of all the rest.

CHORUS.
What royal sorrow hast thou here to tell!

MESSENGER.
Dead are they! and the living own their death.

CHORUS.
Who is the slayer? who hath fallen? Speak.

(Eurydike opens the doors.)

MESSENGER.
Hæmon is dead! no stranger shed his blood.

CHORUS.
Was it his father's, or his own hand slew him?

MESSENGER.
His own—his father's deed of death incensed him.

CHORUS.
O seer, how soothfast thou hast made thy words!

MESSENGER.
This done, the rest demands your best advice.

(Eurydike comes from the palace gates attended.)

ΧΟΡΟΣ.

καὶ μὴν ὁρῶ τάλαιναν Εὐρυδίκην ὁμοῦ
δάμαρτα τὴν Κρέοντος· ἐκ δὲ δωμάτων
ἤτοι κλύουσα παιδὸς ἢ τύχῃ πάρα.

ΕΥΡΥΔΙΚΗ.

ὦ πάντες ἀστοὶ, τῶν λόγων ἐπῃσθόμην
πρὸς ἔξοδον στείχουσα, Παλλάδος θεᾶς   1150
ὅπως ἱκοίμην εὐγμάτων προσήγορος.
καὶ τυγχάνω τε κλῇθρ᾽ ἀνασπαστοῦ πύλης
χαλῶσα, καί με φθόγγος οἰκείου κακοῦ
βάλλει δι᾽ ὤτων· ὑπτία δὲ κλίνομαι
δείσασα πρὸς δμωαῖσι, κἀποπλήσσομαι.   1155
ἀλλ᾽ ὅστις ἦν ὁ μῦθος, αὖθις εἴπατε.
κακῶν γὰρ οὐκ ἄπειρος οὖσ᾽ ἀκούσομαι.

ΑΓΓΕΛΟΣ.

ἐγώ, φίλη δέσποινα, καὶ παρὼν ἐρῶ,
κοὐδὲν παρήσω τῆς ἀληθείας ἔπος.
τί γάρ σε μαλθάσσοιμ᾽ ἂν, ὧν ἐς ὕστερον   1160
ψεῦσται φανούμεθ᾽; ὀρθὸν ἀλήθει᾽ ἀεί.
ἐγὼ δὲ σῷ ποδαγὸς ἑσπόμην πόσει
πεδίον ἐπ᾽ ἄκρον ἔνθ᾽ ἔκειτο νηλεὲς
κυνοσπάρακτον σῶμα Πολυνείκους ἔτι·
καὶ τὸν μὲν, αἰτήσαντες ἐνοδίαν θεὸν,   1165
Πλούτωνά τ᾽, ὀργὰς εὐμενεῖς κατασχέθειν,
λούσαντες ἁγνὸν λουτρὸν, ἐν νεοσπάσι
θαλλοῖς ὃ δὴ λέλειπτο συγκατῄθομεν,
καὶ τύμβον ὀρθόκρανον οἰκείας χθονὸς

CHORUS.

Ah! poor Eurydike, I see her come,
Consort of Kreon: she has left the palace,
Hearing her son's disaster, or by chance.

EURYDIKE

O all ye citizens, I heard the tidings
As I was coming forth to bear my greeting
Of supplication to the goddess Pallas.
Just as I loosed the bolt of the closed door,
Tidings of mine own sorrow pierced my ears,
And, horrified, I fell into the arms
Of these my followers, and my senses fled.
Whate'er the story was, tell it again.
To hear of sorrow is not new to me.

MESSENGER.

I, dear my Queen,—for I was there—will speak,
And nought extenuate the truth's disclosures.
Why should I smooth with words, when after-hours
Would prove me false? The truth stands fast in all things.
I waited on my Lord, to guide his steps
To the high upland mead, where still was lying,
Most piteously rent and torn by dogs,
The corse of Polyneikes. Him, with prayers
To Pluto and the Goddess of the Way,
That they would change their wrath to graciousness,
We washed with pure lavations, and with boughs
Torn from the living olive, all together
We joined in burning what remained of him;
And heaping high for him a funeral mound

χώσαντες, αὖθις πρὸς λιθόστρωτον κόρης 1170
νυμφεῖον Ἅιδου κοῖλον εἰσεβαίνομεν.
φωνῆς δ' ἄπωθεν ὀρθίων κωκυμάτων
κλύει τις ἀκτέριστον ἀμφὶ παστάδα,
καὶ δεσπότῃ Κρέοντι σημαίνει μολών·
τῷ δ' ἀθλίας ἄσημα περιβαίνει βοῆς 1175
ἕρποντι μᾶλλον ἆσσον, οἰμώξας δ', ἔπος
ἵησι δυσθρήνητον· Ὦ τάλας ἐγώ,
ἆρ' εἰμὶ μάντις; ἆρα δυστυχεστάτην
κέλευθον ἕρπω τῶν παρελθουσῶν ὁδῶν;
παιδός με σαίνει φθόγγος. ἀλλά, πρόσπολοι, 1180
ἴτ' ἆσσον ὠκεῖς, καὶ παραστάντες τάφῳ,
ἀθρήσαθ' ἁρμὸν χώματος λιθοσπαδῆ,
δύντες πρὸς αὐτὸ στόμιον, εἰ τὸν Αἵμονος
φθόγγον ξυνίημ', ἢ θεοῖσι κλέπτομαι.—
τάδ' ἐξ ἀθύμου δεσπότου κελεύσμασιν 1185
ἠθροῦμεν· ἐν δὲ λοισθίῳ τυμβεύματι
τὴν μέν, κρεμαστὴν αὐχένος, κατείδομεν
βρόχῳ μιτώδει σινδόνος καθημμένην·
τὸν δ', ἀμφὶ μέσσῃ περιπετῆ προσκείμενον,
εὐνῆς ἀποιμώζοντα τῆς κάτω φθορὰν, 1190
καὶ πατρὸς ἔργα, καὶ τὸ δύστηνον λέχος.
ὁ δ' ὡς ὁρᾷ σφε, στυγνὸν οἰμώξας, ἔσω
χωρεῖ πρὸς αὐτὸν, κἀνακωκύσας καλεῖ·
Ὦ τλῆμον, οἷον ἔργον εἴργασαι; τίνα
νοῦν ἔσχες; ἐν τῷ ξυμφορᾶς διεφθάρης; 1195
ἔξελθε, τέκνον· ἱκέσιός σε λίσσομαι.—

Of natal earth, straightway from thence we sought
The vaulted chamber paved with blocks of stone,
Where Death had wooed the maiden as his bride.
And while it still was distant, some one hears
The voice of lamentations, treble-toned,
Peal from the porch of that unhallowed cell,
And bears the tale right hastily to Kreon.
But as the King drew near there floated round him,
In accents indistinct, the wail of woe.
Then he, his words by weeping interrupted,
Exclaimed, "Ah me! unhappy that I am!
And was my soul prophetic! Is this road
Which now I tread most fraught with wretchedness
Of all my paths? 'Tis my son's voice that greets me!
Quick then, ye slaves, draw nearer to the tomb,
And, standing hard beside it, drag away
The closely-fitting stones which block the passage;
Then, creeping to the very mouth, discover
Whether 'tis Hæmon's voice I recognize,
Or heaven has robbed my senses of themselves."
We did as our desponding Lord enjoined,
And, in the farthest corner of the tomb,
We saw *her* hanging by the neck, fast bound
With noose of linen finely-spun, and *him*
With arms enfolded clinging to her form,
Bemoaning his lost bride, his father's deeds,
And his ill-starred betrothal. When the sire
Espied his son, he raised a piteous cry,
And entering the tomb approached him there:
Then lifting up his voice he wept, and said:
"O my poor boy, what hast thou done! what thoughts
Possessed thee! what ill fate has wrought thy ruin!
Come forth, my son,—a suppliant, I entreat thee."

ΑΝΤΙΓΟΝΗ.

τὸν δ' ἀγρίοις ὄσσοισι παπτήνας ὁ παῖς,
πτύσας προσώπῳ, κοὐδὲν ἀντειπών, ξίφους
ἕλκει διπλοῦς κνώδοντας· ἐκ δ' ὁρμωμένου
πατρὸς φυγαῖσιν, ἤμπλακ'· εἶθ' ὁ δύσμορος   1200
αὑτῷ χολωθείς, ὥσπερ εἶχ', ἐπεντάθεις
ἤρεισε πλευραῖς μέσσον ἔγχος, ἐς δ' ὑγρὸν
ἀγκῶν' ἔτ' ἔμφρων παρθένῳ προσπτύσσεται·
καὶ φυσιῶν ὀξεῖαν ἐκβάλλει πνοὴν
λευκῇ παρειᾷ φοινίου σταλάγματος.   1205
κεῖται δὲ νεκρὸς περὶ νεκρῷ, τὰ νυμφικὰ
τέλη λαχὼν δείλαιος †ἐν γ' Ἅιδου δόμοις,
δείξας ἐν ἀνθρώποισι τὴν ἀβουλίαν,
ὅσῳ μέγιστον ἀνδρὶ πρόσκειται κακόν.

ΧΟΡΟΣ.

τί τοῦτ' ἂν εἰκάσειας; ἡ γυνὴ πάλιν   1210
φρούδη, πρὶν εἰπεῖν ἐσθλὸν ἢ κακὸν λόγον.

ΑΓΓΕΛΟΣ.

καὐτὸς τεθάμβηκ'· ἐλπίσιν δὲ βόσκομαι,
ἄχη τέκνου κλύουσαν, ἐς πόλιν γόους
οὐκ ἀξιώσειν, ἀλλ' ὑπὸ στέγης ἔσω
δμωαῖς προθήσειν πένθος οἰκεῖον στένειν.   1215
γνώμης γὰρ οὐκ ἄπειρος, ὥσθ' ἁμαρτάνειν.

ΧΟΡΟΣ.

οὐκ οἶδ'· ἔμοιγ' οὖν ἥ τ' ἄγαν σιγὴ βαρὺ
δοκεῖ προσεῖναι, χἠ μάτην πολλὴ βοή.

ΑΓΓΕΛΟΣ.

ἀλλ' εἰσόμεσθα, μή τι καὶ κατάσχετον
κρυφῇ καλύπτει καρδίᾳ θυμουμένη,   1220

[1207] λείπ. γ'.

With fierce regards the stripling glared on him—
His looks spoke hatred though he answered not.
Then forth he pulled his double-hilted sword,
And, as his father 'scaped the blow by flight,
On this, poor wretch, in choler with himself,
He leant upon his blade, and fixed it deep
Between his ribs; and then with languid arm
He claspt the maid in his last consciousness,
And in his sharp expiring gasp he threw
A purple drop upon her pallid cheek.
Dead by the dead, he finds, unhappy youth,
His marriage rites consummate in the grave,
And shows to all the world that ill advice
Is far the worst of ills that fall on man.

(*Eurydike rushes into the palace.*)

CHORUS.

What would'st thou say of this? the Queen is gone,
'Ere she a word, or good or bad, has spoken!

MESSENGER.

I shudder at it too: but still the hope
Sustains me, that these tidings having heard
Of her son's sad mishap, she may not deign
To let the city look into her moan,
But will, within, impose upon her menials
This office of domestic lamentation.
She is not strange to sense that she should err.

CHORUS.

I wot not, I: meseems that over-silence
Threatens no less than wailing uncontrolled.

MESSENGER.

Entering the palace we shall soon discover
Whether she veils within her storm-tost heart

δόμους παραστείχοντες. εὖ γὰρ οὖν λέγεις·
καὶ τῆς ἄγαν γάρ ἐστί που σιγῆς βάρος.

ΧΟΡΟΣ.

καὶ μὴν ὅδ᾽ ἄναξ αὐτὸς ἐφήκει
μνῆμ᾽ ἐπίσημον διὰ χειρὸς ἔχων,
εἰ θέμις εἰπεῖν, οὐκ ἀλλοτρίαν   1225
ἄτην, ἀλλ᾽ αὐτὸς ἁμαρτών.

ΙΔ. ΚΟΜΜΟΣ ΔΕΥΤΕΡΟΣ.

ΚΡΕΩΝ.

Ἰὼ
φρενῶν δυσφρόνων ἁμαρτήματα   στροφὴ α΄.
στερεά, θανατόεντ᾽,
ὦ κτανόντας τε καὶ
θανόντας βλέποντες ἐμφυλίους.   1230
ὤμοι ἐμῶν ἄνολβα βουλευμάτων.
ἰὼ παῖ, νέος νέῳ ξὺν μόρῳ
  αἰαῖ, αἰαῖ,
 ἔθανες, ἀπελύθης,
ἐμαῖς, οὐδὲ σαῖσι δυσβουλίαις.   1235

ΧΟΡΟΣ.

οἴμ᾽, ὡς ἔοικας ὀψὲ τὴν δίκην ἰδεῖν.

ΚΡΕΩΝ.

 οἴμοι,
ἔχω μαθὼν δείλαιος· ἐν δ᾽ ἐμῷ κάρᾳ
θεὸς τότ᾽ ἄρτι τότε μέγα βάρος μ᾽ ἔχων

Something she may not speak. Thou say'st it well:
There *is* a sort of threat in over-silence.

(Kreon enters from the right, bearing the body of his son, and followed by a retinue of attendants.)

(Anapæstic Movement.)

CHORUS.

Lo! he approaches, the monarch himself, and he
Bears in his arms a sign too distinct; if the
Truth may be spoken, he rues his own error,
Not a mischief inflicted by others.

XIV. SECOND KOMMOS.

KREON.

STROPHE I.

ALAS, alas! the sins of senseless minds—
Saddening, deadening—
Ah! ye that see us both of kindred blood—
The slain beside his slayer.
My ill-starr'd counsels!—out upon them!
O my son, my son,
In years not yet mature, by a fate premature—
—Ah! woe, woe!—
Thou art dead, thou art gone!
'Twas not thy folly, 'twas mine own!

CHORUS.

Alas!—too late meseems the right thou seest.

KREON

Ah me!
Sorrow hath taught me! then, oh then descending
With heavy tread upon my head—the God

ἔπαισεν, ἐν δ' ἔσειπεν ἀγρίαις ὁδοῖς,
οἴμοι, λακπάτητον ἀντρέπων χυράν.
φεῦ, φεῦ, ὦ πόνοι βροτῶν δύσπονοι.

ΕΞΑΓΓΕΛΟΣ.

ὦ δέσποθ', ὡς ἔχων τε καὶ κεκτημένος,
τὰ μὲν πρὸ χειρῶν τάδε φέρων, τὰ δ' ἐν δόμοις
ἔοικας ἥκειν καὶ τάχ' ὄψεσθαι κακά.

ΚΡΕΩΝ.

τί δ' ἔστιν αὖ κάκιον, ἢ κακῶν ἔτι;

ΕΞΑΓΓΕΛΟΣ.

γυνὴ τέθνηκε, τοῦδε παμμήτωρ νεκροῦ,
δύστηνος, ἄρτι νεοτόμοισι πλήγμασιν.

ΚΡΕΩΝ.

ἰώ,
ἰὼ δυσκάθαρτος Ἅιδου λιμήν.   ἀντιστ. α'. 1250
  τί μ' ἄρα, τί μ' ὀλέκεις;
  ὦ κακάγγελτά μοι
προπέμψας ἄχη, τίνα θροεῖς λόγον;
αἰ, αἰ, ὀλωλότ' ἄνδρ' ἐπεξειργάσω.
τί φής; τίνα λέγεις νέον μοι *νέῳ,
  αἰαῖ, αἰαῖ,
  σφάγιον ἐπ' ὀλέθρῳ
γυναικεῖον ἀμφικεῖσθαι μόρον;

ΕΞΑΓΓΕΛΟΣ.

ὁρᾶν πάρεστιν. οὐ γὰρ ἐν μυχοῖς ἔτι.

¹²⁵⁵ γρ. νέον μοι λόγον.

Spurned me and cast me on my cruel ways.
—Ah me!
He overturned and trampled on my joy.
Fie, fie!—the toilsome toils of mortal men.

ATTENDANT.
(*From the house.*)

O sire, as having both in hand and store,
Thou bringest home this sorrow in thine arms;
But other sorrow soon will greet thee here.

KREON.

What greater, or what other grief is that?

ATTENDANT.

The Queen, with wounds fresh-gaping, lieth dead,
Hapless! in life and death her son's true mother.

KREON. ANTISTROPHE 1.

Alas, alas! insatiate gulf of Hades,
Why, ah why destroy me thus?
O thou who hast companionéd
These woes of evil tidings,
What are the words thou speakest?
Woe, ah woe!
Already dead, thou hast again undone me.
What say'st thou? What is this thou tellest,
(Ah woe, woe!)
That a new bloody death—my wife's—is added to
This desolation still too new?

CHORUS.

That may'st thou see—the wall no longer hides her.

(*The scene opens, and the body of Eurydike is discovered lying on a couch, with a sacrificial knife just fallen from her hand.—The slaves stand around her.*)

ΚΡΕΩΝ.

οἴμοι· 1260
κακὸν τόδ' ἄλλο δεύτερον βλέπω τάλας.
τίς ἄρα, τίς με πότμος ἔτι περιμένει;
ἔχω μὲν ἐν χείρεσσιν ἀρτίως τέκνον,
τάλας, τὸν δ' ἔναντα προσβλέπω νεκρόν.
φεῦ, φεῦ μᾶτερ ἀθλία, φεῦ τέκνον. 1265

ΕΞΑΓΓΕΛΟΣ.

ἡ δ' ὀξύθηκτος ἥδε βωμία † πτέρυξ
λύει κελαινὰ βλέφαρα, [*προσπίπτει δ' ἐκεῖ
σφάγιον ὅπως βωμοῖσι,] κωκύσασα μὲν
τοῦ πρὶν θανόντος Μεγαρέως κλεινὸν †λάχος,
αὖθις δὲ τοῦδε, λοίσθιον δὲ σοὶ κακὰς 1270
πράξεις ἐφυμνήσασα τῷ παιδοκτόνῳ.

ΚΡΕΩΝ.

αἰαῖ, αἰαῖ, στροφὴ β'.
ἀνέπταν φόβῳ. τί μ' οὐκ ἀνταίαν
ἔπαισέν τις ἀμφιθήκτῳ ξίφει;
δείλαιος ἐγώ, 1275
φεῦ, φεῦ,
δειλαίᾳ δὲ συγκέκραμαι δύᾳ.

ΕΞΑΓΓΕΛΟΣ.

ὡς αἰτίαν γε τῶνδε κἀκείνων ἔχων
πρὸς τῆς θανούσης τῆσδ' ἐπεσκήπτου μόρων.

ΚΡΕΩΝ.

ποίῳ δὲ κἀπελύσατ' ἐν φοναῖς τρόπῳ; 1280

[1266] γρ. πέριξ.   [1267] λείπ. προσπίπτει, κ.τ.λ.   [1269] γρ. λέχος.

KREON.

Ah me!
I do indeed behold this second woe.
What—ah! what destiny awaits me still!
While yet my arms enfold my child, unhappy!
I see before mine eyes that bleeding corse!
Alas, ill-fated mother! O my son!

ATTENDANT.

(Standing by Eurydike, and taking up the knife which has fallen from her hand.)

'Twas this sharp sacrificial altar-knife
That closed her eyes in darkness, and she fell,
As falls the victim at the altar-steps:
But first she wailed the glorious destiny
Of Megareus, dead before; and then *his* fate;

(Pointing to the body of Hæmon.)

And, last of all, repeated imprecations
She heaped on *thee*—the murderer of thy sons.

KREON.

STROPHE II.

Alas, Alas!
Fear thrills me: wherefore hath not one of you
Thrust me straight to my heart,
With falchion double-edged!
Ah! pity me, a piteous bondage
On every side surrounds me.

ATTENDANT.

She charged thee, dying, as the guilty cause
Of both the present and the former death.

KREON.

Say—by what mode of bloodshed did she die!

ΕΞΑΓΓΕΛΟΣ.

παίσασ' ὑφ' ἧπαρ αὐτόχειρ αὐτὴν, ὅπως
παιδὸς τόδ' ᾔσθετ' ὀξυκώκυτον πάθος.

ΚΡΕΩΝ.

ὤμοι μοι, τάδ' οὐκ ἐπ' ἄλλον βροτῶν
ἐμᾶς ἁρμόσει ποτ' ἐξ αἰτίας.
ἐγὼ γάρ σ' ἐγώ †σ' ἔκανον, ὦ μέλεος. 1285
ἐγώ· φάμ' ἔτυμον. ἰὼ πρόσπολοι,
ἄγετέ μ' ὅτι †τάχιστ' ἄγετέ μ' ἐκποδὼν,
τὸν οὐκ ὄντα μᾶλλον ἢ μηδένα.

ΧΟΡΟΣ.

κέρδη παραινεῖς, εἴ τι κέρδος ἐν κακοῖς·
βράχιστα γὰρ κράτιστα τἀν ποσὶν κακά. 1290

ΚΡΕΩΝ.

*αἰαῖ, αἰαῖ,   ἀντιστ. β'.
φανήτω μόρων ὁ κάλλιστ' ἐμῶν,
ἐμοὶ τερμίαν ἄγων ἡμέραν
    ὕπατος· ἴτω, ἴτω,
*φεῦ, φεῦ,   1295
ὅπως μηκέτ' ἆμαρ ἄλλ' εἰσίδω.

ΧΟΡΟΣ.

μέλλοντα ταῦτα. τῶν προκειμένων τι χρὴ
πράσσειν· μέλει γὰρ τῶνδ' ὅτοισι χρὴ μέλειν.

ΚΡΕΩΝ.

ἀλλ' ὧν †ἐρῶμεν, ταῦτα συγκατηυξάμην.

ΧΟΡΟΣ.

μὴ νυν προσεύχου μηδέν· ὡς πεπρωμένης 1300
οὐκ ἔστι θνητοῖς ξυμφορᾶς ἀπαλλαγή.

¹²⁸⁵ λείπ. σ'.   ¹²⁸⁷ γρ. τάχος.   ¹²⁹¹ γρ. ἴτω, ἴτω.
¹²⁹⁵ λείπ. φεῦ. φεῦ.   ¹²⁹⁹ γρ. ἐρῶ μὲν.

ATTENDANT.
(Examining the corpse.)

On the right side below the bosom—here—
Her own hand smote her, after she had heard
Her son's mishap—fit source of bitter wailing!

KREON.

Ah me, me! Of other mortals none
Can fit his steps into these guilty ways,
And set me free
'Twas I, 'twas I that killed thee.
Wretched! 'twas I!
Ah 'tis too true. Ye ministering slaves,
Lead me with all speed,
Lead me far away—
For I am nothing now—
More than nothingness.

CHORUS.

Thou biddest well, if ill has any well:
For present ills are always best when shortest.

KREON.   ANTISTROPHE II.

Alas, alas! appear of fates to me
The fairest, the last—
That bringest a closing day.
O come, O come,
And let me ne'er behold to-morrow's light.

CHORUS.

All this will be: the present needs our care:
Those whom it most behoves will rule the future.

KREON.

I joined in prayers for that which we desire.

CHORUS.

Pray not at all!—when fate has fixed it so,
'Tis not in mortals to escape disaster.

ΑΝΤΙΓΟΝΗ.   [1302—1313.

ΚΡΕΩΝ.

ἄγοιτ' ἂν μάταιον ἄνδρ' ἐκποδών,
ὅς, ὦ παῖ, σέ τ' οὐχ ἑκὼν †κατέκανον,
σέ τ' †αὖ τάνδ', ἰὼ μέλεος, οὐδ' ἔχω
ὅπα θῶ *πρότερον· *ἰώ· πάντα γὰρ   1305
λέχρια τᾶν χεροῖν, τὰ δ' ἐπὶ κρατί μοι
πότμος δυσκόμιστος εἰσήλατο.

ΧΟΡΟΣ.

πολλῷ τὸ φρονεῖν εὐδαιμονίας
πρῶτον ὑπάρχει· χρὴ δ' ἐς †τὰ θεῶν
μηδὲν ἀσεπτεῖν· μεγάλοι δὲ λόγοι   1310
μεγάλας πληγὰς τῶν ὑπεραύχων
    ἀποτίσαντες,
γήρᾳ τὸ φρονεῖν ἐδίδαξαν.

1303 γρ. κατέκτανον.   1304 γρ. ὃς σέ τ' αὐτὰν ὤμοσι.
1305 ὅπα πρὸς πότερον ἴδω. τᾶ καὶ θῶ.
1309 γρ. δὲ τά τ' εἰς θεούς.

KREON.

Remove from all eyes a man weak and guilty,
Who slew thee, my son! and thee, too, my wife!
It was not my will!
Wretched me! I know not
Whither first to turn my steps.
Alas! in my hands all here is out of joint,
And there hath leapt on my head
A fate whose heavy tread
Is a load all too weary.

(*Exit Kreon, supported by his attendants.*)

(*Final anapæstic Movement.*)

CHORUS.

Wisdom is first of the gifts of good fortune:
'Tis a duty, be sure, the rites of the Gods
Duly to honour: but words without measure, the
Fruit of vain-glory, in woes without number their
Recompense finding,
Have lesson'd the agéd in wisdom.

CRITICAL AND EXPLANATORY

NOTES.

SOPH. ANT. K

CRITICAL AND EXPLANATORY NOTES.

1. Ὦ κοινὸν αὐτάδελφον Ἰσμήνης κάρα.] The version: "Ismene, dear in very sisterhood," conveys the full force of this periphrastic greeting, so far as the English language can express it without straining. It is well known to scholars that κοινός is frequently used to signify consanguinity[1]; the Scholiast on Eurip. *Phœn.* 1565 renders it συγγενικός, and it is employed in the same sense in other passages of this play. I have pointed out an extension of this use of the word in a note on Pind. *O.* II. 49, 50. For its combination here with αὐτάδελφος, (lit. "from the self-same womb," i. e. of the same mother, *N. Crat.* p. 236,) commentators have aptly compared Æsch. *Eum.* 89: σὺ δ' αὐτάδελφον αἷμα καὶ κοινοῦ πατρὸς Ἑρμῆ. The circumlocution Ἰσμήνης κάρα (κασίγνητον κάρα infr. 874, 890, similarly δέμας,) is very common in Greek, and is not without its parallel in other languages. Perhaps our nearest approach to it in English is our old-fashioned address "dear life," and our combinations "no-body," "some-body:" compare also the frequent use of *lip* (leib) in the *Nibelungen Lied,* and the word *poll,* "an individual," in *polling, catch-poll,* &c. The termination *hood* in *sisterhood,* is originally "head;" but of course

---

[1] Properly speaking, κοινός implied any sort of society or communion, but relationship implied communion in the highest degree: ἔστι δ' ἀδελφοῖς μὲν καὶ ἑταίροις πάντα κοινά, ἑτέροις δὲ ἀφωρισμένα. Arist. *Eth. Nic.* IX. 9, 10.

the compound is not used here for the purpose of expressing the Greek periphrasis.

2, 3. ἆρ' οἶσθ' ὅτι—τελεῖ;] This reading is now established in the favour of critics. Hermann, Böckh, Wunder, and Dindorf, have all adopted it, and there appears to be little reason to doubt that it is better than the old ὅ, τι. The sentiment is that which is expressed in Eurip. *Troad.* 792: τί γὰρ οὐκ ἔχομεν, τίνος ἐνδέομεν μὴ οὐ πασσυδίᾳ χωρεῖν ὀλέθρου διὰ παντός; In the passages quoted in support of the construction, we have τί κακὸν οὐχὶ πασχόντων (Dem. *De Coronâ*, p. 241); τίνα οὐ προσπεμπόντων (id. *Energ. et Mnesib.* p. 1152, 12); τίν' οὐ δρῶν, ποῖα δ' οὐ λέγων ἔπη (Eurip. *Phœn.* 892); ᾧ τίς οὐκ ἔνι κηλὶς κακῶν ξύνοικος; (Soph. *Œd. Col.* 1135); ὅπου τίς ὄρνις οὐχὶ ἀλαγγαίνει (Fr. apud Strab. XV. 687): and this is the natural form of the exclamation. But Heindorf has pointed out instances in which the correlatives ὅπως and ὁπότερος are substituted for πῶς and πότερος (ad Plat. *Lys.* p. 212, c. § 21); and ὁποῖον is here put for ποῖον by a sort of anticipative attraction to the ὁποῖον of v. 5. Emper suggests the following explanation of the construction: ἆρ' οἶσθ' ὅ, τι [τοιοῦτόν ἐστι] ὁποῖον, κ τ.λ. No doubt the transition from the interrogative to the correlative presumes some sort of antecedent, but we do not mend the matter by merely stating this: for ἆρ' οἶσθ' ὅ,τι equally presumes ἆρ' οἶσθα τοῦτο ὅ,τι.

3. νῷν ἔτι ζώσαιν.] Schäfer, Seidler, Wex, Dindorf, Wunder, and Böckh, consider these words as genitives: Hermann, following the Scholiast, takes them as datives dependent on τελεῖ. The addition of ἔτι shows that the poet is speaking here emphatically of the accomplishment of all these misfortunes in the life-time of the two sisters, and not of the limitation of their effects to the sisters themselves: so in the passage which the commentators quote, Soph. *Trach.* 305: μηδ' εἴ τι δράσεις τῆσδέ γε ζώσης ἔτι. At the same time it is clear that Antigone is made to speak of these misfortunes as particularly belonging to herself and her sister,

(v. 6: τῶν σῶν τε κἀμῶν κακῶν) and that which takes place in our life-time does take place, in a certain sense, *for us*. Accordingly, as τελεῖν is properly construed with the dative, (cf. *Œd. Col.* 1437: τάδ᾽ εἰ τελεῖτέ μοι,) I agree with Hermann and the Scholiast that νῷν is dative here. Böckh has introduced *uns* into his version, as a *dativus incommodi* "auf welcher kein starker Ton fällt." This is all that is required, but this is inconsistent with the position that Sophocles has not used the dative here.

4—6. οὐδὲν γάρ———κακῶν.] We have here the main difficulty of this introductory speech. Hermann, Gaisford, Böckh, and Dindorf, think that the difficulty may be surmounted by a liberal interpretation of the accumulated negatives. I cannot permit myself to doubt that ἄτης ἄτερ is corrupt. Schäfer, Wunder, and Emper, acquiesce in Coray's emendation of ἄγης for ἄτης; but it appears to me that the proper opposition is between the ἄλγος and the ἄτη. The former is the inward pain of the individual, the latter is the principle of mischief which makes his misfortunes objective. There is the same antithesis between the αἰσχρόν and the ἄτιμον in the next line: the former implies the sense of shame which results from disgraceful conduct (αἰσχύνη), the latter is the outward degradation, the humiliation in the eyes of the world, the loss of civic franchise and social privilege, which is another and concomitant effect of the same cause (ἀτιμία). We have abundant exemplifications of these antitheses in the play before us. Not to go farther than Ismene's answer: she has had no μῦθος, whether ἡδύς or ἀλγεινός (v. 12): she does not know that she is more εὐτυχοῦσα or ἀτωμένη (v. 17), where she gives the contraries as well as the synonyms of the adjectives in v. 4. It seems to me, therefore, that Porson came near to the truth, when he surmised that ἄτερ arose from the gloss ἀτηρ" for ἀτηρόν, written over the words in the text as an explanation of some periphrase with ἄτη: only I do not agree with him that the lost reading was ἄτης ἔχον, which I should have some difficulty in explaining. Supposing that the word, which was used with ἄτη, in some degree resembled the gloss ἀτηρ"—and this is a reasonable supposition—it remains to discover some such word, which would at the same time suit the meaning required. The emendation ΑΓΗΣ for ΑΤΗΣ is based on the resemblance between ΑΤ and ΑΓ, and I think that the true reading is ΑΓΟν for ΑΤΕΡ. The verb ἄγω, which with the preposition εἰς or πρὸς signifies to lead into or tend to something, may be used with the same word, in the accusative without the preposition, to signify much the same thing: thus we may have ἄγειν εἰς, or πρὸς ἄτην, "to lead into or towards mischief," and also ἄγειν ἄτην, "to bring or cause mischief," the former being predicated more especially of the person who is led into mischief, and the latter being a more general expression of the tendency. Compare infra 434: ἐς κακὸν τοὺς φίλους ἄγειν with Fr. 323 Dind.: ὅτῳ δ' ὄλεθρον δεινὸν ἀληθεῖ' ἄγει. Accordingly, as we have, infra 616: ὅτῳ φρένας θεὸς ἄγει πρὸς ἄταν, we may be allowed to expect here ἄτην ἄγον, and we have another example in Sophocles of the same participle used in conjunction with adjectives: cf. the well-known Fragment on love (Fr. 678 Dind.) v. 6: ἐν κείνῃ τὸ πᾶν, σπουδαῖον, ἡσυχαῖον, ἐς βίαν ἄγον. The abundance of negatives in this passage need create no difficulty. It has been sufficiently illustrated by grammarians and commentators.

10. στείχοντα.] The word is similarly used here and in v. 185: τὴν ἄτην στείχουσαν ἀστοῖς. According to its etymology, στείχω should signify "to go up;" cf. Sanscr. *Stighnâmi*, Russ. *Stignu*, Lith. *Staigios*, Germ. *Steigen*. The Hebrew עָלָה "to go up," is also used to signify a hostile attack, as in 1 *Reg.* xxii. 12.

17. οὔτ' εὐτυχοῦσα—οὔτ' ἀτωμένη.] In *Ajax* 262, ἀτᾶσθαι is a synonym of νοσεῖν; below, 314, it is opposed to σώζεσθαι; and here to εὐτυχεῖν. The ἄτη referred to by Ismene is the death of her two brothers, the εὐτυχία is the defeat and departure of the enemy. When ἄτη is regarded as a cause, it stands naturally in opposition to the δαίμων τύχης. The translation implies that it is to be

taken here in its causative sense. In general, I have translated ἄτη, wherever it occurs in this play, by our word "mischief," which seems to be its exact counterpart. Whether ἄτη is personified or not, it is, as Hamlet says, "miching mal-hecho; it means *mischief*" (Act III. Sc. 2). South has given its full force in his use of the verb "*mischieve:*" "generally in Scripture, Temptation denotes not only a bare trial, but such an one as is attended with a design to hurt or *mischieve* the people so tried." It has not, I think, been generally observed that the concluding petition of the Lord's Prayer involves this distinction; *Matth.* VI. 13: μὴ εἰσενέγκῃς ἡμᾶς εἰς πειρασμόν, ἀλλὰ ῥῦσαι ἡμᾶς ἀπὸ τοῦ πονηροῦ. That this is only one petition is clear from the opposition between μή and ἀλλά; indeed, the latter clause is omitted in the best MSS. of *Luke* X. 4. It is also clear that τοῦ πονηροῦ is masculine (*Matth.* XIII. 9, 38. *Eph.* VI. 16. 2 *Thess.* III. 3).

19. ἐξέπεμπον.] The Scholiast, and after him, the commentators, understand this as equivalent to μετεπεμπόμην. I believe, that, as προπέμπω means to accompany a man forth on his journey—to conduct him forwards—to bring him on his way, so ἐκπέμπω here signifies to accompany a person out of doors—to bring him out with you. In the passages which the commentators quote (infra v. 161, *Œd. Col.* 1461), the simple πέμπω bears its ordinary meaning. For the alteration of οὕνεκα into εἵνεκα, see *New Cratylus*, p. 358.

20. καλχαίνουσ' ἔπος.] Of the three interpretations proposed by the Scholiasts for this use of the verb καλχαίνω, which properly signifies "to look a dark purple colour" (κάλχη, *murex*, "the purple fish,") the first is the most accurate: καλχαίνουσα: ἀντὶ τοῦ, πορφύρουσα καὶ τεταραγμένως φροντίζουσα. Similarly Hesychius: καλχαίνει, ταράσσει [l. ταράσσεται, Photius: ἐκ βάθους ταράσσεται vel omitte; vide infra], πορφύρει, στένει, φροντίζει, ἄχθεται, κυκᾷ, ἐκ βυθοῦ ταράσσεται. The use of the synonym πορφύρει, which Hesychius here quotes in expla-

nation of καλχαίνω, shows how the latter might pass from its original sense to that which it bears in the passage before us. Homer uses πορφύρω in speaking of the sea, when the dead unbroken swell presages a storm, and this too in a simile, in order to describe a mind in a state of doubt or suspense—the τὸ ὁρμαίνειν; *Il.* XIV. 16 sqq.:

ὡς δ' ὅτε πορφύρῃ πέλαγος μέγα κύματι κωφῷ,
ὀσσόμενον λιγέων ἀνέμων λαιψηρὰ κέλευθα
αὔτως, οὐδ' ἄρα τε προκυλίνδεται οὐδετέρωσε,
πρίν τινα κεκριμένον καταβήμεναι ἐκ Διὸς οὖρον·
ὣς ὁ γέρων ὥρμαινε, δαϊζόμενος κατὰ θυμὸν
διχθάδι· ἢ μεθ' ὅμιλον ἴοι Δαναῶν ταχυπώλων
ἠὲ μετ' Ἀτρείδην Ἀγαμέμνονα ποιμένα λαῶν.

From this simile or comparison arose a metaphorical use of the word πορφύρω by itself, as a synonym of ὁρμαίνω, to represent the same fluctuating and disturbed state of mind; compare *Il.* XXI. 551:

αὐτὰρ ὅ γ' ὡς ἐνόησεν Ἀχιλλῆα πτολίπορθον,
ἔστη, πολλὰ δέ οἱ κραδίη πόρφυρε μένοντι,

with *Od.* VII. 82:

πολλὰ δέ οἱ κῆρ ὥρμαιν' ἱσταμένῳ:

and so in other passages. Although the synonym καλχαίνω does not occur in Homer, yet the participial name of the seer Kalchas indicates an equally early employment of this verb, or of its primitive form, κάλχημι (cf. βαίνω with ἔβην as from βημί, and φαίνω with φημί). For if the name of Κάλχας (-ντ-ς) is significant, like that of other old seers (*Polyidus, Melampus*, &c.), it can only refer to the deep, perturbed, anxious pondering which preceded the interpretation of a portent: cf. Pind. *O.* VIII. 41: ἄντιον ὁρμαίνων τέρας. *O.* XIII. 73: παρκείμενον συλλαβὼν τέρας. v. 84: ὁρμαίνων ἕλε φάρμακον. That in the time of the Tragedians καλχαίνω was a synonym of ὁρμαίνω or πορφύρω, is clear from Eurip. *Heracl.* 40: ἐγὼ μὲν ἀμφὶ τοῖσδε καλχαίνω τέκνοις. It is certain then that καλχαίνω is not a transitive verb: so that καλχαίνουσά τι ἔπος can only mean "profoundly stirred by meditation on some ἔπος." Now I cannot think, with Wex, that ἔπος is used here, like the Hebrew דָּבָר, to signify *aliquid* or *res*. The word often means "news," "tidings," "intelligence;" infr. 277, 1159. *Œd. Col.* 302: τίς δ' ἔσθ' ὁ κείρῳ τοῦτο τοὔπος ἀγγελῶν; Eurip. *Hec.* 217: νέον τι πρὸς σὲ σημανῶν ἔπος, whence κατειπεῖν τινός "to tell *news* of any one," i.e. "to inform against him," as distinguished from κατηγορεῖν, which implies a more public accusation. And I think it is clear that Antigone is here represented as deeply moved by the intelligence which she is about to communicate to Ismene respecting the indignities offered to their brother's corpse.

21. οὐ γὰρ τάφου κ.τ.λ.] It may seem hardly necessary to remark that τάφου is dependent on both προτίσας and ἀτιμάσας, and is the genitive of relation. Properly speaking, there had been no τάφος in the case of Polyneikês, but the Greeks did not need to be told that in the world of sense abnegations are merely relative. The opposition between the treatment of the two brothers is here emphatically set forth—the extra-honours paid to the one being contrasted with the non-burial of the other. The commentators seem to have no difficulty in believing that νῷν is dative here. I have been obliged to use a paraphrase to give its full force. The collocation τὼ κασιγνήτω τὸν μὲν—τὸν δέ—is as common as those with the genitive.

24. προσθεὶς δίκαια.] Various attempts have been made to explain the vulgate χρησθεὶς δικαίᾳ, but, as it appears to me, without the least success. Hermann would write χρησθεὶς in the sense of παραγγελθείς, as if the reference were to the request of Eteokles that Kreon would bury him and leave his brother unburied (Triclinius: Ἐτεοκλῆς ὅτε πρὸς πόλεμον ἐξῄει παρήγγειλεν Κρέοντι αὐτὸν μὲν θάπτειν, Πολυνείκην δ' οὔ. cf. Eurip. *Phœniss.* 1660). But Antigone would hardly call this a just request. In fact, she expressly contradicts the supposition that Kreon's edict would have been agreeable to the wishes of Eteokles; infra 515. Wunder and Dindorf get over the difficulty by omitting the line as spurious. But Emper will not relin-

quish the hope that the corrupt words χρησθείς δικαία, may be set right by emendation. Now the emendation in the text appears to me to be not only so true but so easy, that I wonder it has never been suggested before: especially as more than one of the commentators has quoted from the *Electra* 47: ἄγγελλε ὅρκῳ προστιθείς, in illustration of the supposed construction of these words. In the case of Eteokles, Kreon had not been content with observing the ordinary δίκη and νόμος—he had made additions to the conventional usages, but they were righteous and justifiable additions—they did not, at all events, contravene any δαιμόνων δίκη. If instead of burying Eteokles with the customary rites, he had pre-eminently honoured him (προτίσας, v. 22), it was merely by bestowing upon him those additional obsequies, which were due to one who had gained the ἀριστεία in fighting for his father-land (see infra 194—197)—it was an augmentation to him, but no depreciation to any one else; and Antigone herself had willingly joined in the splendid ceremony (infra 875, 6). It seems to me therefore most natural, that Antigone should be made to speak of the funeral of Eteokles, as the corrected text makes her speak. That προστίθημι may be properly used of additional honours paid to a tomb is clear from the *Electra* 933:

> οἶμαι μάλιστ' ἔγωγε τοῦ τηθνηκότος
> μνημεῖ' Ὀρέστου ταῦτα προσθεῖναι τινά.

With regard to the interchange of the letters, I am convinced that many a true reading lies hid under a confusion between γρ, χρ, and πρ (written χϱ, χϱ, and ϖρ), and even between τ, χ. and π: thus we shall see below that παρείρων has been written for γεραίρων, v. 366, and γ' ὑπ' for πρός, v. 640; and I can hardly doubt that in Æsch. *Suppl.* 877, where we have ηπρογα συλασκεις, the true reading is *ἄγρια *γάρ σὺ λάσκεις. It may be added, that the ὡς λέγουσι in v. 23 is quite unintelligible, unless there were some addition to the usual honours in the case of Eteokles: that he had been buried, was well known to Antigone. But she was not necessarily cognizant of the further distinctions decreed by Kreon.

29. οἰωνοῖς—βορᾶς.] Böckh has remarked, that εἰσορᾶν here means " to look with greediness." I have explained and illustrated the phrase πρὸς χάριν βορᾶς in the *New Cratylus*, pp. 359, 360. That θησαυρὸς here means " a store of food," and not ἕρμαιον, as the Scholiast renders the word, appears to me quite clear. Pollux distinguishes between the θησαυρὸς as a receptacle of money and the ταμιεῖον as the granary for corn (*Onomast.* IX. § 44); and Plato perhaps intends the same distinction, (*Resp.* VIII. p. 548, A.); but it is well known that θησαυρὸς was also used in the latter sense; see Aristot. *Œcon.* II. § 39.

35, 36. ἀλλ᾽ ὃς ἄν—ἐν πόλει.] There is the same mixture of the *oratio obliqua* and *directa* in the recital of the edict of Xerxes, in Æsch. *Pers.* 364—373: πᾶσιν προφωνεῖ τόνδε ναυάρχοις λόγον· εὖτ᾽ ἂν φλέγων ἥλιος λήξῃ...τάξας νεῶν στῖφος κ.τ.λ. ὡς εἰ μόρον φευξοίαθ᾽ Ἕλληνες κ.τ.λ. πᾶσιν στερεῖσθαι κρατὸς ἦν προκείμενον. τοσαῦτ᾽ ἔλεξε.

38. εἴτ᾽ εὐγενὴς πέφυκας, εἴτ᾽ ἐσθλῶν κακή.] This apparent confusion in terms is well illustrated by Eurip. *Electr.* 367, sqq.:

φεῦ·
οὐκ ἔστ᾽ ἀκριβὲς οὐδὲν εἰς εὐανδρίαν·
ἔχουσι γὰρ ταραγμὸν αἱ φύσεις βροτῶν·
ἤδη γὰρ εἶδον ἄνδρα γενναίου πατρὸς
τὸ μηδὲν ὄντα, χρηστά τ᾽ ἐκ κακῶν τέκνα. κ.τ.λ.

40. λύουσ᾽ ἂν ἢ 'φάπτουσα.] Böckh has explained this proverbial expression by a reference to *Ajax* 1304: εἰ μὴ ξυνάψων ἀλλὰ συλλύσων πάρει. It is doubtful, however, whether there is the precise double reference which he suggests; namely, that the λύουσα refers to an interruption of Kreon's proceedings, and the ἐφάπτουσα to the εἰ ξυμπονήσεις καὶ ξυνεργάσει of the following verse. I should be rather disposed to understand it generally, as I have expressed it in the translation.

44. ἀπόρρητον.] That this adjective is masculine, appears from the next line, and from 404: ὃν οὐ τὸν νεκρὸν ἀπεῖπας.

46. ἀδελφόν·—ἁλώσομαι.] Wunder, following Didymus, omits this line, which interrupts the στιχομυθιά. I do not agree with him.

48. τῶν ἐμῶν.] This genitive is masculine. Cf. *Œd. Col.* 830, *Electr.* 536, quoted by Wunder, and infra 1040, cited by Wex. The μ' added by Brunck is quite unnecessary; it is fully implied in the construction.

50. δυσκλεής.] Cf. *Œd. Col.* 305: πολὺ γάρ, ὦ γέρον, τὸ σὸν ὄνομα διήκει πάντας.

56, 57. αὐτοκτονοῦντε—ἐπαλλήλοιν χεροῖν.] For αὐτοκτοῦντε = ἀλληλοκτονοῦντε, and ἐπάλληλος = ἀλληλοφόνος, see *New Cratylus*, pp. 220, 221. For the latter, which is due to Hermann, who has substituted it for the vulgate ἐπ' ἀλλήλοιν, Boissonade reads ὑπ' ἀλλήλοιν, and Emper, ὑπ' ἀλλήλων. I think Hermann's is the only change required. For κοινὸν μόρον, see above ad v. 1.

63, 64. ἔπειτα δέ—ἀλγίονα.] The commentators are not agreed as to the construction of this passage. Wex, and after him Wunder, would understand οὕνεκα here in its causative sense, and supply δεῖ or χρή, with ἀκούειν. I take οὕνεκα as a synonym for ὅτι, a sense in which Sophocles often uses the word: e. g. *Philoct.* 232: ἀλλ', ὦ ξέν', ἴσθι τοῦτο πρῶτον, οὕνεκα Ἕλληνές ἐσμεν. And the construction is ἀλλ' ἐννοεῖν χρὴ τοῦτο μὲν ὅτι ἔφυμεν γυναῖκε, ὡς, κ.τ.λ. ἔπειτα δὲ οὕνεκα (= ὅτι) ἀρχόμεσθα [ὥστε] ἀκούειν. For the apposition of the infinitive without ὥστε, I find a reason in the peculiar signification of the verbs ἔφυμεν and ἀρχόμεσθα, which naturally reject the aid of ὥστε, a particle only required to strengthen a comparison. Hermann supposes that a line has fallen out between κρεισσόνων and καί— such as—ὥστ' οὐδὲν ἂν γένοιτο νῷν ἄκος τὸ μὴ οὔ.—This would be more necessary if ἀκούειν meant "to obey." I conceive it bears its ordinary meaning: the ἄλγος of the edict primarily affected the *ears* (infr. 319): and as for the necessity of their *obedience*, that is asserted by Ismene in v. 62.

70. ἐμοῦ γ' ἂν ἡδέως δρῴης μέτα.] Dindorf finds fault with Brunck's version: *lubens te utar adjutrice*, and prefers the rendering *lubens mecum facies*. This seems to me to make nonsense of the passage. As ἡδέως is constantly used with ἂν and the opt. in the sense of *lubenter*, it might have been better if Sophocles had written ἐμοίγε, as in 436: ἡδέως ἐμοίγε κἀλγεινῶς ἅμα. But it is clear that this is the meaning: οὐκ ἂν ἐμοίγε ἡδέως μετ' ἐμοῦ δρῴης.

71. ἴσθ' ὁποία σοι δοκεῖ.] The majority of the commentators read ὁποία, and understand ἴσθι as the imperative of οἶδα. I have followed Hermann, because I think that the reference is to v. 38.

83. μή 'μοῦ.] I think the emphatical antithesis of τὸν σὸν πότμον renders this reading necessary.

86, 87. πολλὸν ἐχθίων ἔσει σιγῶσ', ἐὰν μὴ πᾶσι κηρύξῃς τάδε.] This epexegesis, (which in the present case is equivalent to ἐχθίων σιγῶσα ἢ κηρύξασα,) is found not only in negative appositions, as here and *Œd. Tyr.* 57: ἔρημος ἀνδρῶν μὴ ξυνοικούντων ἔσω, but also where the explanation is positive, as in Æsch. *Choeph.* 742: ἡ δὴ κλύων ἐκεῖνος εὐφρανεῖ νόον, εὖτ' ἂν πύθηται μῦθον.

88. θερμὴν—ἔχεις.] Ψυχρὸς here refers to the chill of fear; cf. Æsch. *Sept. c. Theb.* 816: κακόν με καρδίαν τι περιπιτνεῖ κρύος. *Eumen.* 155: πάρεστι μαστίκτορος δαίου δαμίου βαρύ τι περίβαρυ κρύος ἔχειν. *Prom.* 692: οὐδ' ὧδε δυσθέατα καὶ δύσοιστα πήματα, λύματα, δείματα ἀμφήκει κέντρῳ ψύχειν ψυχὰν ἐμάν. See also Hom. *Il.* IX. 2, XIII. 48. Pind. *P.* IV. 73. *I.* I. 37.

94. ἐχθρᾷ—δίκῃ.] We agree with Emper in accepting the emendation which he attributes to Lohrs. As he rightly observes, δίκη by itself is an awkward and languid termination to the line, and ἐχθρὰ δίκη is *jus inimicorum*, so that the meaning is *jure inimicorum apud mortuum eris*. And he compares *Sept. c. Theb.* 397: δίκη δ' ὁμαίμων κάρτα νιν προστέλλεται.

96. τὸ δεινὸν τοῦτο.] Sophocles uses δεινὸς, and its derivative δεννάζω of threatening language: cf. *Ajax.* 650, (for which see my note on Pind. *O.* VI. 82), 312; infra 750 compared with 743, 744. Eurip. *Heracl.* 542: ἐμοὶ γὰρ ἦλθες δείν' ἀπειλήσων ἔπη.

100—101. *Parodos.* The following schemo will explain the metres of this ode.

στροφή ά.

1. ‒ ∪ ‖ ‒ ∪ ∪ ‖ ‒ ∪ | ‒ ‖
2. ‒ ∪ ‖ ‒ ∪ ∪ ‖ ‒ ∪ | ‒ ‖
3. ‒ ‒ ‖ ‒ ∪ ∪ ‖ ‒ ∪ | ‒ ‖
4. ∪ ‒ | ‒ ∪ ‖ ‒ ∪ ∪ | ‒ ‖
5. ‒ ∪ ‖ ‒ ∪ ∪ | ‒ ‖
6. ‒ ‒ ‖ ‒ ∪ ‖ ‒ ∪ ∪ | ‒ ∪ | ‒ ∪ ‖
7. ‒ ‒ ‖ ‒ ∪ | ‒ ∪ ∪ | ‒ ‖
8. ‒ ∪ | ‒ ∪ ‖ ‒ ∪ ∪ ‖ ‒ ‖
9. ∪ ∪ ∪ | ∪ ∪ ∪ ‖ ‒ ∪ ∪ | ‒ ‖
10. ‒ ‒ ‖ ‒ ∪ ∪ | ‒ ‒ . ‖

σύστημα ά.

Three anapæstic dimeters and a parœmiac; followed by a dimeter, a basis, and a parœmiac.

στροφή β'.

1. ‒ ∪ ∪ | ‒ ∪ ∪ | ‒ ∪ ∪ ‖ ‒ ∪ | ‒ ‒ ‖
2. ‒ ∪ ∪ | ‒ ∪ ∪ | ‒ ∪ ∪ ‖ ‒ ∪ | ‒ ‒ ‖
3. ‒ ‒ ‖ ‒ ∪ ∪ | ‒ ‖
4. ‒ ‒ ‖ ‒ ∪̄ ‖ ‒ ∪ ∪ ‖ ‒ ‖
5. ‒ ∪ | ‒ ‖ ‒ ∪ | ‒ ‖
6. ‒ ∪ ∪ | ‒ ‖ ‒ ∪ ∪ | ‒ ‖ ‒ ∪ ∪ | ‒ ‖ ‒ ∪ ∪ | ‒ ‒ ‖
7. ‒ ∪ ∪ | ‒ ‒ ‖

σύστημα β'.

Seven anapæstic dimeters followed by a parœmiac.

I have explained elsewhere the principles which I consider applicable to the scansion of the Chorusses of Sophocles, and also some of my objections to the system of compound feet, as they are called (*Varronianus*, pp. 175, 176; 275, 276). Whether we divide the lines as I have done, and consider the first two as one line, the rhythm will remain the same,— namely, a basis, and a dactyl followed by a cretic, considered as the ultimate form of a trochaic dipodia. The first syllable of χρυσέας is made short; see Böckh, *de Metris Pindari*, p. 289; Hermann, *Dial. Pind.* p. ix.; and *El. Doctr. Metr.* p. 44.; Elmsley, *ad Med.* 618. Στρ. ά. 10, β'. 1, β'. 7, are special metres, called the *Pherecrateus*, *Praxilleus*, and *Adonius*. On the antispast in α' 4, as expressing the rising of the sun, and the sudden departure of the Argive host, see note on the ὀρχηστικόν infra v. 1111.; and for the *trochæi semanti* in α' 5, 6, β' 4, see Hermann *El. Doctr. Metr.* p. 660.

105. Διρκαίων ὑπὲρ ῥεέθρων μολοῦσα.] As the Dirke, a little river, flowing from several fountains, ran to the west of Thebes (see the passages quoted by Müller, *Orchom.* p. 487), Sophocles has made an error in taking it as the *gnomon* of sun-rise, unless we understand him as speaking rather of the sun's course than of his point of rising. Cf. Xen. *Mem.* III. 8, § 9: οὐκοῦν ἐν ταῖς πρὸς μεσημβρίαν βλεπού σαις οἰκίαις τοῦ μὲν χειμῶνος ὁ ἥλιος εἰς τὰς παστάδας ὑπολάμπει, τοῦ δὲ θέρους ὑπὲρ ἡμῶν αὐτῶν καὶ τῶν στεγῶν πορευόμενος σκίαν παρέχει. See, however, the Introduction, §7.

106. Ἀργεῖον.] I have adopted Böckh's reading as the best of the means proposed for completing the measure of this line. Brunck suggested ἐξ Ἀργόθεν, which does not mend the metre, Erfurdt, ἀπ' Ἀργόθεν, and Hermann, whom Dindorf follows, Ἀργόθεν ἐκ scil. ἐκβάντα. The reading Ἀργόθεν is perhaps due to some scholiast who did not understand the participle βάντα, which, being placed without the article, cannot be descriptive, but must be a secondary predicate, connected in the construction with πανσαγίᾳ only:

cf. infra 127—130. He speaks of "the Argive *man*," instead of the "Argive host," on account of the simile of the eagle which immediately follows; and also with a special reference to the flight of Adrastus on his horse *Arion*, as described in the Cyclic Thebais: hence the φυγάδα πρόδρομον ὀξ. χαλίνῳ. See the Introduction note (32). For φώς, in the sense of "brave man," or "warrior," see Hom. *Il.* IV. 194; XXI. 546; and *Od.* XXI. 26, where it is applied to Hercules. In *Pers.* 90, ῥεῦμα φωτῶν means "a stream of warriors."

109, 110. ὀξυτέρῳ κινήσασα χαλίνῳ.] I have sufficiently illustrated this metaphor in the *New Cratylus*, p. 225. Emper has seen the full force of the comparative ὀξυτέρῳ. He says, "the defeated Argives marched off during the night. The rays of the rising sun, which the Chorus here addresses, drive the Argives to a more rapid flight, i. e. more rapid than their former flight during the night; for the danger of being pursued became more imminent after daybreak."

110 sqq. ὃν ἐφ' ἁμετέρᾳ γᾷ κ. τ. λ.] The accusative ὃν, without any verb to account for it, and the loss of a dipodia in the anapæstic system, shew that there is a lacuna in these lines. Dindorf indeed would get over the former difficulty by assuming an *anacoluthon*. In his opinion, the poet wrote ὃν as if ἤγαγε had followed, but substituted for this verb the fuller description ἀρθείς—αἰετὸς ἐς γᾶν ὑπερέπτα. Wunder, who sets at nought the metrical difficulty, would read ὃς and Πολυνείκους, with Scaliger and others: he interprets ἀρθείς by the phrase αἴρειν στόλον. I think that in this parodos the equilibrium of the anapæstic systems must be strictly maintained, for the reasons given in the Introduction, § 8; and I agree with Erfurdt and Wex that a verb is required: for although the participles suggested by Hermann and Böckh would obviate the difficulty occasioned by the accusative ὃν, it seems to me that, as they would refer the image of the white-winged eagle to Polyneikes, and not to the white-shielded host of the Argives, which is undoubt-

odly the ground of the comparison, they would only introduce a partial correction into the passage before us. The following are the readings proposed:

Erfurdt: [ἐπόρευσε· θοῶν δ'] ὀξέα κλάζων.
Hermann: ὡς [συναγείρας] ὑπερέπτα.
Böckh: [ἀγαγὼν θούριος] ὀξέα κλάζων.
Wex: [ἤγειρεν· ὁ δ'] αἰετὸς εἰς γᾶν ὥς.

With a slight change in the order of words I have received the last of these. Wex has derived the verb, which, in common with Hermann, he has selected as that proper to the passage, from the words of the Scholiast, supported by an apt quotation from Homer. The Scholiast writes: ὅντινα στρατὸν Ἀργείων ἐξ ἀμφιλόγων νεικέων ἀρθεὶς ἤγαγεν ὁ Πολυνείκης; and Wex suggests that Ἀργείων is a corruption of ἀγείρων, so that the Scholiast was explaining the ἤγειρεν of the text by the periphrasis ἀγείρων ἤγαγε. Thus Homer *Il.* IV. 377:

ξεῖνος ἅμ' ἀντιθέῳ Πολυνείκεϊ λαὸν ἀγείρων
οἵ ῥα τότ' ἐστρατόωνθ' ἱερὰ πρὸς τείχεα Θήβης.

cf. *Œd. Col.* 1306:

ὅπως τὸν ἑπτάλογχον ἐς Θήβας στόλον
ξὺν τοῖσδ' ἀγείρας κ.τ.λ.

where Polyneikes is speaking. As there does not appear to be any particular reason for departing from the usual practice of keeping the dipodiæ separate, and as the Scholiast recognizes the position of the ὡς after αἰετός, I have written:

ἤγειρεν· ὁ δ' εἰς γᾶν, αἰετὸς ὥς,
ὀξέα κλάζων ὑπερέπτα.

The parœmiac, which I have thus introduced here and in the corresponding verse of the antisystem, seems to me to be quite in accordance with the usual practice in the case of the parodus. The pauses in the march-time are similarly indicated in the parodus of the *Ajax*, the *Supplices* of Æschylus, the *Persæ*, and the *Agamemnon*. It is scarcely necessary to mention that I have endeavoured to express in the version the play of words in the original.

114. λευκῆς χιόνος πτέρυγι στεγανός.] This construction of the genitive has been fully illustrated by grammarians and commentators: see Matthiä, *G. Gr.* § 316 f. and the note on Pind. *P.* XI. 33, 34. The philological explanation of the idiom is given in the *New Cratylus*, p. 379. The poet may have had various reasons for comparing the Argive host to a snow-white eagle. The white shields of the Argives are mentioned by Æschylus (*Sept. c. Theb.* 90) and Euripides (*Phœn.* 1115): the great ἀσπις covering the whole body would suggest the broad wing of the eagle, when let down, as it is constantly seen in archaic art: and the image of the eagle itself would be derived from the almost proverbial hostility of the αἰετός and the δράκων (see the passages quoted by Wunder on v. 124, and by Orelli on Horace, IV. *Carm.* 4, 11,) combined with the legendary origin of the Thebans. Moreover, I would venture to suggest that the white Argive eagle and the argent shield of the Argive warriors may have had some reference to the name of the people—namely, that they were ἀργαῦντες because Ἀργεῖοι. At any rate, the two eagles which represented the brother kings of Lacedæmon and Argos are described by Æschylus *Agam.* 114 as ὁ κελαινός ὅ τ' ἐξόπιν ἀργᾶς. That the Atreidæ bore a Saturnian sceptre is stated in the tradition (Homer *Il.* II. 102 sqq.), and the Saturnian sceptre was surmounted by an eagle (Pind. *P.* I. 6). There is an obvious reason for the black shield assigned to Menelaus by Æschylus. But the Spartans might have been distinctively μελάγχλαινοι, like the Scythians so called.

115, 116. πολλῶν μεθ' ὅπλων ξύν θ' ἱπποκόμοις κορύθεσσιν.] As Sophocles might have said πολλοῖς ξὺν ὅπλοις as well as ξὺν ἱπποκόμοις κορύθεσσιν, (cf. Pind. *N.* I. 51: Καδμείων ἀγοὶ χαλκέοις ἀθρόοι σὺν ὅπλοις ἔδραμον,) and as there was no metrical reason to prevent him from doing so, we must suppose that there was some cause which induced this subtle and accurate writer to employ two different prepositions in the present passage. Although μετά and ξύν both signify connexion or conjunction, and although μετά with the genitive is often used in a signification which corresponds, in part at least, to that of ξύν with the dative, the force of these prepositions in composition with verbs may show us that μετά implies rather juxtaposition, or placing side by side, in company or participation, (and this is, in fact, the force of the genitive case with which it is combined in this signification,) and that ξύν denotes a closer union and a more complete conjunction. I believe then that Sophocles, in reference to the wings of the eagle, uses ὅπλον here in the proper and original sense—namely, to signify the ἀσπις only. And this is implied in the etymology of the word: for the ὅπλον, or "thing moved about in defence" (ἕπω), and the ῥόπ-αλον, or "thing brought down heavily to strike" (ῥέπω), would form the two arms offensive and defensive of the primitive warrior. As then he had spoken before of the πανσαγία or πανοπλία of this warrior-host, he here takes its two principal parts, the shield and helmet, and says that the Argives came with many shields *by their sides* and with many helmets, as a part of them, *on their heads*. The student of ancient art is aware that the heavy-armed combatants on the Æginetan pediment have only the large shield and helmet, while the bowmen are in mail. See Müller's *Denkmäler*, I. no. 28. The spears are mentioned immediately afterwards in v. 119. Æschylus expresses the whole equipment of a Greek hoplite in the words: ἔγχη σταδαῖα καὶ φεράσπιδες σάγαι.

117. στὰς—φονώσαισιν.] The στὰς ὑπὲρ μελάθρων probably refers to the position of the Argive camp on the Ismenian hill. Struve did not think of this when he proposed to read πτάς. The conjecture, of φονώσαισιν for φονίαισιν, which is claimed by both Böckh and Hermann, is undoubtedly required by the sense and the metre, and appears to have existed in the text as read by one of the Scholiasts, who writes: ταῖς τῶν φόνων ἐρώσαις λόγχαις; for φονᾶν is de-

fined by the glossographers as equivalent to φόνου ἐπιθυμεῖν, or ἑτοίμως πρὸς τὸ φονεύειν ἔχειν.

124—126. τοῖος—δράκοντι.] It seems to me very surprising that any doubt should be entertained about the meaning of these words. The construction obviously is: τοῖος πάταγος Ἄρεος ἀμφὶ νῶτα [τοῦ αἰετοῦ] ἀντιπάλῳ δράκοντι δυσχείρωμα ἐτάθη. The clatter of the pursuing host was prolonged in the rear of the flying Argives: and as these were represented by the eagle, so the Thebans are described as the dragon or serpent, which had proved his match in the fight. Now this war-clatter, or the onset of a pursuing host which had shown itself ἀντίπαλος in the battle, was a δυσχείρωμα to the defeated army, for the very same reason that made a defeated army itself εὐχείρωτον (Æsch. Pers. 458). The word δυσχείρωμα, therefore, which is predicated secondarily, or through ἐτάθη, is well placed before the causative case δράκοντι, and after the epithet ἀντιπάλῳ, which contributes so much to its meaning. For ἀντίπαλος cf. Æschyl. Sept. c. Theb. 417: τὸν ἀμὸν νῦν ἀντίπαλον εὐτυχεῖν θεοὶ δοῖεν.

130. χρυσοῦ, καναχῇ θ᾽ ὑπερόπλους.] In the two passages in the *Persæ* of Æschylus, in which we find ῥεῦμα used to signify the advance of an army, it is coupled with a genitive explanatory of the metaphor: thus, v. 90: δόκιμος δ᾽ οὔτις ὑποστὰς μεγάλῳ ῥεύματι φωτῶν, and v. 414: τὰ πρῶτα μὲν δὴ ῥεῦμα Περσικοῦ στρατοῦ. And although this assistance is less necessary in the case before us, I think it makes the metaphor more picturesque, if we take the genitive χρυσοῦ, which stands so awkwardly in this line, as a complement of the πολλῷ ῥεύματι, which precedes. The epithet πολλῷ merely refers to the common collocation πολὺς ῥεῖ: so in the more direct expression of the metaphor before us in Æschyl. *Sept. c. Theb.* 80: ῥεῖ πολὺς ὅδε λεὼς πρόδρομος ἱππότας, where the nature of the stream is clearly stated. I believe that the χρυσὸς refers to the helmets which were adorned with this metal; for while the breast-

plate was chiefly of bronze (whence the epithet χαλκομίτρης), and the greaves of tin, the helmet often had a gold or gilded crest (cf. Hom. *Il.* XVIII. 612), whence the epithet χρυσεοπήληξ. Now as the helmets, and their crests waving backwards and forwards, gave the idea of the fluctuating surface of a stream when an army was advancing in order of battle, it seems to me neither forced nor unpoetical to say, that an advancing army πολὺς ῥεῖ χρυσῷ, or, what is the same thing, προσνίσσεται πολλῷ ῥεύματι χρυσοῦ: cf. Strabo, p. 625: ῥεῖ δ' ὁ Πακτωλὸς ἀπὸ τοῦ Τμώλου καταφέρον τὸ παλαιὸν χρυσοῦ ψῆγμα πολύ. On the other hand, I think that καναχή refers to the heavy tramp of the armed multitude, coupled with the clang of their hollow shields against each other: cf. *Il.* XVI. 794, with *Od.* VI. 82. The emendation ὑπερόπλους seems to me required by the sense. All the MSS. have ὑπεροπτίας, over which the correction ὑπερόπτας is written in the oldest Laurentian MS. I consider these corruptions as having been suggested by ὑπερέπτα in the corresponding verse of the *antisystema*. We have other instances in this play of corruptions which have arisen in precisely the same manner. See below v. 606, and elsewhere. Hermann and some others adopt the Laurentian correction ὑπερόπτας; Brunck proposed ὑπεροπλίαις; Emper suggests ὑπεροπλῆτας; and Böckh has substituted ὑπεροπλτείαις.

131. βαλβίδων.] Hermann justly remarks, that βαλβίδων "de extremo loco in quo quis consistit, et hic quidem de summa parte muri dicitur." The prep. ἐπί here bears its proper sense with the gen.—i. e. it denotes parallelism at a certain height from the ground.

133. ὁρμῶντα.] Wunder's translation, *aliquem qui parabat*, may be added to the numberless instances of inaccurate syntactical knowledge on the part of professed scholars in Germany. The participle thus placed without the article can never signify *aliquem qui parabat*, but must mean *quum pararet*, scil. he ὃς τότε ἐπέπνει. The antecedent is omitted because the story of Kapaneus was well known: the participle itself merely indicates the moment at which the bolt struck him.

133. ἀλαλάξαι.] Schol.: παιωνίσαι.

134. ἀντιτύπᾳ.] I agree with Neue, Wunder, and Dindorf, in adopting Porson's correction of the common reading ἀντίτυπα, which other commentators attempt to defend.

135. πυρφόρος,] I can see no reason for removing the comma after this word. As a secondary predicate it may as well be referred to πέσε, as to ἐπέπνει. See some good remarks in K. O. Müller's *Kleine Deutsche Schriften*, I. p. 310. The reference is to the γυμνὸν ἄνδρα πυρφόρον on the shield of Kapaneus (Æsch. *Sept. c. Theb.* 417), and perhaps to the name of this mythological warrior (Καπανεύς, καπ-νός, κάϝω, κάβειρος); and the meaning is, that πυρφόρος as he was, down he went before the mightier fire of Zeus.

135—137. ὅς—ἀνέμων.] For ῥιπαὶ ἀνέμων, see below on v. 904. I think we have here another allusion to the name Καπανεύς; cf. Æsch. *Sept. c. Theb.* 340: ἄλλος δ᾽ ἄλλον ἄγει τὰ δὲ καὶ πυρφορεῖ· καπνῷ χραίνεται πόλισμ᾽ ἅπαν. μαινόμενος δ᾽ ἐπιπνεῖ Λαοδάμας μιαίνων εὐσέβειαν Ἄρης.

139, 140. εἶχε δ᾽ ἄλλᾳ τὰ μὲν—δεξιόσειρος.] I have not scrupled to adopt Böckh's emendation, and I think with him that the τὰ δὲ must be considered as a marginal gloss on ἄλλα, which has crept into the text. The meaning appears to be: "some things happened in one way," i.e. Kapaneus was destroyed by Zeus, as the chorus has just mentioned: "but mighty Ares, acting as an additional horse on the right, where his aid was most required, bestowed other things, in the way of a rough handling, on others," i.e. our warriors, with the assistance of the god of war, gained the victory in other parts of the field. I cannot agree with some of the commentators in thinking that εἶχε is here used in the sense of ἐπεῖχε. It appears to me to be merely the verb of relation, as in Æsch. *Sept. c. Theb.* 799: καλῶς ἔχει τὰ πλεῖστ᾽ ἐν ἐξ πυλώμασιν· τὰς δ᾽ ἑβδόμας κ.τ.λ. For the phrase ἄλλῃ ἔχει, cf. *Philoct.* 22 sq.: σήμαιν' εἴτ' ἔχει χῶρον πρὸς αὐτὸν τόνδε γ' εἴτ' ἄλλῃ κυρεῖ—for σήμαινε εἴτε οὕτως ἔχει εἴτε ἄλλῃ.

Στυφελίζω, from στυφελός, or στυφλός (a synonym for χέρσος, τραχύς, σκληρός, χαλεπός, *Schol. Apoll. Rhod.* II. 1007. cf. infra, v. 250), is used by Homer to signify the infliction of hard blows with stones, spears, or other weapons, (*Il.* V. 437; VII. 261; XII. 405; XVI. 774.) Whence στυφελός is an epithet of a warrior: Æsch. *Pers.* 80: ὀχυροῖσι πεποιθὼς στυφελοῖς ἐφέταις.

Bœkh, and after him Wunder, understand the first part of the compound δεξιόσειρος, as referring to δέξιος Ἄρης, *Mars adjutor.* I think this unnecessary. The Greeks used to place the strongest horse on the right side, and as an outrigger, because in the δρόμος the gallop went to the left about (see Hermann *Opuscula*, Vol. I. p. 69). And as σειραφόρος signifies "an assistant" in general (Æsch. *Ag.* 850), δεξιόσειρος would mean "an assistant on the right hand, where he was most needed." Now the Greeks in battle were always anxious to be covered on the right side (see Thucyd. V. 71). Consequently, there is a double propriety in the metaphor. See below on vv. 291, 662.

The person who stood on the right hand of the chorus was called δεξιοστάτης, (cf. Pollux, *Onom.* II. 161; IV. 106). As there was an intimate connexion between the arrangements of the chorus and the phalanx, it is by no means improbable that this name, as well as παραστάτης, was applied to soldiers in battle. If so, the full force of the compound δεξιόσειρος would at once be felt by any one of the original audience.

141. ἕπτα λοχαγοί.] It would seem from this that Sophocles did not reckon Kapaneus among the seven. But see Wunder on *Œd. Col.* 1308 sq.

143. Ζηνὶ—τέλη.] Böckh rightly remarks, that we must not understand weapons hung up as an offering in the temple, but πανοπλίαι arranged as trophies, as appears from the phrase Ζηνὶ τροπαίῳ. I would venture to suggest that they decorated the scene in this Tragedy.

144. πλὴν τοῖν στυγεροῖν.] As each was victorious, there was no one to offer up the trophy to Zeus. This shows the true force of the δικρατεῖς λογχάς, which Brunck rightly translated *utrinque victrices*. Passow makes a strange blunder, when he supposes that the reference is to large spears hurled with both hands. As we shall see directly, they did not throw, but thrust at one another.

145. καθ' αὑτοῖν.] Above on v. 56.

146. λόγχας στήσαντε.] It will be observed that the poet makes his combatants thrust at one another with their lances, according to the fashion of soldiers in his own time, and according to the plan recommended by Nestor to his chariot-warriors, *Il.* IV. 306, 7. Similarly, Virgil departs from the Homeric type in many respects. The word *foine*, which I have introduced in the translation, was commonly employed in our language to express the push of the pike or spear, at a time when these weapons were in constant use: e. g. Berner's *Froissart*, Vol. II. c. 317: "they began to *foine* with spears, and strike with axes and swords." Chaucer, *Knight's Tale*, v. 1656:

"And after that with sharpe speares strong,
They *foinden* eche at other wonder long."

Mort d'Arthur, Part I. c. 134: "they went to battle again, tracing, racing, and *foining*, as two boars."

147. κοινοῦ θανάτου.] Above v. 1.

149. ἀντιχαρεῖσα.] "Sharing in her joy and congratulating her upon her success." Schol.: ἴσον αὐτῇ χαρεῖσα. On the personification of places, see *ad Pind.* O. III. 9, VI. 84; and Böckh on the latter passage for the epithet πολυάρματος.

153. ἐλελίχθων.] i. e. with dancing, as the Scholiast rightly explains it.

155—161.] Κρέων—συντυχίαις.] As I believe with Böckh that this antisystem should agree in number of lines with the last system of anapæsts, and as I think the supplement which he has introduced is as likely as any other to convey the intended meaning of the poet, I have allowed it to appear in the text, and have expressed it in the translation. On the synizesis in κρέων, the student may consult Dindorf *ad Œd. Col.* 1073.

158. τίνα δὴ μῆτιν ἐρέσσων.] With Hermann, I prefer the interrogative here. That Kreon had *some* plan was clear from his convocation of the Gerusia. For ἐρέσσων, see below on v. 231.

159, 160. ὅτι σύγκλητον τήνδε γερόντων προύθετο λέσχην.] The Prytanes at Athens were said προθεῖναι ἐκκλησίαν, not προθέσθαι. But Kreon, as a sovran ruler, could call a meeting, not to hear *their* suggestions, but to communicate *his* will, and therefore would naturally use the middle voice with that distinction of meaning, which is well known in the opposition between θεῖναι and θέσθαι νόμον. In Lucian's *Necyomantia*, c. 19, we find the following obvious discrimination of προθεῖναι and προθέσθαι: οὐ γὰρ οἶδ᾽ ὅπως, περὶ τούτου λέγειν προθέμενος, παμπολὺ ἀπεπλανήθην ἀπὸ τοῦ λόγου· διατρίβοντος γάρ μου παρ᾽ αὐτοῖς, προύθεσαν οἱ πρυτανεῖς ἐκκλησίαν περὶ τῶν κοινῇ συμφερόντων. Hemsterhuis concludes an excellent note on these words by a reference to the passage in the text. "Nunc liquido patet unde duxerit Sophocles in *Antig.* 165: ὅτι σύγκλητον—πέμψας· solemne est ingeniosissimo poëtæ phrases a suæ gentis moribus derivatas aliorsum apte traducere: cui, præter illud προθέσθαι λέσχην, hisce lectis non statim ἐκκλησία σύγκλητος in memoriam venit? neque obscurum est perito linguæ Græcæ, quare cùm in superioribus exemplis προθεῖναι conspiciatur, ipse medium usurparit." The commentators ought to have remarked, that, by using λέσχη, instead of βουλή, the poet has told us that this was a private co.. rence, and not a public convocation. The inconsiderable number of persons in the chorus partly implied this: it is expressly stated below, in v. 164, that this was a very select council; and it appears from v. 821 that they were the wealthy men of Thebes—the ἄνακτες, as they are termed in v. 955. The κοινῷ κηρύγματι πέμψας is explained by the πομποῖς ἔστειλα ἰκέσθαι of v. 164, and implies that a message was sent to each of them Cf. for πομπός, Œd. T. 289, Œd. Col. 70, and for κοινός, Phil. 1130, Œd. Col. 61. By κήρυγμα, he does not mean a public proclamation in the market-place, but the herald's summons at the house of each of the elders. Similarly, the members of the Roman *curiæ* were summoned by the thirty lictors of the *curiæ*, and the *comitia curiata* were thence termed the *comitia calata*, "the called or summoned assembly," in contradistinction to the *comitia centuriata*, which were convened by the sound of trumpet. In general, it is to be observed that κήρυξ and κηρύσσω refer to a call by the voice (cf. γηρῦς, κράζω, κραυγή, &c.), as distinguished from any other means of summoning. It is worthy of remark, that in the passage in the book of *Daniel*, in which the Greek is seen through a very transparent covering, the borrowed term כָּרוֹז (κήρυξ) is placed by the side of the genuine Semitic קְרָא (III. 4), with which it has an undoubted affinity. The aphel verb which occurs in *Dan.* V. 29, is clearly nothing more than a derivation from this foreign root. If there were no other Greek words in *Dan.* III. 4, we might compare the Sanscrit *Krus* and the Zend *Khresio*, which are adduced by Gesenius.

162. πολλῷ σάλῳ—πάλιν.] The phrase σάλῳ σείσαντες is well illustrated by Œd. T. 22; Plut. Phoc. c. III. Fab. Max. c. XXVII., which are cited by Wex. The verb ὀρθόω here and v. 166, and the secondary predicate ὀρθῆς in v. 190, are borrowed from the same reference to a ship, which is called ὀρθή when it does not heel over to either side. With the Greek rowing-galleys, no less than with our steamers, it was very desirable to maintain the proper trim.

174. γένους κατ' ἀγχιστεία.] The more common ἀγχιστεία is thus explained by the author of the λέξεις ῥητορικαί (*Bekker. Anecd.* p. 413): ἀγχιστεία: συγγένεια. καὶ ἀγχιστεῖς οἱ ἀπὸ ἀδελφῶν καὶ ἀνεψιῶν καὶ θείων

κατὰ πατέρα καὶ μητέρα ἐγγυτάτω τοῦ τελευτήσαντος· οἱ δὲ ἔξω τούτων συγγενεῖς μόνον. οἱ δὲ κατ' ἐπιγαμίαν μιχθέντες τοῖς οἴκοις οἰκεῖοι λέγονται. And yet Thucydides says (I. 9) κατὰ τὸ οἰκεῖον of the very relationship referred to in the text—that between Atreus and Eurystheus. In Pindar (P. IX. 64), and Æschylus (*Agam.* 237), ἄγχιστος signifies merely "nearest at hand to protect," like the *præsens numen* of the Romans: cf. *Œd. T.* 919. In this sense I have introduced the word in v. 939 infra.

176. ψυχήν τε καὶ φρόνημα καὶ γνώμην,] It would be an injustice to Sophocles to suppose that he used these three words as idle synonyms. The connexion by means of τε καί shows an intimate union; but there is still a difference, which it was important to mark. By ψυχή is meant the fabric of a man's mind and character; by φρόνημα, that mind as it manifests itself in the general tenour of his outward actions, especially in relation to politics; and by γνώμη, the dogmatical expression of the meaning in words; so that φρόνημα and γνώμη are distinct and successive manifestations of the ψυχή—the former being the προαίρεσις or *will*, a unity of which contributes to the formation of a political party, and which by itself regulates the enactments of a ruler: and the latter being the *meaning* or *sentiment*, which expresses in words, or justifies to the reason, that which is already felt to be a sufficient motive for the will and choice. See above, v. 169, below, v. 207, for φρόνημα. The whole speech, as an exposition of the φρόνημα which springs from the ψυχή of Kreon, is his γνώμη. For ἐκμανθάνω cf. Eurip. *Med.* 220: ὅστις, πρὶν ἀνδρὸς σπλάγχνον ἐκμαθεῖν σαφῶς στυγεῖ δεδορκώς.

178. ἐμοὶ γάρ,] The particle γάρ, and in prose γοῦν, are frequently used thus at the beginning of a narrative or exposition: see below, vv. 238, 405, 983. The English particle "for" is rarely an adequate representative of γάρ. Our phrases "in fact," "the fact is," "in point of fact," "if you come to that," &c., are much better equivalents in very many cases.

185—190. οὔτ' ἂν σιωπήσαιμι—ποιούμεθα.] There

is a parallelism in this passage, which has not, I think, been sufficiently noticed: Kreon says that he would not purchase his own *safety* by winking at that which would bring mischief on his people: and that he would not select a *friend* from among the enemies of his country: for that our *safety* depends on the security of our country, and that *friends* are naught, except when our native land is in prosperity. Emper has pointed out the proper interpretation of ἀντὶ τῆς σωτηρίας. For although there is nothing in the words themselves to prevent us from referring the σωτηρία to the same object as the ἄτη (cf. infra v. 314, 439), it is clear that Kreon is here opposing the individual σωτηρία to the public ἄτη, and is arguing for the fact that no individual is really safe unless his country is so likewise: for ἥδ᾽ ἐστὶν ἡ σώζουσα. The article, in τὴν ἄτην and τοὺς φίλους, must not be neglected. By τὴν ἄτην is meant *the* mischief which always comes upon the citizens of a free state, when a man, through fear of his ἑταῖροι, or intimate associates, acquiesces in their corrupt or seditious designs: and τοὺς φίλους implies that those are not friends, in any true sense of the term, whose friendship tends to an interference with the state's equilibrium. For the nautical sense of σώζω, σωτηρία, I may refer to my note on Pind. O. VIII. 20—27.

196. ἐφαγνίσαι.] This is, no doubt, the true reading. I believe the word refers to honours paid at the tomb *subsequently* to the regular sepulture—those ἐναγίσματα τῶν κατοιχομένων which Pindar calls αἱμακουρίαι, O. I. 90. See above on v. 25.

205, 206. ἐᾶν δ᾽ ἄθαπτον—ἰδεῖν.] There is no good reason for the alteration αἰκιστόν τ᾽, or for the reading αἰκισθέν τ᾽. The construction is, αἰκισθέντα ἰδεῖν δέμας πρὸς οἰωνῶν καὶ πρὸς κυνῶν ἐδεστόν.

208. προέξουσ᾽] Hermann proposes προσέξουσ᾽, with what signification it is difficult to see. The hiatus may be excused by the aspirate: cf. αὐτοέντης. Sophocles makes Kreon represent any honour paid to Polyneikes as a diminution of those due to Eteokles: below v. 512.

212. τὸν—πόλει.] Dindorf proposes καὶ τὸν εὐμενῆ. I agree with Hermann, Wex, and Böckh, that no alteration is necessary.

213. νόμῳ—σοι.] Böckh thinks that the omission of either που or γε will be detrimental to the ethos of this passage. He conceives that the Chorus is intended to express dissatisfaction coupled with a sort of gentle irony. It appears to me, that this is quite inconsistent with the tenour of the play, so far as the Chorus is concerned. From first to last the elders not only admit, but maintain, the authority of the king. The vulgate παντί πού τ' is obviously corrupt. Hermann writes παντὶ πάντ', which is harsh. Erfurdt suggests πού γ', which is not a Greek collocation. I agree with Dindorf, that τ' ἔνεστι should be changed into πάρεστι; and I have ventured upon a further change of παντὶ που into πανταχοῦ. In the first place, the collocation πάρεστι χρῆσθαι νόμῳ, without the addition of παντί, appears to me most in accordance with the spirit of the Greek language: cf. *Trach.* 60: ὥστ' εἴ τί σοι πρὸς καιρὸν ἐννέπειν δοκῶ, πάρεστι χρῆσθαι τἀνδρὶ τοῖς τ' ἐμοῖς λόγοις. Then, in an admission of Kreon's authority, the adverb πανταχοῦ or πανταχῇ is strictly in its place. In v. 625 infra, we have in this sense: ἢ σοὶ μὲν ἡμεῖς πανταχῇ δρῶντες φίλοι; In the passage before us, the reading που points to an original πανταχοῦ. In the *Ajax*, 1348: ὡς ἂν ποιήσῃς πανταχοῦ χρηστός γ' ἔσει, we find the various reading πανταχῇ. In the following we find only πανταχοῦ; *Ajax* 1252: ἀλλ' οἱ φρονοῦντες εὖ κρατοῦσι πανταχοῦ. *Phil.* 1041: νικᾶν γε μέντοι πανταχοῦ χρῄζων ἔφυν. And there can be no doubt that although πανταχῇ *might be used* in the same, or a very similar sense, πανταχοῦ is strictly the more appropriate adverb.

215. ὡς ἂν σκοποὶ νῦν ἦτε] I am surprised that any scholars should be found to whom Dindorf's emendation πῶς ἂν σκοποὶ νῦν εἶτε; could appear even probable. That such a strong expression of a wish should proceed from the sovran ruler, is quite inconsistent with the general accuracy of this

poet. The collocation ὡς ἄν with the subjunctive is by no means uncommon, and though there is a good deal of syntactical refinement in its usage, every Greek scholar is aware that in a final sentence it indicates an *eventual* conclusion— one in which an additional hypothesis is virtually contained: e. g. Æschyl. *Prom.* 670—672: ἔξελθε πρὸς Λέρνης βαθὺν λειμῶνα, κ.τ.λ. ὡς ἂν τὸ Δῖον ὄμμα λωφήσῃ πόθου, "in order that the eye of Jove may, *as in that case it will*, be freed from passion." Soph. *Electr.* 1495, 6: χώρει δ᾽ ἔνθα περ κατέκτανες πατέρα τὸν ἁμόν, ὡς ἂν ἐν ταὐτῷ θάνῃς, "in order that you may, *as by going there you will*, die in the very place where you murdered him." (Hermann's note on this passage seems to me very surprising.) Now the only difference in the case before us is, that the main verb is omitted. If the Chorus had asked Kreon:

τί δ᾽ ἔστιν, ἀνθ᾽ οὗ τόνδ᾽ ἀνήλωσας λόγον;

the answer in the text would be quite in accordance with the common usages of the language: "in order that you may, as by having heard my words you will, be careful to see to their observance by others." But this or a similar basis for the sentence being fully implied in the tenour of what has preceded, its omission need not offend here any more than in Æsch. *Choeph.* 981: ὡς ἂν παρῇ μοι μάρτυς ἐν δίκῃ ποτέ, where I think there is, properly speaking, an omission of the antecedent clause. Cf. Thucyd. VI. 91. On the whole, I conceive that there are only three modes of dealing with this passage, in which a scholar can acquiesce: (1.) the supposition that a line has fallen out, in which the Chorus asked why they had been summoned; (2.) the supposition that Kreon is interrupted by the Chorus, who mistake his use of the word σκοποί; (3.) the supposition that the subjunctive with ὡς ἄν has here an imperative force, the antecedent clause being implied. As I consider this the most reasonable supposition, I have merely changed νῦν into νυν, a change which the second supposition would also demand.

222. τὸ κέρδος.] For the agency here attributed to κέρδος, "the love of lucre," cf. Pind. *P.* III. 54, *N.* IX. 33.

225. φροντίδων ἐπιστάσεις.] Cf. Plutarch. de Profect. Virt. Sent. 76, c: οὕτως ἄν τις ἐν φιλοσοφίᾳ τὸ ἐνδελεχὲς καὶ τὸ συνεχὲς τῆς πορείας καὶ μὴ πολλὰς διὰ μέσου ποιούμενον ἐπιστάσεις, εἶτ᾽ αὖθις ὁρμὰς καὶ ἐπιπηδήσεις, ἀλλά, κ.τ.λ. τεκμήριον ἑαυτῷ ποιήσαιτο προκοπῆς. Plato Resp. VI. p. 511, n: τὰς ὑποθέσεις ποιούμενος οὐκ ἀρχὰς ἀλλὰ τῷ ὄντι ὑποθέσεις, οἷον ἐπιβάσεις τε καὶ ὁρμάς. The plural ὁδοῖς, which follows, shews that he is speaking of a number of fresh starts, or recommencements of one and the same journey.

231. τοιαῦθ᾽ ἑλίσσων—ταχύς.] This emendation, which Erfurdt and Hermann have derived from the Scholiast, seems to me necessary. The common reading, βραδύς, is obviously a marginal gloss. It may be perhaps as well to remark, that ἑλίσσων refers to the thoughts, and not to the turns, which the Sentinel took on his journey; compare *Ajax*, 351: ἅλιον ἑλίσσων πλάταν, with v. 158 supra: τίνα δὴ μῆτιν ἐρέσσων.

233, 234. τέλος γε μέντοι—ὅμως.] For ἐνίκησεν (sc. ἡ γνώμη) see below v. 274. *El.* 245. The words which follow have not found favour in the eyes of some of the critics. Wunder would read σοί τ᾽ εἰ, or κεί σοι. Emper proposes ὡς, κεί τὸ μηδὲν ἐξερῶ, φράσων ὅμως. I think that the vulgate is genuine, and that it is sufficiently supported by the passage which Erfurdt quotes from the *Œd. T.* 545, 6: λέγειν σὺ δεινός· μανθάνειν δ᾽ ἐγὼ κακὸς σοῦ. δυσμενῆ γὰρ καὶ βαρύν σ᾽ εὕρηκ᾽ ἐμοί. The terror of the Sentinel, and the anger of Œdipus, justify this emphatic position of the personal pronoun. Cf. infra v. 681: τὸ γὰρ σὸν ὄμμα δεινὸν ἀνδρὶ δημότῃ λόγοις τοιούτοις οἷς σὺ μὴ τέρψει κλύων.

235. δεδραγμένος.] One MS. has πεπραγμένος: others, πεφραγμένος, for which Dindorf has substituted the Attic form πεφαργμένος. The Scholiast obviously read δεδραγμένος, a strong metaphorical word, well adapted to the character of the speaker. The later writers seem to use the word in very much the same signification, and it must have extended its

applications in the ordinary language of Athens, in which the commonest coin, the δράχμη, was so called because it was a handful of κέρματα, i. e. ὀβολοί. Cf. Herod. III. 13: ταύτας (τὰς μνέας) δρασσόμενος αὐτοχειρίῃ διέσπειρε τῇ στρατιῇ.

241. εὖ γε—κύκλῳ.] I have adopted the correction στεγάζει, which Emper has suggested, of the vulgate στοχάζει. The latter has no signification which suits the context: the former, which means "you roof yourself in," or "cover yourself over-head," is the proper correlative to ἀποφάργνυσαι κύκλῳ, "you surround yourself with a hedge." In the next line, I have given νέον its common euphemistic force.

253. ὁ πρῶτος—ἡμεροσκόπος.] This is a note of time. The day-watches had just commenced, for it was shortly after sun-rise.

259, 260. λέγοι—φύλακα.] The participial sentence is a secondary predication, or explanatory apposition to the main verb. It is, in fact, equivalent to an adverb. Cf. Æsch. Prom. 200. Eurip. Bacch. 1084, where see Elmsley.

260. κἂν ἐγίγνετο.] The imperfect is used here instead of the aorist, because, in the eagerness of his narrative, the Sentinel reproduces the scene, and represents it as going on. Consequently, he has used the imperfect or present throughout, instead of the aorist, which is the regular historical tense. Similarly, in a shorter clause, Œd. Col. 272 (cf. 952):

καί τοι πῶς ἐγὼ κακὸς φύσιν,
ὅστις παθὼν μὲν ἀντέδρων, ὥστ᾽ εἰ φρονῶν
ἔπρασσον, οὐδ᾽ ἂν ὧδ᾽ ἐγιγνόμην κακός.

The other passages which Neue quotes (ad Œd. Tyr. 125), and which present an aorist in the apodosis, are not to the point. He might have found one precisely similar in Thucyd. I. 75: καὶ γὰρ ἂν αἱ ἀποστάσεις πρὸς ὑμᾶς ἐγίγνοντο.

263. ἀλλ' ἔφευγε μὴ εἰδέναι.] The common reading inserts τὸ before μή. This is not required by the sense, and spoils the metre. As it is clear that the imperfect must stand, it seems much better to omit the article, than to substitute the aorist. The poet has here used φεύγω, which commonly signifies "to be defendant in a suit," as opposed to διώκω, in the sense of ἀρνοῦμαι, or "to put in a plea." In the same sense the word is used by Æschyl. *Suppl.* 393:

δεῖ τοι σὲ φεύγειν κατὰ νόμους τοὺς οἴκοθεν
ὡς οὐκ ἔχουσι κῦρος οὐδὲν ἀμφὶ σοῦ.

Demosth. *adv. Aph.* p. 813, § 1: ἐπειδὴ δ' οὗτος τοὺς μὲν σαφῶς εἰδότας τὰ ἡμέτερα ἔφυγε μηδὲν διαγνῶναι περὶ αὐτῶν. These passages, which are quoted by Wex, sufficiently justify the construction, and although the repetition of εἴ τις, through οὐδεὶς, may seem a little harsh, it is not without precedent; and there certainly does not appear to be any necessity for the emendations ἔφλεγε for ἔφευγε, or ἐπεῦκτο for ἔφευγε τό, proposed by Hermann and Bergk, or for Dindorf's insertion of πᾶς before ἔφευγε, and his omission of εἰδέναι at the end of the line.

269, 270. ἐς πέδον κάρα νεῦσαι.] Not that they threw themselves on the ground like Oriental mourners, but merely that they hung their heads—a sign of embarrassment, which has been ingeniously expressed by Tennyson in his new poem, *The Princess*, p. 26:

" At those high words, we, conscious of ourselves,
Perused the matting."

See below, v. 439.

280. πρὶν ὀργῆς καί με.] With many of the commentators, I have adopted Seidler's correction of the common reading κἀμέ. The καί throws an emphasis on ὀργῆς.

289. ἀλλὰ ταῦτα—ἐμέ.] In these lines there are several points which previous Editors have overlooked. In the first place, the καὶ πάλαι has seemed to one of them inconsistent with the short duration of time which had elapsed

since Kreon came to the throne. But πάλαι does not imply of necessity any particular lapse of time. The Chorus had just used the same adverb to express a short cogitation (above v. 275). The ἄνδρες πόλεως are the ἀστοί, δημόται, or *lower* citizens: see below v. 681, and cf. Pind. *P.* I. 84: ἀστῶν ἀκοὰ κρύφιον θυμὸν βαρύνει[1]. *P.* XI. 30: ὁ δὲ χαμηλὰ πνέων ἄφαντον βρέμει. The adverb δικαίως is used here in a sense which has escaped the commentators, but which I have expressed in the version, and have explained in the *New Cratylus* (p. 371). Lastly, ὡς στέργειν ἐμέ, does not refer to the filial affection of the people for their King, but to Kreon's approbation of the sentiments and conduct of the lower orders. For the meaning of the verb, see above v. 273, and *Phil.* 456: τούτους ἐγὼ τοὺς ἄνδρας οὐ στέρξω ποτέ; and for the post-position of the subject ἐμέ, see Eurip. *Hecub.* 730: σὺ δὲ σχολάζεις ὥστε θαυμάζειν ἐμέ. Æsch. *Pers.* 513: ὡς στένειν πόλιν Περσῶν ποθοῦσαν φιλτάτην ἥβην χθονός. Any other way of construing these words seems to me impossible. Kreon merely says that he would have liked them to be implicitly obedient; for their love he cared nothing: *oderint, dum metuant*, is the tyrant's motto. For the force of ὡς c. infin. vide infra v. 303, and the passage quoted above from the *Persæ*.

303. χρόνῳ ποτ'—δίκην.] The King says that they have at last brought their dislike to an overt act, which will ensure their punishment. The χρόνῳ ποτε belongs therefore to ἐξέπραξαν, of which the effect is ὡς δοῦναι δίκην.

318. ῥυθμίζεις.] For this use of the word, see Blomfield's *Glossar. in Prom.* 249.

320. ἄλημα.] With most of the Editors, I have adopted

[1] The poet means: "not only is prolixity tiresome in all matters, but it is especially so when another's glory is being proclaimed in the hearing of his fellow-citizens of the lower orders." I cannot but think that ἀστῶν here is governed by κρύφιον θυμόν: for the ἀκοά is clearly the glory of Hiero (cf. v. 90), and ἀστοί are the lower citizens (cf. *P.* III. 71), who were generally envious (cf. *O.* VI. 7.)

Schneider's suggestion, that Sophocles wrote ἅλημα here, as in the *Ajax*, 381, 389, and not the vulgate λάλημα. The Scholiast translates the word in this passage just as he translates ἅλημα in the *Ajax*, and the context requires it.

324. κόμψευε.] Ruhnken has sufficiently illustrated the use of this word (*ad Tim.* p. 154), which here refers to the Sentinel's punning refinements on δοκεῖ, δοκεῖν, and δόκησις. An English writer, who was celebrated for τὰ κομψὰ ταῦτα, εἴτε ληρήματα χρὴ φάναι εἶναι εἴτε φλυαρίας; has used the verb "to prate," as their best description: "he would be bold with himself, and say, when he preached twice a day at St. Giles', he *prated* once." Buckeridge's *Funeral Sermon on Bishop Andrewes*, p. 295. *Lib. Angl. Cath. Theology.* And with reference to the ἅλημα of v. 320, this verb very appropriately expresses the egotistical vulgarity of the special-pleading coxcomb. So in the *Pursuits of Literature*, the notorious egotism of Lord Erskine is similarly described:

Octavius. This of yourself?
Author. 'Tis so.
Oct. You're turn'd plain fool,
   A vain, pert *prater* of the Erskine school.

332—373. *First Stasimon.* The metres are as follows:

στροφὴ ά.

1. –́ ⏑ ⏑ ‖ –́ ⏑ | –́ ⏑ | – ‖
2. – – ‖ –́ ⏑ ⏑ ‖ –́ ⏑ | – ‖
3. –́ ⏑ ‖ –́ ⏑ ⏑ ‖ –́ ⏑ | – ‖
4. – – ‖ –́ ⏑ ⏑ | –́ ⏑ | – ‖
5. – ‖ –́ ⏑ ‖ –́ ⏑ ⏑ | –́ – ‖
6. ⏑ ‖ –́ ⏑ | – ⏑ | –́ ‖
7. ⏑ ‖ –́ ⏑ | – ⏑ | –́ ⏑ | – – ‖
8. –́ ⏑ ⏑ | –́ ⏑ ⏑ | –́ ⏑ ⏑ | –́ ⏑ ⏑ ‖
9. –́ ⏑ ⏑ | –́ ⏑ ⏑ | –́ ⏑ ⏑ | –́ ⏑ ⏑ ‖
10. – – ‖ –́ ⏑ | – ⏑ | –́ ⏑ ‖

στροφὴ β'.

1. $- \parallel \acute{-} \cup \cup \mid \acute{-} \cup \cup \parallel \acute{-} \cup \parallel$
2. $\acute{-} \cup \cup \mid \acute{-} \cup \cup \parallel \acute{-} \cup \parallel$
3. $\acute{-} \cup \cup \mid \acute{-} \cup \cup \parallel \acute{-} \cup \mid - - \parallel$
4. $\cup \parallel \acute{-} \cup \mid - \parallel \acute{-} \cup \mid - \parallel$
5. $\cup \parallel \acute{-} \cup \mid - \parallel \acute{-} \cup \mid - \parallel$
6. $\acute{-} \cup \cup \mid \acute{\cup} \parallel$
7. $\cup \parallel \acute{\cup} \cup \cup \mid - \cup \mid \acute{-} \cup \mid - \parallel$
8. $\cup \parallel \acute{-} \cup \mid - \parallel \acute{-} \cup \mid - \parallel$
9. $\acute{-} \cup \mid - \cup \mid \acute{-} \cup \mid - \parallel$
10. $\cup \parallel \acute{-} \cup \mid - \cup \mid \acute{-} \cup \mid - \parallel$
11. $\acute{-} \cup \mid - - \parallel$

The whole of this ode should be scanned as dactylico-trochaic. It seems to me most unreasonable to suppose that iambic rhythms should find a place in such a scheme: and instead of imagining, with Dindorf, iambic verses mixed up with cretics, trochees, and Bacchei, I have merely marked the anacrusis in στρ. ά. 5, 6, 7. στρ. β'. 4, 5, 7, 8, 10. That universal metre, the Saturnian, may teach us that the anacrusis is most properly in its place at the beginning of trochaic rhythms (see *Varronianus*, p. 173 sqq.). Στρ. ά. 8, 9, 10, may be considered as a dactylic octameter resting on a spondee, and followed by a trochaic tripodia.

332. πολλὰ τὰ δεινά.] Some years ago I suggested (*ad Pind. O.* I. 28), that it would be as well to make πολλά the subject here, as it is in the passage of Pindar, because it seemed more natural that δεινά should be the subject as δεινότερον is. In this conjecture, I now see, I had been anticipated by Neue, who is confidently followed by Wunder. I should not have thought it worth while to alter the text, even if there were any great force in the reasons mentioned

above. But there seems to be truth in what Emper says, that if we translate καὶ by *und doch*, "and yet," the inversion of the propositions will give greater emphasis to the passage. For the meaning of δεινός here, the student may compare infra 1013: βροτῶν χοἰ πολλὰ δεινοί, with the definition in Aristotle, *Eth. Nic.* VI. 12. § 9: ἔστι δή τις δύναμις ἣν καλοῦσι δεινότητα κ.τ.λ. ἂν μὲν οὖν ὁ σκοπὸς ᾖ καλός, ἐπαινετή ἐστιν, κ.τ.λ.

340. ἰλλομένων ἀρότρων.] The Aldine and one of the MSS. have παλλομένων, which appears to me unintelligible. I am unable to see any difficulty in the text according to the above reading, which I consider indisputably genuine. The sense is suggested by the word πολεύων which follows, and the words before us must mean, "as the ploughs are being moved backwards and forwards in a zig-zag course," alluding, naturally, to the continuance from furrow to furrow; from which the Greeks derived their phrase, "to write as the oxen turn" (βουστροφηδὸν γράφειν i.e. ἐπὰν ὁμοίως τοῖς ἀροτριῶσι βουσὶ τὰς ἀντιστροφὰς ποιῇ τις. Hesych.). That ἴλλω may be used in this sense, is clear from the line in Nicander quoted by Buttmann, (*Lexil.* II. 156): φεῦγε δ᾽ ἀεὶ σκολιήν τε καὶ οὐ μίαν ἀτραπὸν ἴλλων, with which we might compare Virgil's description of the flight of Turnus, *Æneid* XII. 742, 743:

> Ergo amens diversa fuga petit æquora Turnus,
> Et nunc huc, inde huc, incertos implicat orbes.

And another passage, (*Ibid.* XII. 482):

> Haud minus Æneas tortos legit obvius orbes
> Vestigatque virum, et disjecta per agmina magna
> Voce vocat—

might be used to explain Xenophon's phrase, (*Venat.* VI 15): αἱ δὲ [κύνες] ὑπὸ χαρᾶς καὶ μένους προϊᾶσιν ἐξιλλοῦσαι τὰ ἴχνη, ὡς πέφυκε, διπλᾶ, τριπλᾶ, προφορούμεναι παρὰ τὰ αὐτά, διὰ τῶν αὐτῶν ἐπηλλαγμένα, κ.τ.λ. Buttmann's opinion seems to have coincided with this: but he speaks doubtfully, and quotes nothing in support of his suggestion, except the line from Nicander.

340. ἱππείῳ γένει πολεύων.] I prefer πολεύων, the *constructio ad sensum*, to πωλεῦον, which agrees more strictly with τοῦτο. Immediately afterwards we have ἀμφιβαλών. By the ἱππείῳ γένει the Scholiast rightly understands not horses, which were rarely used with the plough, but mules, which were preferred for that employment in very ancient times; he says: ἱππείῳ γένει πολεύων· ταῖς ἡμιόνοις

αἱ γάρ τε βοῶν προφερέστεραί εἰσιν
ἑλκέμεναι νειοῖο βαθείης πηκτὸν ἄροτρον.

(Il. X. 352). He adds τινὲς δὲ καὶ ἵπποις χρῶνται εἰς ἀροτριασμόν; but the training of the *horse* for the yoke is not mentioned till afterwards, v. 350. In the same way as Sophocles has here shrunk from mentioning the mule, Simonides addressed the victorious mules of Leophron as "the daughters of storm-footed steeds" (χαίρετ' ἀελλοπόδων θύγατρες ἵππων. *Fragm.* 13. Bergk.).

342. κουφονόων.] The credit of this certain emendation is due to Brunck. We have below, v. 610, ἀπάτα κουφονόων ἐρώτων. The reader of the *Phædrus* does not need to be told, that, in the language of Sophocles and Plato, words referring to the use of wings are employed to denote the purpose of the mind, especially in regard to the fluctuating emotions of love (See *New Cratylus*, p. 68). Here we have the converse metaphor; or rather that, which gave occasion to the metaphor in the other case, is here used in the reversed application: wings expressed the light-mindedness of man, therefore light-mindedness is made an epithet of the winged birds. See Aristoph. *Aves*, 168—170:

ὁ Τελέας ἐρεῖ ταδί·
ἄνθρωπος ὄρνις ἀστάθμητος πετόμενος,
ἀτέκμαρτος, οὐδὲν οὐδέποτ' ἐν ταὐτῷ μένων.

With which compare the *Funeral Service:* "he *fleeth* as it were a shadow, and never *continueth in one stay*." The compound "flighty-purposed," by which I have rendered κουφόνοις is derived from Shakspere, *Macbeth*, Act IV. Sc. 1:

"The *flighty purpose* never is o'ertook
Unless the deed go with it."

The words φῦλον and ἔθνος are used here with a covert reference to their employment as political terms, denoting classes in a state.

343. θηρῶν—ἔθνη.] Cf. Aristot. *Eth. Nic.* VIII. 1, § 3 : τοῖς πλ. τῶν ζώων καὶ τοῖς ὁμοέθνεσι πρὸς ἄλληλα.

350. ὀχμάζεται—ζυγῶν.] This emendation, which Franz sent to Böckh, is referred by Wolff (in the *Zeitschrift für Alterthumswissenschaft*, 1846, p. 746,) to Schöne (*Allg. Schulztg.* 1833, II. p. 948); and I agree with Emper in thinking it by far the most probable of those which have been proposed. Phavorin. p. 1406: κυρίως δέ ἐστιν ὀχμάσαι τὸ ἵππον ὑπὸ χαλινὸν ἀγαγεῖν ἢ ὑπὸ ὄχημα. So Eurip. *El.* 817 : ὅστις ταῦρον ἀρταμεῖ καλῶς ἵππους τ' ὀχμάζει. The middle here has its proper force. *Antholog. Palat.* IX. No. 19 : νῦν κλοιῷ δειρὴν πεπεδημένος, οἷα χαλινῷ καρπὸν ἐλᾷ Δηοῦς ὀκριόεντι λίθῳ.

352. καὶ φθέγμα καὶ ἠνεμόεν φρόνημα καὶ ἀστυνόμους ὀργάς.] Most students of Sophocles have sought in vain for a precise and consistent explanation of these words. Without discussing the opinions of previous commentators, whether I partially agree with, or wholly differ from, their views, I will state what appears to me the meaning of the poet. In speaking of the δεινότης or *power* of man, he enumerates the following exemplifications of it : (1) navigation : (2) agriculture : (3) fowling, hunting, and fishing : (4) domestication of wild cattle, and taming and training the ox and the horse : (5) the three particulars in the verses before us : (6) architecture : (7) medical skill. In such a complete specification, it seems scarcely possible that a highly educated Athenian would omit : (*a*) language applied to poetry and oratory : (*b*) speculative reasoning or philosophy : and (*c*) political science. And I believe that these are the three particulars here mentioned as φθέγμα, ἠνεμόεν φρόνημα, and ἀστυνόμοι ὀργαί. The first word,

φθέγμα, has no epithet, and as it cannot mean that man taught himself (ἐδιδάξατο) mere utterance, it must imply language in its higher sense, or as applied to oratory and poetry. The other words, φρόνημα and ὀργαί, are defined by their epithets. In themselves, they are general terms referring, the one to that mixture of intellect and will which was placed by the Greeks in the breast (φρήν) of man, and which formed the basis of his political predilections and of his philosophical bias (see above, v. 176); the other, to that complex of longings and likings, which, regulated by the mind, constituted the distinctive character or disposition of an individual (see below, v. 850, 929). How φρόνημα and ὀργή differ, and at the same time how far they agree, may be seen by a comparison of the following passages; above, v. 169: μένοντας ἐμπέδοις φρονήμασιν. *Ajax* 640: οὐκέτι συντρόφοις ὀργαῖς ἔμπεδος. What then are the ἠνεμόεν φρόνημα and the ἀστυνόμοι ὀργαί which man has *taught himself* (ἐδιδάξατο)? With regard to the former, it is to be observed that we have twice in this play the phrase φρονεῖν διδάσκεσθαι, or διδάσκειν τὸ φρονεῖν, (infra vv. 717, 1313), where φρονεῖν means "wisdom" considered as a sort of experience (ἐμπειρία), and the ὀργαί, which a man teaches himself, can only be regarded as habitudes, or ἕξεις, which he acquires by practice. Accordingly, the very idea, which must be attached to the word φρόνημα in this passage, is inconsistent with one of the versions proposed for the epithet ἠνεμόεν, namely, "swift as the wind:" for φρόνημα must here be considered as something fixed and stable, not as something fleeting and changeable. Moreover, it does not appear that ἠνεμόεις is used in this sense by the more ancient poets: we have ἀελλάδες ἵπποι in *Œd. T.* 463, and conversely, Βορέας ἄμιππος, infra v. 952: but the passages quoted by Erfurdt are all of them from later poets. With regard to the *animorum incredibiles motus celeritasque ingeniorum* of Cicero (*pro Archia*, VIII. § 17), this does not settle the meaning of Sophocles in this passage, but only shows what he might have said. The ῥιπαὶ ἐχθίστων ἀνέμων, supra v. 137, and the τῶν αὐτῶν ἀνέμων αὗται ψυχῆς ῥιπαί, infra v. 904, obviously refer to passion, and not to intellect. We must have recourse therefore to the other and more ancient sense of ἠνεμόεις, i.e. "*ventosus eâ significatione quâ dicuntur loca ventosa*" (II. Steph. in v.). By a very natural application of the word in this sense it means "lofty"—(cf. *luft, lift, luff,* &c.) "up in the air," "exposed to the winds:" thus Pindar calls Ætna ἶπον ἀνεμόεσσαν Τυφῶνος. If therefore φθέγμα refers to poetry, as by implication and in part it does, there is the same juxtaposition, that we find here, in Eurip. *Alcest.* 962: ἐγὼ καὶ διὰ μούσας καὶ μετάρσιος ᾖξα (where for the verb cf. *Hecub.* v. 31). The epithet ἀστυνόμος is not to be explained by a mere reference to the phrase ἄστη νέμειν, *urbes incolere*. For although this is no doubt the origin of the compound, it had established itself in the time of Sophocles as an independent word, which conveyed a special signification. It referred, namely, to the internal care and management of a town—the repair of houses, the police and cleansing of the streets, and the superintendence of the fountains, harbours, &c. The performance of these duties was called ἀστυνομία (Arist. *Pol.* VI. 8. § 5); and in order to its proper performance at Athens, there was a board of officers called ἀστυνόμοι, five for the city and five for the Piræus (Aristot. *apud Harpocr.* s. v.). Plato thought, that, in proportion as his citizens were properly educated, they would the less need regulations of this kind (*Resp.* IV. p. 425, D.)—that is, they would of themselves be sufficiently under the influence of ἀστυνόμοι ὀργαί;—but in his *Laws* (VI. p. 763, C.), he is careful to appoint a board of three ἀστυνόμοι and five ἀγορανόμοι. If, from the legal use of the word in the prose writers, we turn to its tropical use in the poets, we shall find, as here, a direct reference to the primary application. Thus, Pindar prays on behalf of the city of Ætna, that Jupiter will bestow upon the inhabitants μοῖραν εὔνομον, ἀγλαΐαισιν δ᾽ ἀστυνόμοις ἐπιμίξαι λαόν (*N.* IX. 31). And Æschylus distinguishes between the Gods as ἀστυνόμοι, ὕπατοι, χθόνιοι, οὐράνιοι, and ἀγοραῖοι (*Agam.* 88). I think therefore that this adjective and its converse ἀγρονόμος (*Œd. T.* 1103. infra 775. Æschyl. *Agam.* 140) ought to be paroxytone, like the word denoting the offices of town and country police. In conclusion, I will remark that if, as is probably the case, Sophocles is referring here by covert allusion to his friend Pericles, the connexion between the ἠνεμόεν φρόνημα and the ἀστυνόμοι ὀργαί will be particularly emphatic; for there was nothing better known about this great statesman, than that he combined with his ἀστυνομία the μετεωρολογία which he got from Anaxagoras; cf. Plato, *Phædrus*, p. 270, A. (where τὸ ὑψηλόνουν is the prose version of ἠνεμόεν φρόνημα), with Cic. *Orator*. 34, § 119, who says, "quem etiam quo grandior sit et quodammodo *excelsior* (ut de Pericle supra dixi) ne physicorum quidem ignarum esse volo. Omnia profecto, quum se a coelestibus rebus referet ad humanas, *excelsius* magnificentiusque et dicet et *sentiet*."

354. δυσαύλων.] As the poet is here speaking of architectural contrivances as a shelter against the inclemency of the weather, it is obvious that this epithet must be taken in its most pregnant meaning, namely, "frosts which make a mere hut, or any thing except a walled house, very comfortless." Although αὐλή is used poetically to signify a complete house (*Trach.* 897), and even a treasure-house entirely walled in (infra v. 920), its proper meaning was "a partial shelter"—such as a court-yard or cattle-pen without a roof, or a hut without side walls. According to Athenæus (V. p. 189, B), it was essential to the proper definition of the term, that the place to which it was applied left a free access for the wind: ἔτι τοίνυν οὐδ᾽ ἡ αὐλὴ ἁρμόττει ἐπὶ τοῦ οἴκου, ὁ γὰρ διαπνεόμενος τόπος αὐλὴ λέγεται· καὶ διαυλωνίζειν φαμὲν τὸ δεχόμενον ἐξ ἑκατέρου πνεῦμα χωρίον. ἔτι δὲ αὐλὸς μὲν τὸ ὄργανον ᾧ διέρχεται τὸ πνεῦμα κ.τ.λ. As people who lived in the country, watching the flocks and herds, were obliged to trust to their clothing for a defence against the weather, and had only αὐλαί to retire to, we read of their ἀγρονόμοι αὐλαί (infra 775). Electra sends word to her brother οἵοις ἐν πέπλοις αὐλίζομαι (Eurip. *Electr.* 304), and her rustic husband speaks similarly of his own cottage: τίνος δ᾽ ἕκατι τάσδ᾽ ἐπ᾽ ἀγραύλους πύλας προσῆλθον (*ib.* 342); in-

deed, so completely was this phraseology adopted by the Athenians, that their rustic deity, whom they worshipped in the spring as a daughter of *Kekrops*, was called *Agraulus*, or *Aglaurus*, vide Photius, s.v. καλλυντήρια, p. 127, Porson. By a not unnatural transition, the wild animals are called ἀγρονόμοι (Æsch. *Agam.* 140), or ἄγραυλοι (supra v. 348); and the poor shelter of the soldier's *biouac* is termed his δυσαυλία (Æsch. *Agam.* 541). With so many implied references, it is obvious that the epithet δύσαυλος is best rendered by the converse of the English word "comfortable," which is almost equally comprehensive, and equally untranslatable. The idea, which Sophocles wished to convey, is partly expressed by the *sparso triste cubile gelu* of Propertius, *Lib.* III. *El.* 13. v. 26.

355, 6. πάγων ὑπαίθρεια καὶ δυσομβρα φεύγειν βέλη.] The metre indicated a corruption in the old reading; with Dindorf, I have introduced Böckh's emendation; cf. Æsch. *Agam.* 355; and, for the lengthening of the penultima, such forms as ἐπινύμφειος, ἐπινίκειος, κ.τ.λ. For the force of this epithet of the frost, see Soph. *Tr.* 162 : πάγου φανέντος αἰθρίου; and cf. Horat. III. *Carm.* 10, 8 : " positas ut glaciet nives *puro* numine Jupiter." For the application of βέλη to the frost, see *Psalm* CXLVII. 17 : מַשְׁלִיךְ קַרְחוֹ.

357, 8. ἄπορος ἐπ' οὐδὲν ἔρχεται τὸ μέλλον.] Hermann, whom most of the commentators repeat, connects the words ἐπ' οὐδέν with τὸ μέλλον, remarking: " Non recte Scholiasta explicat, ἐπ' οὐδὲν τῶν μελλόντων. Aliud est enim ἐπ' οὐδὲν μέλλον, *ad nullam rem futuram*, infinito dictum, quam finito, *ad eorum, quæ futura sunt, nihil*. Quorum alterum est, *ad nihil, si quid futurum est*: alterum, *ad nihil, quod est futurum.*" With all submission to this veteran scholar, I must beg to doubt whether the Greek syntax would bear such a construction as ἐπ' οὐδὲν τὸ μέλλον. The passage referred to by Wunder is not at all parallel: infra v. 719 : μηδὲν τὸ μὴ δίκαιον. This is, of course, to be explained by what precedes, and Hæmon means μηδὲν διδάσκου τὸ μὴ δίκαιον, "be not in any respect instructed by me in what is not just." In the passage before us, as I have elsewhere stated (*New Cratylus*, p. 385), I take τὸ μέλλον as a sort of adverb, analogous to τὸ πρίν, τὸ νῦν, &c. In v. 605 infra, it is undoubtedly used in this way; and the construction of this passage requires a similar usage: τὸ μέλλον, ἄπορος ἔρχεται ἐπ' οὐδέν, "in regard to the future, he comes to nothing without resources."

360. φεῦξιν ἐπάξεται.] Here ἐπάγομαι bears its common sense "of calling in succours" (Thucyd. I. 3); with which is coupled the notion of getting aid of any kind; see Plato, *Menex.* p. 238, B: ἄρχοντας καὶ διδασκάλους αὐτῶν ἐπηγάγετο [ἡ γῆ], Thucyd. I. 81: ὧν δέονται, ἐπάξονται. There is no need, therefore, for Heindorf's correction ἐπεύξεται (in his note on Plato, *Sophist.* p. 235, c: οὐ—μήποτε ἐκφυγὸν ἐπεύξηται τὴν—μέθοδον).

362. σοφόν τι—ἔχων,] i.e. τὸ μηχανόεν τῆς τέχνης σοφὸν ἔχων, Scholiast. The reference is of course to the use of the verbs μηχανῶμαι and τεχνῶμαι, and not to mechanical art in its modern sense: cf. μηχανορράφος *Œd. T.* 387. τέχνημα *Phil.* 916.

366. γεραίρων.] With Ellendt, I have received the old conjecture of Reiske and Musgrave, which seems to me far more probable than any of the more recent emendations. For the palæographical considerations, see on v. 24, supra.

370, 3. τόλμας χάριν—ἔρδει.] As the pause in the strophe is at τὸ μέλλον, I have placed a similar stop at ξύνεστι, especially as the position of the words τόλμας χάριν is very awkward, if they are to be referred to what precedes. It seems much more reasonable to suppose that they furnish a sort of preface to the deprecation which follows. For the use of τόλμη, cf. *Trachin.* 582:

κακὰς δὲ τόλμας μήτ' ἐπισταίμην ἐγώ,
μήτ' ἐκμάθοιμι, τάς τε τολμώσας στυγῶ.

Pind. *P.* II. 83: οὐ οἱ μετέχω θράσεος. For the use of

χάριν in this collocation, see *Œd. T.* 883 sqq: εἰ δέ τις ὑπέροπτα χερσὶν ἢ λόγῳ πορεύεται, Δίκας ἀφόβητος, οὐδὲ δαιμόνων ἔδη σέβων, κακά νιν ἕλοιτο μοῖρα δυσπότμου χάριν χλιδᾶς, εἰ μή κ.τ.λ. For the general idea cf. Æschyl. *Eumen.* 344: Ζεὺς—ἔθνος τόδε λέσχας ἇς ἀπηξιώσατο. For ἴσον φρονῶν, see above on 176, and compare Hom. *Il.* IV. 361: τὰ γὰρ φρονέεις ἅ τ᾽ ἐγώ περ. That ἔρδω is often used in a bad sense, is well known: see especially *Phil.* 684.

374. δαιμόνιον τέρας.] The adjective δαιμόνιος, which refers to the influences of an intermediate deity (δαίμων), often expresses that which is more than would be expected without such intervention: hence it means "strange," "surprising," "wonderful"—and this is the signification which it bears in the compellation ὦ δαιμόνιε: see *ad Pind. O.* VI. 8, 9.

378. ἀπάγουσι.] I have adopted the emendation of Böckh: for this reference to the ἀπαγωγή, while it might easily perplex a scribe, would be very much in its place here.

385. ἄναξ—ἀπώμοτον.] Probably a tacit reference to Archilochus, *Fr.* 69, 1. Bergk: χρημάτων ἄελπτον οὐδέν ἐστιν οὐδ᾽ ἀπώμοτον. cf. below 390. The same fragment seems to have been in his memory when he wrote *Œd. Col.* 615.

388. ἐξηύχουν.] Unless we ought to read ἐξηύχησα, as in *Phil.* 851, we must explain this imperfect by the common use of the same tense with οὐ, and without ἄν; so that the construction suggested by Matthiä, § 598, A, is the true one; σχολῇ ποθ᾽ ἥξειν δεῦρ᾽ ἂν ἐξηύχουν being equivalent to οὐκ ἐξηύχουν ἥξειν. One of the MSS. and the margin of Turnebus give σχολῇ γ᾽ ἄν for σχολῇ ποθ᾽, and this is adopted, after Erfurdt and Hermann, by most of the critics. Precisely the same construction is found in *Œd. Tyr.* 434, where, however, we have the aorist ἐστειλάμην; and if ἐξηύχησα

were read here, I should prefer σχολῇ γ' ἂν after ἐπεί. In nearly all the passages quoted by Blomfield (*Gloss. Prom.* 710), we have οὔ ποτε with the imperfect of αὐχέω or ἐξαυχέω, and he tacitly introduces the same tense into the line from the *Philoctetes*. In *Agam.* 508 (470), the herald says οὐ γάρ ποτ' ηὔχουν—μεθέξειν; and if any one wishes to have the same construction here, he might read σχολῇ ποθ' ἥξειν δεῦρ' ἂν ἐξηύχουν ἐγώ. It must be remarked that the Sentinel is more likely to be made to refer to what he *did* say (supra v. 329), than to what he *would have* said.

395. θούρμαιον.] I have been obliged to render this word by an English phrase, which is more expressive than elegant. The word *Godsend* is used with a different application, and the exclamations "a prize, a prize!" or "found, found!" could not be introduced in a descriptive passage, although the latter is the best representative of the Greek εὕρηκα, which has become a descriptive word in the proper name *Hurreekee*, still given to a place on the Indus, where Alexander's Indian conquests ceased, and where our dominion was consummated.

429. χοαῖσι τρισπόνδοισι.] i. e. milk, wine, and honey. Hom. *Od.* xi. 26. The verb στέφει perhaps refers to the libations being poured round the body: the Scholiast says στέφει· κοσμεῖ, περιρραίνει. For the full force of ἄρδην in the preceding line, and for the shape of the *prochus*, see the figure of Victory in Müller's *Denkmäler der alten Kunst*, Heft I. Taf. 13. No. 47.

434. ἄμ'.] I have adopted Dindorf's ΑΜ for ΑΛΛ.

448—450. οὐ γάρ τι—νόμους.] The third of these lines has caused a good deal of perplexity to the Editors: some propose to emend it by writing ἦ for οἵ, or τοιοῦσδ' for οἵ τουσδ', and changing ὥρισαν into ὥρισεν. And Dindorf, who is followed by Wunder and Emper, adopts the favourite expedient of omitting the line altogether. It appears to me that the intention of the poet has not been understood. Kreon asks Antigone if she knew the *proclamation* (τὰ κηρυχθέντα), and then expresses his surprise that she should venture to transgress *these laws* (τούσδε νόμους), meaning, of course, his own enactments. She replies, that she did not consider his proclamations as emanating from Zeus, the supreme God, or from that justice which regulated the rights of the dead, who, she says, have established *these laws*, namely, the laws of sepulture, which do not need any enactment, but have their ὅροι set up in the human heart; "and I did not," she continues, "think *your* κηρύγματα superior to νόμιμα, which had the Gods for their authors." The whole Play turns upon the opposition between *his* laws and those which she thought it right to obey. And this speech in particular is entirely upon that text. The last words, σοὶ δ᾽ εἰ δοκῶ—ὀφλισκάνω, are another expression of the same antagonism. "If my obedience to the laws of heaven in defiance of the laws of man, seems to you foolish, I consider your opposition to the laws of heaven, on behalf of your own ordinances, equally void of sense." The signification of τούσδε νόμους in v. 450 is partly suggested by the ἡ ξύνοικος τῶν κάτω θεῶν which precedes, and partly by the ὥρισαν ἐν ἀνθρώποις which follows. The laws, which infernal justice regulated, and which had their ὅροι, not as outward marks, but as records in the heart, could need no further description in their opposition to the κηρύγματα of Kreon. It is because they are so implicitly defined, that the article which Böckh would place before ἄγραπτα is unnecessary, and has been omitted by the poet. Moreover, it will be remembered that δίκη and νόμος, in their relation to funeral rites, have a natural title to stand in juxtaposition: cf. above v. 23, 24. I think, therefore, that the proposal to reject line 450, must be considered as one proof, among many, of the necessity of general exegesis to sound criticism.

507. σοὶ δ᾽ ὑπίλλουσι στόμα.] The Scholiast has correctly explained these words: γιγνώσκουσι καὶ οὗτοι· διὰ δὲ σὲ τὸ στόμα συστέλλουσι καὶ σιωπῶσιν. Ὑπίλλω applies to that action of the mouth in resolute silence, which is produced by the pronunciation of the word *mum*, and I have

used the word in the translation as it is employed by Shakspere, *Richard III.* Act III. Sc. 7:

"Now, by the Holy Mother of our Lord,
The citizens are mum, say not one word."

509. τοὺς ὁμοσπλάγχνους.] See 1034 infra.

513. οὐ μαρτυρήσει—χθονός.] The common reading is, ταῦθ' ὁ κατθανὼν νέκυς. In one MS. and in the margin of Turnebus, we have ὁ κατὰ χθονὸς νέκυς, which Brunck adopted, without a due regard to the metre. I believe that I have restored the true reading, which was lost partly by the copyists looking back to v. 510, χὠ κατ[άντιον] θανών, where also we have the various reading κατὰ χθονός, and partly by some confused reference to vv. 24 and 26, where Eteokles is described as κατὰ χθονός, and his brother spoken of as τὸν ἀθλίως θανόντα Πολυνείκους νέκυν. I think also that the καὶ was required here as in v. 510, and that the reference to Eteokles would not be sufficiently distinct if the old reading were retained.

519. τίς οἶδεν—εὐαγῆ τάδε.] Scholiast: τίς οἶδεν, εἰ καθ' Ἅιδην ἀλλήλοις διαλλάσσοντες ἡγοῦνται εὐσεβῆ τάδε; cf. *Œd. Tyr.* 921: ὅπως λύσιν τιν' ἡμῖν εὐαγῆ πόρῃς. Κάτωθεν for κάτω 'στίν, is suggested by the Scholiast, from whom Dindorf has borrowed it.

554. ἀλλ' οὐκ—λόγοις.] Matthiä's explanation of these words (586 γ.) appears to me inadmissible. He translates them, "not without my having spoken," and quotes Eurip. *Ion.* 237: ἐπὶ δ' ἀσφάκτοις μήλοισι δόμων μὴ πάριτ' ἐς μυχόν. But the omission of the article in the latter passage makes a great difference, and it seems impossible to translate the line before us, without considering ἀρρήτως as a secondary predicate, or adjective used adverbially. The construction is the same as the πρὸς ἰσχύοντας τοὺς ἐχθροὺς of Thucyd. I. 36, which is explained in *New Crat.* p. 384.

557, 8. θάρσει—ὠφελεῖν.] Wunder entertains a

strange notion as to the meaning of these words: he says, "nemo non perspexisset sensum hujus loci, si scripsisset poeta: ὥστε τοῖς ζῶσι μηκέτ' ὠφελεῖν, ita ut vivis nihil jam utilis sim. Idem significavit iis verbis quæ posuit. Nam mortuis necessario incipit utilis esse, qui vivis esse desierit." The sense in which I understand the passage is very different from this. Ismene had said: "Nay, our sin is equal; for if you were the agent, I was privy before the fact," (Scholiast: ὅτι σὺ μὲν ἔπραξας ἐγὼ δὲ συνῄδειν, cf. Hec. 857: σύνισθι—συνδράσῃς δὲ μή). To which Antigone replies: "Never mind —you live; that is the difference,—and my life has been long ago sacrificed in my attempt to help (i. e. bury) the dead." The idea which attached itself to the phrase ὠφελεῖν τοῖς θανοῦσι, may be derived from a comparison of Æsch. Pers. 842: ὡς τοῖς θανοῦσι πλοῦτος οὐδὲν ὠφελεῖ, with Eurip. Alcest. 56: κἂν γραῦς ὄληται πλουσίως ταφήσεται.

563. ξὺν καλοῖς πράσσειν κακά.] Although it is clear from the τοῖς κακῶς πράσσουσιν of the preceding verse, and from the word βιώσιμον in the answer of Ismene, that the reference is to suffering rather than to sin, Böckh has translated these words, als Böses du mit Bösen thatst.

570. ὦ φίλταθ'—πατήρ.] I subscribe to the opinion of Böckh and Süvern, who, following the old Editions, have restored this verse to Antigone. I have also adopted Böckh's suggestion that 572, 574, should be assigned to the Chorus, and not to Ismene.

573. Ἅιδης—ἔφυ.] As I believe that the phrase "to forbid the banns," however connected with our Church usages, is derived from the signification of the words themselves, I have not hesitated to imitate Ford in this reference to "the churchman's part."

575. καὶ σοί γε κἀμοί.] The poet is again playing with the different usages of δοκεῖν. He means ἐμοὶ δέδοκται, ὡς καὶ σοὶ δοκεῖ, scil. τήνδε κατθανεῖν.

576, 7. ἐκ δὲ τοῦδε—ἀνειμένας.] Dindorf, who is followed by Wunder, thinks this reading inadmissible, and proposes instead, εὖ δὲ τάσδε χρὴ γυναῖκας εἶλαι μηδ᾽ ἀνειμένας ἐᾶν. His arguments have failed to convince me that this emendation is either necessary or in good taste. Any person who will take the trouble to compare *Ajax* 286: ὁ δ᾽ εἶπε πρός με βαί᾽· ἀεὶ δ᾽ ὑμνούμενα, γύναι, γυναιξὶ κόσμον ἡ σιγὴ φέρει: *Tr.* 61: ἄλλως τε καὶ κόρη τε κἀργεία γένος, αἷς κόσμος ἡ σιγή τε καὶ τὰ παῦρ᾽ ἔπη, with *Electr.* 516: ἀνειμένη μὲν, ὡς ἔοικας, αὖ στρέφει. οὐ γὰρ πάρεστ᾽ Αἴγισθος, ὅς σ᾽ ἐπεῖχ᾽ ἀεί, μή τοι θυραίαν γ᾽ οὖσαν αἰσχύνειν φίλους: supra 61: γυναῖχ᾽ ἔφυμεν, 484: ἡ νῦν ἐγὼ μὲν οὐκ ἀνήρ, αὕτη δ᾽ ἀνήρ, and the passages quoted by Poppo on Thucyd. II. 45 fin., will see that the emphatic use of γυναῖκας in this passage, as a predicate opposed to ἀνειμένας, is quite in accordance with the spirit of the Greeks, and of their language.

580—617. *Second Stasimon.* The metres are as follows:

στροφὴ ά.

1. – ‖ – ∪ ∪ | – ∪ ∪ | – ∪ ‖ – ∪ | – – ‖
2. – ∪ ‖ – – ‖ – ∪ ∪ | – ∪ ∪ | – – ‖
3. – ∪ | – – ‖ – ∪ ∪ | – ∪ ∪ ‖ – ∪ | – – ‖
4. ∪ ‖ – ∪ | – ∪ | – ∪ | – ‖
5.   – ∪ | – ∪ | – ∪ | – ‖
6. – ‖ – ∪ | ∪ ∪ ∪ | ∪ ∪ ∪ | ∪ ∪ ∪ ‖ – ∪ | – ∪ | – – ‖
7.   – ∪ | – ∪ | – – ‖
8.   – ∪ | – ∪ | – ∪ | – ‖
9. ∪ ‖ – ∪ | – ∪ ‖ – ∪ | – ∪ | – – ‖

στροφὴ β´.

1. ∪ – ‖ – ∪ ∪ ‖ – ∪ | – – ‖
2. ∪ ‖ – ∪ ∪ ‖ – ∪ | – – ‖
3. – ‖ – ∪ ∪ | – ‖ – ∪ ∪ ‖ – ∪ | – – ‖
4.   – ∪ ∪ ‖ – ∪ | – ῡ ‖

5. $\bar{} \cup \cup \mid \bar{} \parallel \bar{} \cup \cup \parallel \bar{} \cup \mid - \parallel \bar{} \cup \cup \parallel \bar{} \cup \mid - - \parallel$
6. $\bar{} \cup \cup \parallel \bar{} \cup \mid - - \parallel$
7. $\cup \cup \parallel \bar{} \cup \mid - \cup \mid \bar{} - \parallel$
8. $- \parallel \bar{} \cup \cup \mid \bar{} \cup \mid - \parallel$
9. $\bar{} \cup \cup \mid - \cup \mid \bar{} - \parallel$
10. $- \parallel \bar{} \cup \cup \mid \bar{} \mid \bar{} \cup \cup \parallel \bar{} \cup \mid - - \parallel$

In my judgment, the previous arrangements of this ode have been altogether unsatisfactory. The critics have not shrunk from a medley of iambics, trochees, and antispasts; and even a senarius, with unequally resolved arsis, has been allowed to appear. It is nothing but dactylico-trochaic verse, the trochaic rhythm appearing chiefly as dipodia and ithyphallicus. There is a *trochœus semantus* (vide Herm. *El. Doctr. Metr.* p. 660) in στρ. *ά* 1, which makes an *incisio* in the line. Στρ. *α'* 6 is the metre which I have restored in v. 943 infra, namely, two trochaic *dipodiæ cum anacrusi* followed by an *ithyphallicus*, which is repeated in the following line, and follows a single *dipodia cum anacrusi* in the last line of the Strophe.

580. αἰών.] Sophocles opposes to γενεά, considered as representing the whole series of generations which make up the existence of a family, the αἰών here, or γένος v. 591, i. e. the existing generation for the time being. If mischief (ἄτη) once gets into a family, no single generation (αἰών, γένος) can exhaust it, but it must have its play; just as the waves, which the wind raises on the surface of a narrow sea or bay, such as that between Eubœa and Attica, must affect the whole mass of water until they reach the shingle at the bottom. The Chorus in the *Ajax* 629 holds to a different opinion. He speaks of a father's hearing παιδὸς δύσφορον ἄταν, ἃν οὔπω τις ἔθρεψεν αἰὼν Αἰακιδᾶν ἄτερθε τοῦδε. The inherited evils of the Labdakidæ are the leading idea in the one case; the exception, which Ajax furnished to the general prosperity of his race, is prominently brought forward in the other passage. See Pind. *P*. III. 86: αἰὼν δ᾽ ἀσφαλὴς

οὐκ ἔγεντ' οὔτ' Αἰακίδᾳ παρὰ Πηλεῖ οὔτε παρ' ἀντιθέῳ Κάδμῳ. Schiller has fully caught the spirit of Greek tragedy in his *Piccolomini* (Act II. Sc. 7, of Coleridge's version; III. Sc. 9, of the original): " Es geht ein finstrer Geist durch unser Haus," u. s. w. "There's a dark spirit walking in our house," &c. See a Greek version of the passage in Hermann's *Opuscula*, V. p. 356.

586, 7. βυσσόθεν κελαινὰν θῖνι καὶ δυσάνεμον.] The commentators have, strangely as it appears to me, mistaken the meaning of this passage. Wunder adopts the explanation of the Scholiast: " nomen δυσάνεμον recte explicat Scholiasta: τὴν ὑπὸ ἀνέμων ταραχθεῖσαν. Similiter, supra 356, δύσομβρα dictum est." Jacobs, who is followed by Erfurdt, proposes δυσανέμῳ, scil. στόνῳ. Ellendt, who retains δυσάνεμον, would join the word adverbially to βρέμειν. It seems to me that the context leads to a very obvious interpretation. When mischief begins in a family, it goes on ἐπὶ πλῆθος γενεᾶς: similarly, when the wind in the Euripus blows hard upon the surface for a given time, the undulatory motion continues till the shingle at the bottom is stirred; now this shingle being in the ἔρεβος ὕφαλον—i. e., as Jacobs explains it, τὸ μέλαν τῆς θαλάσσης βάθος—is itself black and gloomy for want of light (κελαινά); and being covered by a bulk of water, it is also δυσάνεμος, or not easily affected by the wind. I should therefore explain δυσάνεμος in the same way as the adjectives δυσήνιος, δυσθαλπής, δυσθεράπευτος, δυσθήρατος, &c. &c., which all signify a defiance of that which is expressed by the main part of the compound. Accordingly, the poet is not here speaking of the alluvial mud cast up along the shore, which Aristotle calls ὁ θὶς ὁ μέλας, but of the general deposits at the bottom of the sea: thus also Aristoph. *Vesp.* 696: τί λέγεις; ὡς μοῦ τὸν θῖνα ταράσσεις, on which the Schol.: ἐκ βυθοῦ με κινεῖς. Hesych.: θῖς· τὸ κάτω βάθος τῆς θαλάσσης. Pind. *P.* VI. 12—14: οὔτ' ἄνεμοι ἐς μυχοὺς ἁλὸς ἄξαισι παμφόρῳ χεράδι τυπτόμενον. In general, we may compare with this metaphor that which has been explained above, v. 20.

588. ἀντιπλῆγες ἀκταί.] The poet speaks as an Athenian, who had taken his stand on the East Coast of Attica, and looked towards Euboea while a violent gale was blowing from the North-East. It would first touch the surface of the sea, but at length would so affect the whole mass of water, that the windward coast of Euboea, no less than the lee shore of Attica, would be lashed by the waves. That ἀκτή is particularly applied to the sea-coast of Attica, which derived its name from this use (Ἀττική=Ἀκτική), is well known. See Suidas *s.v.*; *Anecd. Bekkeri*, p. 370, 8; Strabo (quoting Sophocles) IX. p. 392. And that the term was also applied to Euboea, is clear from v. 1100 infra, and from *Trach.* 236: ἀκτή τις ἐστ' Εὐβοΐς.

589, 90. ἀρχαῖα—πίπτοντ'.] For the construction see the *New Cratylus*, p. 385. The necessary emendation φθιτῶν is due to Hermann. Dindorf has pointed out a similar corruption in Eurip. *Alcest.* 100.

593—597. νῦν γάρ—Ἐρινύς.] Hermann's insertion of ὁ before τέτατο is required by the metre, and recognized by the Scholiast. He subsequently adopted a more extensive change, writing ὅπερ for ὑπέρ, and ἐτέτατο: but the preposition seems necessary, and, as well as the relative, was read by the Scholiast. For the phrase ὁ τέτατο φάος, I have elsewhere compared *Phil.* 817 sq.: ὄμμασι δ' ἀντίσχοις τἄνδ' αἴγλαν ἃ τέταται τανῦν. For the sense of the word ῥίζα the student may refer to *Ajax* 935; Pind. *O.* II. 4; Æsch. *Suppl.* 105; St. Paul, *Rom.* XV. 12; Arist. *Eth. Nic.* VIII. 14. § 3: ὅθεν φασὶ ταὐτὸν αἷμα καὶ ῥίζαν καὶ τοιαῦτα. The phrase κόνις καταμᾷ ῥίζαν may be partly illustrated by *Ajax* 1157: γένους ἅπαντος ῥίζαν ἐξημημένος. I have justified the common reading κόνις against the emendation κόπις, in the *New Cratylus*, p. 294.

597. λόγου τ' ἄνοια καὶ φρενῶν Ἐρινύς.] It is clear that this is predicated of Antigone, whose inconsiderate language to Kreon, coupled with her feeling of resentment at the violation of religious ordinances in the case of

Polyneikes, had led to her condemnation. This is the proper force of the word ἐρινύς, which, as Müller says (*Eumenid.* § 77), denotes "the feeling of *deep offence*, of *bitter displeasure*, when sacred rights belonging to us are impiously violated by persons who ought most to have respected them."

598, 9. τεὰν, Ζεῦ—κατάσχοι.] Some years ago I pointed out the sense of this passage, which had been generally misunderstood. I will repeat here what I wrote in 1836. "The connexion of ideas in this passage is as follows: 'What mortal transgression or sin is Jupiter liable to, Jupiter the sleepless and everlasting God? But mortal men know nothing of the future till it comes upon them.' We should certainly read ὑπερβασία in the nominative case. Τίς ὑπερβασία κατέχει τεὰν δύνασιν; is equivalent to τεὰ δύνασις κατέχει οὔτινα ὑπερβασίαν" (see above on v. 4). "Compare Theognis 743—6, which Sophocles had in his head:

καὶ τοῦτ᾽, ἀθανάτων βασιλεῦ, πῶς ἐστι δίκαιον
ἔργων ὅστις ἀνὴρ ἐκτὸς ἐὼν ἀδίκων,
μή τιν᾽ ὑπερβασίην κατέχων μηδ᾽ ὅρκον ἀλιτρὸν,
ἀλλὰ δίκαιος ἐὼν μὴ τὰ δίκαια πάθῃ;
Theatre of the Greeks, Ed. 4, p. 81."

600—602. τὰν οὔθ᾽ ὕπνος—μῆνες.] These words do not balance the corresponding words in the antistrophe, and various attempts have been made to mend the corruption thus indicated. Moreover, the word παντογήρως has been with justice objected to on its own account. Schneider, in his Lexicon, pronounced it a word of doubtful authority. Emper says, that this epithet is totally inapplicable to refreshing sleep, and that as the gods were supposed to be liable to sleep, they must have been considered liable to grow old, if that was the effect of sleep. He suggests, therefore, that we have in this word an old error of the copyist, whose eye lighted on ἀγήρως, written as a various reading by the side of ἀγήρῳ, and that Sophocles probably wrote παντοδμάτωρ, as in Homer *Il.* XXIV. 5. *Od.* IX.

373, we have the phrase ὕπνος ᾕρει πανδαμάτωρ. I understand that Bamberger (in Schneidewin's *Philologus* I. 4, p. 604), proposes παντόθηρος or παντοθήρως. It appears to me, that the true reading is παγκρατής, which occurs as an epithet of ὕπνος in the *Ajax* 660, and which appears as an epithet of χρόνος in a passage in which Sophocles was obviously influenced by his recollections of what he had written in this chorus: *Œd. Col.* 607 sqq:

ὦ φίλτατ' Αἰγέως παῖ, μόνοις οὐ γίγνεται
θεοῖσι γῆρας, οὐδὲ κατθανεῖν ποτε,
τὰ δ' ἄλλα συγχεῖ πάνθ' ὁ παγκρατὴς χρόνος.

Other commentators have sought to mend the metre by altering the following line. Hermann originally proposed οὔτε θεῶν ἄκμητοι, which Emper adopts with the dialectical change ἄκματοι. Dindorf writes: οὔτ' ἄκοποι θεῶν νιν. Böckh: ἀκάματοι θεῶν οὐ. It appears to me that the corruption lies in θεῶν. What are "the months of the Gods?" The Διὸς μεγάλου ἐνιαυτοί, of Homer (*Il.* II. 134), are by no means a parallel. Although the word θέω does not occur elsewhere in Æschylus or Sophocles, there is no reason why he should not have used it, as I believe he did here, and in v. 1305 infra: and I have written with the greatest confidence ἀκάματοι θέοντες, which suits the metre, and perfectly coincides in construction with *Electra* 164: ὃν ἔγωγ' ἀκαμάτα (vulg. ἀκάματα) προσμένουσ' ἄτεκνος. The use of this adjective, as a secondary predicate or adverb, has been mentioned by Suidas, *s. v.* ἀκάματα or ἀκαμάτα, ἀντὶ ἀκαμάτως, καὶ ἀδιαλείπτως ἢ οὐ κεκμηκότως. For the months as a measure of time, we may compare Catullus XXXIV. 18: "Tu cursu, dea, menstruo, Metiens iter annuum," and for the rapidity of their course (θέοντες), cf. Hor. IV, *Carm.* VI. 39: "celeremque pronos volvere menses." Id. IV. *Carm.* VII. 13: "damna tamen celeres reparant coelestia lunæ."

604—607. τό τ' ἔπειτα—ἄτα.] Of the various methods which have been proposed for correcting this manifestly corrupt passage, the only one which I can accept as partially true, is that which regards the terminations of vv. 606 and 607, as wanting—the words οὐδὲν ἕρπει and ἐκτὸς ἄτας having been transferred from vv. 611 and 617. Supposing then that we have a lacuna, amounting in each case to a trochaic dipodia, at the end of each line, the question is— how can we, without any aid from the MSS., restore the missing words? With regard to v. 606, I think it may be safely concluded: (1) that we have here lost some word governed by ἐπαρκέσει; for although the absolute use of this verb is not unprecedented, as we shall presently see, yet it seems absolutely necessary to connect the law, here mentioned, with the destiny of man, otherwise the immunity of Zeus from mortal transgression will be without its proper antithesis: (2) that the lost words must have borne some palæographical resemblance to what precedes or follows, otherwise their absorption would be hardly explicable. With regard to v. 607, the meaning obviously intended comes so close to that of the intrusive words, that I think we may safely regard them as a marginal illustration of something which stood in the text. To begin then with this second line: I consider the words οὐδὲν ἕρπει as the remains of a gloss on the dative βιότῳ, which was placed on the left-hand margin of this line. The Scholiast wished to illustrate the use of a verb of motion with the dative, and therefore quoted the phrase [εἰδότι δ'] οὐδὲν ἕρπει from v. 611. And I regard the words ἐκτὸς ἄτας as the remains of a gloss upon the whole line, which having been originally [οὐδεὶς ἐν πάσαις ταῖς πόλεσιν πράσσει τὸν βίον ἅπαντα], ἐκτὸς ἄτας, where the illustration was partly borrowed from the phraseology of vv. 616, 617, has ultimately coalesced with the gloss on βιότῳ, so that there remained in the margin only the words οὐδὲν ἕρπει ἐκτὸς ἄτας, which have been equally divided between the two lines in the text. Now the evidence in a case like this is of cumulative probability; and before we can restore v. 607, we must return to the former line. The poet says, that although Zeus is free from sin, as he is a sleepless and everlasting potentate, yet that for the present, the future, and the past, (cf. Eurip. *Iph. T.* 1263), the law, which he is about to mention, will sufficiently describe (ἐπαρκέσει)—what?—of course, the destiny of man. The common use of the verb ἐπαρκέω is well known. It signifies "to ward off"—hence, "to help or aid"—hence, "to supply or furnish." In the first sense it governs the dative of the person and the accusative of the thing—in the second, the dative or accusative of the person—in the third, the genitive of the person and the accusative of the thing, or the dative of the thing only. But besides this common use, there are passages in which ἐπαρκέω seems to approximate in meaning to ἀπαρκέω " to be sufficient," (see *Œd. Col.* 1766: ταῦτ' ἂν ἀπαρκοῖ). Thus Solon writes (*Fr.* 14, Bach. 4, Bergk):

δήμῳ μὲν γὰρ ἔδωκα τόσον κράτος ὅσσον ἐπαρκεῖ,
τιμῆς οὔτ' ἀφελὼν οὔτ' ἐπορεξάμενος,

which shows that the same verb is intended in Æsch. *Agam.* 370: ἔστω δ' ἀπήμαντον ὥστε κἀπαρκεῖν εὖ πραπίδων λαχόντα, for this seems to be an imitation of the former passage. It is true that Coraës would read ἀπαρκεῖ in the fragment of Solon, and that some understand the same verb in the *Agamemnon*. But as Blomfield justly remarks: "ἀπαρκεῖν de rebus dicitur quarum satis est, ἐπαρκεῖν potius de personis"—meaning, I presume, that ἀπαρκέω is used only intransitively, but that ἐπαρκέω always implies an active satisfying of some want, law, or condition: which is the case. Now, I believe that, in this sense, ἐπαρκέω would properly govern the accusative of the person or thing, whose requirements were adequately met and answered, just as ἐξίσταμαι, which, properly and according to the construction of its preposition, would govern the genitive, is used with the accusative when it denotes avoidance from fear, as in the phrase ἐκστῆναι κίνδυνον (see Lobeck, *ad Ajacem*, v. 82). It is easy to see the origin of these changes of construction. If ἐξίσταμαι means, "I get out of the way" of a thing, it might first be used absolutely, to signify "I fear," and then if the object of alarm were expressed, this would naturally be expressed in the accusative. Similarly, if ἐπαρκέω, which signifies to lend our aid in warding off danger, got the accessary meaning of being a sufficient aid or help-mate, and from that passed on to the signification, to be adequate to all the requirements of an object, it might be used absolutely, as in the passage from Solon,—where, however, τὸν δῆμον is immediately supplied by the thoughts of the readers, —or if the object were necessarily expressed, it would stand in the accusative, as in the passage from the *Agamemnon*. Now, as I have already said, the expression of the object is necessary here, and the metre and sense suggest the words ἀνδρὸς αἶσαν as the necessary supplement; see Pind. *P.* III. 59, 60:

χρὴ τὰ ἐοικότα πὰρ' δαιμόνων μαστευέμεν θναταῖς φρασίν,
γνόντα τὰ πὰρ ποδός, οἵας εἰμὲν αἴσας.

Let us now see if this meets the palæographical test which has been suggested—that is, whether these words are sufficiently like what followed to make their absorption probable. We come then to the other lacuna. If the meaning of v. 607 was given in the gloss which we have assumed, —and enough is left of the line to make this nearly certain—the remaining words must have been ἄτα and a verb of motion. Whether we agree or not with Hermann (*Opuscul.* II. 326), that εἶμι may be used as a present tense, I think no one will doubt that it might with propriety be employed here in a general apophthegmatic sentence, dependent on the future verb ἐπαρκέσει: cf. Soph. *Fr. Incert.* 813, Dindorf: τίσις δ' ἄνωθεν εἰσιν αἱματορρόφος. Æsch. *Sept. c. Theb.* 682: μελαναιγὶς δ' οὐκ εἶσι δόμον Ἐρινύς, οὔτ' ἂν ἐκ χερῶν θεοὶ θυσίαν δέχωνται. *Suppl.* 158, 172: χαλεποῦ γὰρ ἐκ πνεύματος εἶσι χειμών. If then εἶσιν ἄτα were the original reading here, we see how the resemblances between the terminations of the five successive lines produced the absorption or loss in two of the intermediate verses. For if the endings were,

ἐπαρκ—έσει
ἀνδρὸς—αἶσαν
εἶσιν ἄτα
[ἐστὶ] [ἄρσει]
αγ-κτος ἐλπίς
ὄν—ασις ἀνδρῶν,

we may perfectly well understand how a blundering copyist,

assisted in his error by confused marginal glosses[1], may have made the omissions, which I have thus endeavoured to supply. I may add, that, as the epithet πάμπολις, like ἄπολις, ὑψίπολις, δικαιόπολις, &c. implies a person or personification, this is an additional reason for concluding that ἄτη was here mentioned in the nominative case.

608—612. ἁ γὰρ δή—προσαύσῃ.] It will be remarked that ὄνασις and ἀπάτα are both predicates. By ἀπάτη ἐρώτων, he means the frustration of a man's longings: so infra 623: ἀπάτη λεχέων "the disappointment of his expectations in regard to marriage." Alciphron (III. 5) speaks of ἐλπίδες ἀπατηλαί. The nominative to ἕρπει is not οὐδέν, which is the accusative after εἰδότι, but, as Wunder has remarked, ἡ ἐλπὶς ἀπάτη γενομένη. On the form προσαύσῃ, it may be sufficient to quote Lobeck, ad Ajacem, p. 358 : " Ex quo colligi licet, αὔειν illud, quo de agimus, idem valere quod αἴρειν, verumque esse quod in Soph. Antig. 615, plerique libri exhibent, πρὶν πυρὶ θερμῷ πόδα τις προσαύσῃ, id est, προσάρῃ, ut in glossa exponitur, sive προσαρμόσῃ." Id. Ῥηματικόν, p. 12 note : " cum Sophoclis illo πρὶν—προσαύσῃ, si quis contulerit Apollinar. Ps. XC. 24 : μήποτε σὸν πόδα λᾶϊ καθάψῃς, non dubium habebit hujusmodi locis grammaticos inductos esse, ut αὖσαι et ἅψασθαι synonyma dicerent." For the general meaning, the reader will find an exact parallel to this passage in Pindar, O. XII. 5—9. Cf. also *Proverbs* XIII. 12.

612, 613. σοφίᾳ—πέφανται.] The parallel passages for this adage are fully given by Ruhnken on Velleius Paterculus II. 57 (265, 266), and by Wyttenbach on Plutarch, *de audiendis poetis*, p. 17, n (pp. 190, 191). The Latin adage, which is still in colloquial use, *quem vult deus perire, dementat prius*, is probably an abridged translation of ὅταν δ' ὁ δαίμων ἀνδρὶ πορσύνῃ κακά, τὸν νοῦν ἔβλαψε πρῶτον ᾧ βουλεύεται.

[1] By a singular coincidence, (which shows the probability of such corruptions,) in the first proof of page 60, the words κατ' αὖ νυν. which I had written in the margin after Οἰδίπου δόμοις, were inserted between οὐδ' ἔχει and λύσιν in v. 502

617. πράσσει—ἄλγους.] I have here written ἄλγους instead of ἄτας, because I think it scarcely possible that Sophocles should have repeated this word without any emphasis, and because the parallelism of the actual ἄλγος and the tendency to ἄτη seems to me to be required here no less than in v. 4 supra. I think the corruption arose from a former Scholiast having written in the margin of v. 607 supra, οὐδεὶς ἐν πάσαις τ. π. πράσσει ἐκτὸς ἄτας, as an explanation to the πάμπολις εἰσὶν ἄτα which he found there. The proper explanation of ὀλιγοστὸν χρόνον here may be derived from the converse πολλοστῷ χρόνῳ Aristoph. *Pax*, 559: on which see *New Cratylus*, p. 206. Πράσσει is used with ἐκτὸς ἄλγους, as it is with the adverbs πῶς, εὖ, κακῶς.

620. τάλιδος.] I agree with Dindorf, that the words τῆς μελλογάμου νύμφης, which appear in the MSS., are a marginal gloss on τάλιδος, and ought to be expunged. The resemblance between τᾶλις and the ταλιθά (טַלְיְתָא) of Mark V. 41, is merely accidental. The latter is simply a Syriac derivative from טַלְה "a young lamb," or "a new-born gazelle."

627, 628. καὶ σύ μοι—ἐφέψομαι.] Hæmon promises only a conditional obedience. "*If* you have for me γνώμαις χρηστάς—and not otherwise—you are my ruler and guide." I consider ἀπορθόω, as nearly as possible, a synonym of ἀπευθύνω, cf. ad 666: cf. Plato, *Legg*. VI. 757, E: ἀπορθοῦν τὸν κλῆρον πρὸς τὸ δικαιότατον, with id. *ibid*. p. 757, B: κλήρῳ ἀπευθύνων εἰς τὰς διανομὰς αὐτήν. Consequently, the words to be supplied here are με γνώμαις, cf. Plato, *Legg*. XII. 946, D: κατὰ τὴν τῶν εὐθύνων γνώμην: and for the use of ἀπευθύνω in Sophocles, see *Œd. T.* 104, *Ajax* 72, and cf. supra 178. The same conditional obedience is promised in the σοῦ καλῶς ἡγουμένου, which follows.

637. πέδας.] This reading is introduced by Wunder on the authority of the Scholiast.

639. πρὸς ἡδονῆς.] The common reading γ' ὑφ' ἡδονῆς is not sanctioned by the best MSS., and the γε is quite out of place. I have therefore adopted the reading proposed by Hermann (see above on v. 24, and for the construction, cf. v. 51).

654—658. ὅστις δ' ὑπερβὰς—τἀναντία.] With Bückh and Dindorf, I have adopted Hermann's original suggestion respecting the transposition of these lines. They were formerly placed after line 662.

655. κρατύνουσιν νοεῖ.] Dindorf has extracted this correction from the best MS.

660. εὖ δ' ἂν ἄρχεσθαι θέλειν.] This second ἂν is, like the former, to be referred to θαρσοίην, and θέλειν governs ἄρχειν as well as ἄρχεσθαι. This is another of those instances, in which it has not been generally observed, that θέλειν is used to signify habitual conduct. Compare Pindar, O. XIII. 9: ἐθέλοντι δ' ἀλέξειν Ὕβριν. Æschyl. Persæ, 176: ὧν ἂν δύναμις ἡγεῖσθαι θέλῃ.

662. παραστάτην.] See note on v. 140 supra, and cf. Aristot. *Pol.* III. 4. § 6: ὥσπερ οὐδὲ τῶν χορευτῶν κορυφαίου καὶ παραστάτου.

666. ὀρθουμένων.] Although ὀρθὸς properly signifies "vertical," and εὐθὺς, "horizontal," they are both used to denote a straight unbroken line, whether horizontal or vertical. Thus, we have seen ἀπορθόω employed as a synonym for ἀπευθύνω (supra v. 627, 628); and we have ὀρθοῦν πόλιν, v. 167, as well as εὐθύνειν πόλιν, v. 178. Here ὀρθούμενοι does not mean *qui erecti stant*, as Wunder takes it, nor *qui se regi patiuntur*, as Emper translates it, but *qui rectam aciem servant*.

667. σώζει.] Hom. *Il.* V. 531: αἰδομένων δ' ἀνδρῶν πλέονες σόοι ἠὲ πέφανται, and the other passages quoted in the *New Cratylus*, p. 406.

668. τοῖς κοσμουμένοις.] Wunder and Emper rightly understand this participle as neuter. For the use of κόσμος, as implying government and military discipline, see *Theatre of the Greeks*, Ed. 4. p. 8.

678, 679. γένοιτο—προσκοπεῖν.] I cannot see the necessity for any alteration here. The sense is made clear by the particles which the poet has used: "although I could not, and do not wish, to arraign the justice of your sentiments, nevertheless (μέντοι) it *might* come to pass, that this censure would proceed with propriety from another," (i. e. γένοιτο καλῶς—ἔχον καὶ ἑτέρῳ λέγειν ὅπως σὺ κ. τ. λ. where καὶ performs that office of emphasis, which is best expressed in English by a stress on the auxiliary). "At all events (οὖν), whether such censure were right or wrong, it is my natural office as your son (πέφυκα), to keep an eye on your behalf," (προ-σκοπεῖν, cf. infra 732: σοῦ γὰρ οὖν προ-κήδομαι), "to all words, thoughts, and censures, which have reference to your conduct." I think, therefore, that Wunder's correction γένοιτο is quite unnecessary, and that Hermann's readings χἀτέρως and σὺ δ᾽ οὐ πέφυκας are detrimental to the sense.

687—689. ἥτις—τίνος.] There is some little difficulty in this passage from the use of μή where we should have expected οὐ. Wunder takes this negative with the infinitives, and explains the use of the prohibitive by referring to the fact—"impedimento fuisse Antigonam, ne insepultus jaceret Polynices, quum sepulturæ honore ipsa cum ornaret." Emper "finds the justification of the μή in the transition from a particular to a general reference : ἥτις refers indeed to Antigone, but by means of the second apodosis (for we have here the figure *protasis inter duplicem apodosin*), the thought receives a general application, οὐχ ἥδε, &c." This is the more correct view of the case. I consider that the special reference to Antigone terminates at φθίνει, and that the words which follow contain a general sentiment in explanation of the epithet εὐκλεεστάτων—"her deeds were most glorious : for, if a woman, when her brother lies unburied, braves every danger to guard his corpse from insult, is she not worthy of the highest glory?" This appears from the use of ἥτις instead of ἥ. Sophocles must have been particularly anxious to show that his reference here was general, for the verb ἐάω would have justified the use of οὐ, even in a conditional clause: see *Ajax* 1131: εἰ τοὺς θανόντας οὐκ ἐᾷς θάπτειν παρών.

709. ἀλλ' εἶκε—δίδου.] I prefer the old reading θυμοῦ to the dative, which has been substituted by many of the Editors. The word θυμοῦ, on which the rhetorical accent falls, is so placed as to qualify the whole sentence: "with regard to your θυμός, εἶκε καὶ μετάστασιν δίδου scil. μετάστασιν αὐτοῦ." That εἶκε θυμοῦ in itself would be good Greek, is clear from Hom. *Il.* IV. 509: ὄρνυσθ' ἱππόδαμοι Τρῶες, μηδ' εἴκετε χάρμης Ἀργείοις. It would be impossible to understand εἶκε θυμῷ otherwise than as equivalent to the phrase διδόναι τόπον τῇ ὀργῇ. Plutarch, *De cohibendâ irâ*, p. 4623. *Rom.* XII. 19. Casaubon *ad Athen.* XIV. p. 652.

711—714. φήμ' ἔγωγε—μανθάνειν.] For the sentiment see Hesiod. *Op. et dies* 291, sqq., and cf. Aristot. *Eth. Nic.* I. 4, § 5—7. According to the ancients, true σοφία was ἐμφυτόν τι,—hence the φῦναι τὸν ἄνδρα ἐπιστήμης πλέων, or κεί τις ἦ σοφός, above 701; and thus Pindar teaches, *O.* IX. 28: ἀγαθοὶ δὲ καὶ σοφοὶ κατὰ δαίμον' ἄνδρες. It is worthy of remark,—indeed, the proper understanding of an important epoch in Athenian history depends upon it—that although the nobles were by birth ἀγαθοὶ καὶ σοφοί, and though καλοκἀγαθός expressed a mixture of good qualities and mental culture, which was generally found in the nobles (see the *New Cratylus*, p. 408), yet in the time of Pindar and Sophocles the καλοί, as a class, were beginning to separate themselves from the nobles or καλοκἀγαθοί, and a middle class was springing up, especially at Athens, who called themselves οἱ καλοί, as distinct from the δῆμος on the one hand, and from the aristocrats on the other. Sophocles could say, as here, καλὸν τὸ μανθάνειν, or τὸ μανθάνειν πόλλ' αἰσχρὸν οὐδέν (above v. 701), and the educated Athenians thought with him, but Pindar delights in invectives directed against the καλοί and μαθόντες. And this reminds me that all the commentators on Pindar P. II. 72,—myself included —have missed the meaning of that passage. I can scarcely doubt, after all, that the true punctuation is:

γένοι' οἷος ἐσσί· μαθὼν καλός τοι πίθων παρὰ παισίν, αἰεὶ καλύς—

It seems most probable that the sentence would be completed in the first three words, which contain an intelligible idea, and are in accordance with the Homeric phrase, and with the passage in Thucyd. III. 14: γίγνεσθε δὲ ἄνδρες οἷουσπερ ἡμᾶς οἵ τε Ἕλληνες ἀξιοῦσι καὶ τὸ ἡμέτερον δέος βούλεται. With regard to the second clause, wherein the men of accomplishment (καλοί), who have acquired their learning (μαθόντες), are opposed to those whose abilities are the gift of heaven, it is sufficient to quote O. II. 86: σοφὸς ὁ πολλὰ εἰδὼς φυᾷ· μαθόντες δὲ λάβροι παγγλωσσίᾳ κόρακες ὥς, κ.τ.λ. Cf. Eurip. *Hippol.* 79.

719, 20. μηδὲν—σκοπεῖν.] Scil. μηδὲν διδάσκου ὃ μὴ δίκαιόν ἐστι. Wunder has rightly explained τἄργα—"opera sua quum spectanda dicit, significat id, quod faciendum suaserit oratione illa, qua patrem de sententia sua demovere studuerit. Non dissimiliter dictum *Phil.* 99: νῦν δ' εἰς ἔλεγχον ἐξιὼν ὁρῶ βροτοῖς τὴν γλῶσσαν, οὐχὶ τἄργα πάνθ' ἡγουμένην, ubi τὴν γλῶσσαν, οὐχὶ τἄργα nobis est, *das Reden, nicht das Thun.*"

722. οὐδ' ἄν—κακούς.] The meaning of this line has been overlooked. The emphasis falls on the first syllable of εὐσεβεῖν. Kreon asks, "Is it the result of your counsels that one should pay respect to—treat with consideration (σέβειν)—those who oppose themselves to the laws?" The son answers: "I would not even bid you to pay religious reverence (εὐσεβεῖν), when the base were the objects of it." And then Kreon asks whether Antigone was not in this predicament—whether she had not, in her anxiety to perform the duties of εὐσεβία (infra 899, 918), taken the enemies of the state as the objects of her undue reverence. There is

the same allusion to the two applications of σέβω in vv. 735, 736, where οὐ γὰρ σέβεις = ἀσεβεῖς γάρ.

727. χρὴ 'πὶ τῆσδ' ἄρχειν χθονός.] Most scholars will agree with Wunder in rejecting the γε of the vulgate. It appears to me that Sophocles must have written the line as I have given it: ἄρχειν is used absolutely, as it generally is, and the collocation ἐπὶ τῆσδε χθονός is very common in Sophocles (cf. Œd. Col. 569, 1258, 1705). The interchange of γ and π has been referred to above on v. 24. The corruption has crept in from the γῆς ἄρχοις of v. 730. The use of the dative after χρή is referred to by Thom. M., and is justified by other examples.

729. οὐ τοῦ κρατοῦντος—νομίζεται;] Cf. Phil. 386, Œd. Col. 38, and see Arist. Eth. Nic. IX. 8, § 6: ὥσπερ καὶ πόλις τὸ κυριώτατον μάλιστ' εἶναι δοκεῖ καὶ πᾶν ἄλλο σύστημα.

747. γυναικός—μὴ κώτιλλέ με.] The verb κωτίλλω seems to be properly applied to the idle small-talk of women: cf. Hesiod. Op. et D. 371: μηδὲ γυνή σε νόον πυγοστόλος ἐξαπατάτω αἱμύλα κωτίλλουσα. Theocr. Id. XV. 87: παύσασθ', ὦ δύστανοι, ἀνήνυτα κωτίλλοισαι. The King here treats Haemon as a παρθενοπίπης, who could not speak like a man, with reference to his saying οὐκ εὖ φρονεῖν, when he meant παραφρονεῖν.

750. χαίρων—δεννάσεις ἐμέ.] Böckh takes ἐπὶ ψόγοισι with χαίρων. Wunder would translate the words reprehendendo, accusando. Emper proposes to read ἔτι for ἐπί. I think that, as δεννάζω signifies to use hard words, threats, and the like, and as Haemon begins with ψόγος (above 680), and is at last supposed by his father to threaten (above 743), the meaning must be, "you shall not, after all your censure, come to threats and abusive language with impunity." I cannot think, with Emper, that this meaning is here out of its place: it seems to me that after the bandying of words in vv. 745, sqq., it is eminently appropriate here.

765. πετρώδει—κατώρυχι.] It is clear from the description here and elsewhere, that the place of Antigone's confinement was one of those partially-subterraneous θάλαμοι or οὐδοί, with dome-shaped top, which the Greeks used as secret chambers, treasure-houses, store-rooms, and prisons: see Müller's *Ancient Art and its remains*, § 48. pp. 22, 23, English Translation. Emper refers to a paper by Col. Mure in the *Rhein. Mus.* 1839, Heft. II. p. 265. See below on v. 1173.

772—783. *Third Stasimon.* The following is the scheme of the metres.

1. ∪ ‖ ⊥ ∪ ǀ – ‖ ⊥ ∪ ∪ ǀ ⊥ ‖
2. ∪ ‖ ⊥ ∪ ǀ – ‖ ⊥ ∪ ∪ ǀ ⊥ ‖ ⊥ ∪ ‖ ⊥ ∪ ∪ ‖ ⊥ ∪ – ‖
3.   ⊥ ∪ ‖ ⊥ ∪ ∪ ‖ ⊥ ∪ ǀ – – ‖
4. – ‖ ⊥ ∪ – ‖ ⊥ ∪ ∪ ǀ ⊥ ‖ ⊥ ∪ ∪ ǀ ⊥ ‖ ⊥ – ‖
5. – – ‖ ⊥ ∪ ∪ ǀ ⊥ ‖ ⊥ ∪ ∪ ǀ ⊥ – ‖
6. – ‖ ⊥ ∪ ∪ ‖ ⊥ ∪ ǀ – – ‖ ⊥ ∪ ∪ ǀ ⊥ ∪ – ῠ.

It is customary to scan this pair of strophes with iambic dipodiæ, Bacchei, and other irregularities, inimical to the rhythm, which is simply dactylico-trochaic. The second and third lines are, in effect, one, as appears not only from the metre, but still more so from the repeated Ἔρως, which, according to the laws of good style, ought to stand in close rhetorical connexion with the two relatives which follow.

773. Ἔρως, ὃς ἐν κτήμασι πίπτεις.] Most of the commentators understand by κτήματα, "the wealthy and powerful," and Propertius is quoted in explanation; I. *El.* 14, 15:

> Nam quis divitiis adverso gaudet amore?
> Nulla mihi tristi præmia sint Venere.
> Illa potest magnas heroum infringere vires:
> Illa etiam duris montibus esse dolor.

Klotz thinks that by κτήματα we must understand "slaves." Emper regards the passage as corrupt. Now the use of ἐμπίπτω, with the dative, to signify the access of an emotion or passion, is exceedingly common, and ἔρως ἐμπίπτει τινί is a phrase of constant occurrence, e. g. Æschyl. *Ag.* 322: ἔρως δὲ μήτις πρότερον ἐμπίπτῃ στρατῷ πορθεῖν ἃ μὴ χρὴ λέρδεσιν νικωμένους. Plato, *Resp.* VI. p. 499, c: πρὶν ἂν τοῖς φιλοσόφοις τούτοις...ἔκ τινος θείας ἐπιπνοίας ἀληθινῆς φιλοσοφίας ἀληθινὸς ἔρως ἐμπέσῃ. Whether this phrase is borrowed from the language of the wrestling school or not (see note on Pindar, *P.* VIII. 81), it is sufficiently expressive and intelligible. What then is the meaning of ἔρως ἐμπίπτει κτήμασι? It does not appear to me to be explicable otherwise than by a reference to the dictum of Plato, that men are the κτήματα of the Gods; see *Phædo*, p. 62, b: οὐ μέντοι ἀλλὰ τόδε γέ μοι δοκεῖ, ὦ Κέβης, εὖ λέγεσθαι, τὸ θεοὺς εἶναι ἡμῶν τοὺς ἐπιμελομένους καὶ ἡμᾶς τοὺς ἀνθρώπους ἐν τῶν κτημάτων τοῖς θεοῖς εἶναι. *Ibid.* p. 62, d, *Legg.* X. p. 902, b, 906, a: ξύμμαχοι δὲ ἡμῖν θεοί τε ἅμα καὶ δαίμονες, ἡμεῖς δ' αὖ κτήματα θεῶν καὶ δαιμόνων. If the reader will compare these passages with that in the *Critias*, p. 109, b, he will see that the mind of man is regarded as influenced by the Deity, in the same way as the flock is guided by its shepherd: οἷον νομῆς ποίμνια κτήματα καὶ θρέμματα ἑαυτῶν ἡμᾶς ἔτρεφον πλὴν οὐ σώμασι σώματα βιαζόμενοι, καθάπερ ποιμένες κτήνη πληγῇ νέμοντες, ἀλλ' ᾗ μάλιστα εὔστροφον ζῷον ἐκ πρύμνης ἀπευθύνοντες οἷον οἴακι πειθοῖ ψυχῆς ἐφαπτόμενοι κατὰ τὴν αὐτῶν διάνοιαν, οὕτως ἄγοντες τὸ θνητὸν πᾶν ἐκυβέρνων. That the poets were in the habit of speaking of the regulated functions of the mind, in phraseology borrowed from that which described the shepherd's office, is clear from the metaphors βουκολεῖν φροντίσι τι (Æsch. *Agam.* 669), or βουκολεῖσθαί τι (*Eumen.* 78); and φρενὸς οἰοβώτης (Soph. *Ajax* 607). I am convinced, therefore, that Sophocles here speaks of love as making men his κτήματα, by his triumphant victories over those whom he attacks; so that κτήματα is here used proleptically. And I think that this interpretation is supported by the context. First, the poet addresses Eros as invincible; then he states that he is not only victor when he combats, but that by attacking he at once enslaves—makes the objects of his attack his κτήματα, the herd which he guides and governs. As the wrestler, who merely threw his adversary, might gain only an incomplete victory, while he who fell upon him would secure his triumph, so love not only conquers, but he falls with his victim undermost, who thenceforth becomes entirely his own. He then expresses the throne of love's supremacy, and the universality of his influence. Of all the commentators on Sophocles, Reisig has, in my opinion, made by far the nearest approximation to the truth. He says (*Enarrat. in Œd. Col.* 315): "κτήματα sunt illi, qui amore sunt capti. Amor, qui in eos irruis quos habes, qui tibi sunt mancipati, κτήμασι σοῖς." Only, it will be observed, that he does not quite see the force of ἐμπίπτω, and takes κτήμασιν as a descriptive phrase, whereas it must be a proleptic word or secondary predicate, so that the phrase may be rendered: *Amor, qui, incidendo jacentibus, debellatos tibi quasi jure mancipi vindicas.*

777. ὁ δ' ἔχων μέμηνεν.] It is in accordance with the idiom of the Greek language to say not only ἔρως ἔχει τινα, but also ἔχει τις ἔρωτα. Thus we have seen above, that the objects of Love's influence are his κτήματα. Pindar says (*I.* VII. 29), ἔρως γάρ ἔχεν. Plato, on the contrary, as here, ἀνήρ ἔχων ἔρωτα (*Phædr.* p. 239, B), and, ὁ Ἔρως ἐν πάσῃ ἀναρχίᾳ καὶ ἀνομίᾳ ζῶν, ἅτε αὐτὸς ὢν μόναρχος, τὸν ἔχοντα—αὐτὸν ὥσπερ πόλιν ἄξει ἐπὶ πᾶσαν τόλμαν (*Resp.* IX. p. 575, A). We have the same inversions in εἰς ἄτην ἄγειν and ἄτην ἄγειν (supra ad v. 4), κατέχειν ὑπερβασίαν and ὑπερβασία κατέχοι (supra ad 598, 9), &c.

778. ἀδίκους.] Schol.: σὺ καὶ δικαίους διαφθείρεις, ὥστε τὰς φρένας αὐτῶν ἀδίκους γενέσθαι.

781. ἐναργὴς βλεφάρων ἵμερος.] For the idea, see *New Cratylus*, p. 583. I need hardly say that my version was suggested by Shakspere; *Love's Labour's Lost*, Act IV. Sc. 3:

"But love, first learned in a lady's eyes,
Lives not alone immured in the brain, &c."

782, 3. τῶν μεγάλων—θεσμῶν.] Dindorf, who is followed as usual by Wunder, alters the vulgate by inserting οὐχὶ before πάρεδρος, and omitting the words ἐν ἀρχαῖς before θεσμῶν. I agree with him so far as to think that the metre is faulty, and that ἐν ἀρχαῖς is a marginal gloss; but I think his insertion of οὐχὶ utterly tasteless. The abnegation of a metaphor, which it was not *necessary* for the poet to use, seems to me at variance with all established rules of good style, and suitable only for the lowest comedy. Dindorf thinks that his view is confirmed by the words which follow: νῦν δ᾽ ἤδη 'γὼ καὐτὸς θεσμῶν ἔξω φέρομαι. It appears to me that these words point to a very different remedy for the corruption of the text: they tell us that the preceding words must have spoken of the power of love as having equal power with the mighty laws of filial piety, in the case of a particular person; for this is the opposition implied in the νῦν ἤδη ἐγὼ καὶ αὐτός. Now as they are speaking of the particular case of Kreon and Hæmon (τόδε νεῖκος ἀνδρῶν ξύναιμον), and as the victory gained by love referred only to Hæmon, I have not hesitated to insert παιδὶ before πάρεδρος. I think that the resemblance of the first two syllables of the latter word has caused the confusion between them and the word which originally preceded. There is perhaps a play upon this last word in the ἐμπαίζει which follows. For the application of this verb, cf. Aristoph. *Thesm.* 975: Ἥραν τὴν τελείαν, ἣ πᾶσι τοῖς χοροῖσιν ἐμπαίζει τε καὶ κλῇδας γάμου φυλάσσει. Love and filial duty take their seats on the bench together, and the vote of love carries the day, because Aphrodite is irresistible in her sport. For the meaning of the μεγαλοὶ θεσμοί, see Pindar *P.* VI. 19—27. For νικᾷ, see above 274, and cf. Æschyl. *Eumen.* 915: νικᾷ δ᾽ ἀγαθῶν ἔρις ἡμετέρα διὰ παντός: and for the phraseology of the version, see *King Lear*, Act III. Sc. 6:

"Thou robed man of justice, take thy place;—
And thou, his yoke-fellow of equity,
Bench by his side:—You are of the commission,
Sit you too."

789—857. *First Kommos.* The metres are as follows:—

στροφὴ ά.

1. ⏑ ‖ –́ ⏑ – ‖ –́ ⏑ ⏑ ‖ –́ ⏑ – ‖
2.   –́ ⏑ ⏑ ‖ –́ ⏑ – ‖
3. – ⏑̆ ‖ –́ ⏑ ⏑̆ ‖ –́ ⏑ | – – ‖
4. – ‖ –́ ⏑ ‖ –́ ⏑ ⏑ | –́ ‖ – ⏑̽ ‖ – ⏑̽ ‖ –́ ⏑ ⏑ | –́ ‖ –́ – ‖
5. – – ‖ –́ ⏑ ⏑ | –́ ‖ ⏑̃
6.   –́ ⏑ ⏑ | –́ – ‖
7. – – ‖ –́ ⏑ ⏑ | –́ – ‖
8. – ‖ –́ ⏑ ‖ –́ ⏑ ⏑ | –́ – ‖ –́ ⏑ ⏑ | –́ – ‖
9. – ‖. –́ ⏑ ‖ –́ ⏑ ⏑ ‖ –́ ⏑ – ‖ –́ – ‖

στροφὴ β'.

1. – ‖ –́ ⏑ – ‖ –́ ⏑ ⏑ ‖ –́ ⏑ – ⏑ –́ – ‖
2. – ‖ –́ ⏑ ⏑ ‖ –́ ⏑ | – – ‖
3.   –́ ⏑ ⏑ | –́ – ‖
4.   –́ ⏑ ⏑ ‖ –́ ⏑ – ‖
5. ⏑̽ – ‖ –́ ⏑ ⏑ | –́ – ‖
6. – –́ – | – –́ – | – –́ – ‖
7. – ‖ –́ ⏑ ⏑ ‖ –́ ⏑ | – – ‖
8. – ‖ –́ ⏑ ⏑ ‖ –́ ⏑ – ‖ –́ – ‖
9. – ‖ –́ ⏑ – ⏑ ‖ –́ ⏑ – ‖ –́ ⏑ – ‖
10. ⏑ ‖ –́ ⏑ – ⏑ | –́ ⏑ – ⏑ | –́ ⏑ – ⏑ ‖ –́ ⏑ –
11. ⏑ –́ | –́ ⏑̽ | –́ ‖
12. ⏑̽ – ‖ –́ ⏑ ⏑ ‖ –́ ⏑ | – – ‖
13. ⏑ ‖ –́ ⏑ – ‖ –́ ⏑ – ⏑ –́ – ‖

The chorus adds three iambic dimeters and a dimeter antispast.

ἐπῳδός.

1. – ‖ –́ ◡ | ◡ ◡ ◡ | ◡́ ◡ ◡ | – ◡ ‖
2. –́ ◡ – ‖ –́ ◡ ◡ | –́ ‖
3. –́ ◡ – | –́ ◡ – ‖
4. –́ ◡ ◡ | –́ ◡ ◡ | –́ ◡ ◡ ‖ –́ ◡ – ◡ ‖
5. ◡́ ◡ ◡ | – ◡ | –́ – ‖
6. –́ ◡ – ‖ –́ ◡ ◡ | –́ ‖ –́ – ‖
7. – ‖ –́ ◡ | – ◡ | –́ – ‖

792—797.] ἀλλά μ᾽ ὁ παγκοίτας—νυμφεύσω.] See Shakspere, *Romeo and Juliet*, Act IV. Sc. 5:

"O son, the night before thy wedding-day
Hath death lain with thy wife:—There she lies,
Flower as she was, deflowered by him.
Death is my son-in-law, death is my heir;
My daughter he hath wedded! I will die,
And leave him all; life leaving, all is death's."

801. ἐπίχειρα.] See *New Cratylus*, p. 223.

805. ξέναν.] The Theban Chorus is made to use this designation of Niobe, because she married Amphion, king of Thebes. On the epithet Φρυγίαν applied to her, see Strabo XII. p. 571.

811.] τέγγει δ᾽.] I agree with Wunder and Emper in accepting Bothe's emendation of the vulgate τέγγει θ᾽, and I have also, in v. 808, adopted Musgrave's change of ὄμβρῳ into ὄμβροι. As Emper justly remarks, there is a confusion here between the person and the thing in the metamorphosis—ὀφρὺς and δειράς being applicable to the rock as well as to Niobe.

815.] τοῖς ἰσοθέοις.] Emper has remarked with truth, that this refers to a nominative τὰ ἰσόθεα, and not to a lower synonym of θεός and θεογεννής, applied to Niobe.

818. οὐκ οὐλομέναν.] With Böckh, I have restored the Homeric form of the common reading ὀλομέναν. It seems to me inconceivable that Sophocles should make Antigone, on the road to the grave, speak of herself as οὐκ ὀλλυμέναν. The passages quoted by Erfurdt and Wunder, from Euripides, prove nothing.

823, 4. ἔμπας—ἐπικτῶμαι.] Wunder would read ἐπαυδῶμαι, which is quite unnecessary. Emper properly remarks that ἔμπας explains ἐπικτῶμαι: "you, at all events, even though I can obtain nothing else."

828. οὔτ'—τοῖσιν.] I have adopted Emper's emendation of this passage. The common reading—οὔτ' ἐν βροτοῖσιν οὔτ' ἐν νεκροῖσιν,—has obviously crept into the text from a marginal gloss.

833. πατρῷον—ἆθλον.] The common reading is ἐκτίνεις. The best Laurentian MS. has ἐκτείνεις, which, by the mere omission of a connecting line, becomes ἐκτελεῖς. And I think there can be little doubt that this is the true reading. For although there is an apparent justification of the phrase, ἐκτίνεις πατρῷον ἆθλον, in Æschyl. *Agam.* 1564: χερὸς πατρῴας ἐκτίνοντα μηχανάς, it must be recollected that this is only apparent; Agamemnon might be said to atone to Ægistheus for the crime of Atreus, but this mode of speaking could not be applied to the case of Antigone, against whom no one entertained inherited animosity. On the other hand, the phrase ἐκτελεῖν ἆθλον is established in common usage: see Hom. *Od.* XXII. 5: οὗτος μὲν δὴ ἄεθλος ἄατος ἐκτετέλεσται, (cf. Theon apud Plutarch. p. 1087, A. Vol. V. Pars II. p. 440, Wyttenb.) *Od.* XXI. 135: ἐκτελέωμεν ἄεθλον. Soph. *Trach.* 1177: τὸ λεκτὸν ἔργον ἐκτελῶν; and especially Hom. *Od.* XI. 279, 280: τῷ δ' ἄλγεα κάλλιπ' ὀπίσσω πολλὰ μάλ', ὅσσα τε μητρὸς Ἐρινύες ἐκτελέουσιν, where the misfortunes of this very family are referred to. So above, v. 2, 3: ἆρ' οἶσθα ὅτι ὁποῖον—οὐχὶ τῶν ἀπ' Οἰδίπου κακῶν Ζεὺς τελεῖ; Pind. *P.* IV. 165: τοῦτον ἄεθλον ἑκὼν τέλεσον.

834—838. ἔψαυσας—Λαβδακίδαισιν.] If ψαύω, in its translated sense of touching upon in words, can be used with the accusative (and this is clear from v. 933: ψαύων τὸν θεόν; cf. supra 544, 5: μηδ᾽ ἃ μὴ 'θίγες ποιοῦ σεαυτῆς), there seems to be no reason for making a difficulty here. Μερίμνας will then be the accusative, and as a train of thoughts rather than a single recollection is awakened by the word πατρῷον (cf. above, 582), the plural is almost required. With Dindorf, I have received Brunck's emendation of οἶτον for οἶκτον. Böckh has justified the use of τριπόλιστον in the sense of τριπόλητον, cf. Pind. *N.* VII. fin. Soph. *Phil.* 1238. The construction ἡμετέρου Λαβδακίδαισιν πότμον is explained by Matthiä (*G. Gr.* § 589 g. 3). For the phraseology of the translation, the reader may compare *Macbeth*, Act IV. Sc. 1:

"Whate'er thou art, for thy good caution thanks;
Thou hast *harp'd* my fear aright."

The epithet "thrice-renowned" is also Shaksperian (*Richard III.* Act IV. Sc. 2. So *thrice-famed. Henry VI. Part II.* Act III. Sc. 2.).

852. ἀ ταλαίφρων.] I have introduced ἀ from v. 842, on account of the cretic rhythm. In v. 854, I have written ἱρόν for ἱερόν, with Wunder and Dindorf.

856. ἀδάκρυτον.] Triclinius: τὸ ἀδάκρυτον σαφηνισμός ἐστι τοῦ οὐδεὶς στενάζει· τὸ γὰρ παρ᾽ οὐδενὸς στεναζόμενον ἀδάκρυτόν ἐστιν, i.e. ἀδάκρυτον is a secondary predicate, equivalent to ὥστε οὐ δακρύουσιν αὐτόν. Cf. *Œd. Col.* 1602: τῶν σῶν ἀδέρκτων ὀμμάτων τητώμενος.

862, 3. ἄφετε—εἴτε χρῇ—ζῶσα τυμβεύειν στέγῃ.] These corrections, which are partly due to the MSS., and partly to Dindorf, have been most properly received by Wunder. The use of χρῇ for θέλει or χρῄζει, is supported by Hesychius and Suidas, and by quotations from Euripides (*apud Cic. ad Att.* VIII. 1. *et Suidam*, s.v. παλαμᾶσθαι), and Cratinus (*apud Suidam*, s.v. χρῇ).

873. φίλη—προσφιλὴς δὲ σοί.] Cf. Eurip. *Hecuba*

982, 3: φίλη μὲν εἶ σύ, προσφιλὲς δέ μοι τόδε στρά-
τευμ' Ἀχαιῶν.

884—887. πόσις μὲν—βλάστοι ποτέ.] In the *Transactions of the Philological Society*, Vol. I. pp. 163, 164, I have stated my reasons for believing that Herodotus (III. 119) has imitated Sophocles in this passage. G. Wolff, who gives the priority to Herodotus, considers this passage as an interpolation by the frigid Iophon (*Zeitschr. f. d. Alterthumsw.* 1846, p. 629 sqq.).

899. τὴν δυσσεβείαν.] So above, v. 185: τὴν ἄτην: below, v. 918: τὴν εὐσεβίαν. The article implies that which is, in the particular case, a mischief, an impiety, an act of religion. The Chorus says above, v. 847: σέβειν μὲν εὐσέβειά τις, meaning that in the conflict between human and divine laws, that which is εὐσέβεια, considered under one aspect, may be regarded from another point of view as an act of δυσσέβεια; and thus the translation given by Dindorf and Wunder in this passage—*impietatis crimen*—truly expresses the force of the construction. It was a charge of impiety—it appeared an impiety to the accuser who judged from his own principles,—but it was not so in itself.

900—903.] ἀλλ' εἰ—ἐκδίκως ἐμέ.] If we read this passage under the influence of those habits of thought which we derive from Christianity, we may be disposed to understand it as spoken in a spirit of self-abasement and charity. But this is very far from the poet's meaning. Antigone says: "If I have done wrong, if the gods, in fact, approve of the conduct of Kreon, by suffering I shall become conscious of my error; the fact of my suffering will prove to me that the award of Heaven is against me: but if Kreon is wrong, I pray that he may not escape an equal amount of anguish." The first two lines have been properly explained by the Schol.: εἰ ταῦτα τοῖς θεοῖς ἀρέσκει, παθόντες τὴν τιμωρίαν, [συγ]γνοίημεν [ἂν] τὴν ἁμαρτίαν. Only we must be careful to remember, what Wex has pointed out, that συγγιγνώσκω here appears in its original sense, as a correlative of σύνοιδα: cf. Herod. V. 91: συγγιγνώσκομεν αὐτοῖσι ἡμῖν οὐ ποιήσασι ὀρθῶς. The two latter lines are properly explained by Wex, in the Appendix to a translation of the *Antigone*, which I have not seen. His explanation is thus given by G. Wolff (*Zeitschrift f. d. Alterthumsw.* 1846, p. 628). Wex supposes that the indicative εἰ μὲν οὖν τάδ᾽ ἐστιν ἐν θ. κ. suggests a subtle irony: "if these things really are as they think:" referring to Plato, *Apol.* p. 37, c. p. 30, B. p. 25, B. *Protag.* 340, E. *Theatet.* 171, D; to which Wolff adds *Œd. Tyr.* 895. He thinks also that the καί in v. 903, indicates the wish on the part of Antigone that Kreon might meet with equal sufferings; and he compares, for the negative periphrase which gives bitterness to this wish, Æsch. *Prom.* 104: αὐθαδία...αὐτὴν καθ᾽ αὑτὴν οὐδενὸς μεῖζον φρονεῖ (Teuffel, *Rhein. Mus.* 1844, 621, quotes Dem. *Ol.* II. 6, p. 23: οὐδένων εἰσὶ βελτίονες, i.e. "as bad as any one"). Aristoph. *Equites* 1252: κλέπτης μὲν οὐκ ἂν μᾶλλον, εὐτυχὴς δ᾽ ἴσως.

905. τήνδε γ᾽.] "The γέ gives the following turn to the thought: 'she at least is still the same (though perhaps Kreon has altered his mind).' This view is nullified by Kreon's words, and then at length the Chorus gives up all hope." Emper.

915. τὴν κοιρανιδῶν.] The reading in the text is due to Emper, who has seen that κοιρανίδαι could not apply to the Chorus, and that βασιλίδα must be a marginal gloss.

919—954. *Fourth Stasimon.* The following scheme will exhibit the very simple metres of these stanzas.

στρ. α΄.

1. $\stackrel{\prime}{-} - \parallel \stackrel{\prime}{-} \cup \cup \mid \stackrel{\prime}{-} \parallel \stackrel{\prime}{-} \cup \cup \mid \stackrel{\prime}{-} \parallel$
2. $\stackrel{\prime}{-} - \parallel \stackrel{\prime}{-} \cup \cup \mid \stackrel{\prime}{-} \parallel \stackrel{\prime}{-} \cup \cup \mid \stackrel{\prime}{-} \parallel \stackrel{\prime}{-} - \parallel$
3. $\stackrel{\prime}{-} \cup \cup \mid \stackrel{\prime}{-} \parallel \stackrel{\prime}{-} - - \parallel \stackrel{\prime}{-} \cup \cup \mid \stackrel{\prime}{-} \cup - \parallel \stackrel{\prime}{-} - \parallel$
4. $\stackrel{\prime}{-} - \parallel \stackrel{\prime}{-} \cup \cup \mid \stackrel{\prime}{-} \parallel \stackrel{\prime}{-} \cup \cup \mid \stackrel{\prime}{-} \parallel \stackrel{\prime}{-} - \parallel$

5. $\acute{-} - \| \acute{-} \cup \cup | \acute{-} \| \acute{-} \cup \cup | \acute{-} \| \acute{-} \cup \cup | \acute{-} \|$
6. $\acute{-} - \| \acute{-} \cup \cup | \acute{-} \| \acute{-} \cup \cup | \acute{-} \| \acute{-} - \|$
7. $- \| \acute{-} \cup | - \cup \| \acute{-} \cup | - \|$
8. $- \| \acute{-} \cup | - \cup \| \acute{-} \cup | - \cup | \acute{-} \bar{\cup} \|$
9. $\acute{-} \cup | - \cup | \acute{-} \underset{\cdot}{\cup} \|$

στρ. β'.

1. $\breve{\cup}\cup\cup \| \acute{-} \cup \cup | \acute{-} \cup \cup | \acute{-} \cup \cup \| \acute{-} \cup \underset{\cdot}{\cup} \|$
2. $- - \| \acute{-} \cup \cup | \acute{-} \cup \cup | \acute{-} - \| \acute{-} \cup - \|$
3. $- \underset{\cdot}{\cup} \| \acute{-} \cup \cup | \acute{-} \| \acute{-} \cup \cup | \acute{-} \|$
4. $- \| \acute{-} \cup - \| \acute{-} - \|$
5. $\acute{-} \cup \cup \| \acute{-} \cup - \underset{\cdot}{\cup} \|$
6. $\bar{\cup} \| \acute{-} \cup | - \| \acute{-} \cup | - \cup | \acute{-} \underset{\cdot}{\cup} \|$
7. $\cup \| \breve{\cup}\cup\cup | - \cup \| \acute{-} \cup | \overline{\cup\cup} \cup \| \acute{-} \cup | - \cup | \acute{-} - \|$
8. $\acute{-} \cup | - \cup | \acute{-} - \|$
9. $- | \acute{-} \cup - \| \acute{-} \cup | - \cup | \acute{-} - \|$

The long syllables which occasionally interrupt the regular progress of the dactylico-trochaic verse in this, and other odes of the same kind (especially the *Dancing Song*, infra), are due to a peculiarity in the music, and indicate distinct successive bars in the accompaniment. In Pindar *P. V.*, Hermann, whom I have followed, assigns to the seventh line of the strophes a single word of three long syllables, or a disyllable followed by an enclitic, remarking (*Opusc.* VII. p. 152): "evanescit omnis difficultas, si incisionis constantia moniti illas tres syllabas credimus, similiter ut trochæum semantum, multo tardiore ductu cantatas singularem vocem fecisse."

920. ἐν χαλκοδέτοις αὐλαῖς.] i. e. in a chamber lined with plates of bronze fixed to the walls by nails of the same metal: see above on v. 354, and cf. Pausan. II. 23. § 7, with

Leake *Morea* II. p. 382, and Dodwell's *Cyclopean Remains*, pl. 10.

922. καί τοι καί.] I have adopted Hermann's insertion of the καί, for the article cannot be omitted in the corresponding verse of the antistrophe.

925. ὄλβος.] This is Erfurdt's undoubtedly true emendation: cf. Bacchylides Fr. 34 Bergk: θνατοῖσι δ' οὐκ αὐθαίρετοι οὔτ' ὄλβος οὔτ' ἄγναμπτος Ἄρης. The vulg. ὄμβρος is quite unintelligible in this collocation.

928. ὀξύχολος.] The MSS. have ὀξυχόλως. I have adopted Scaliger's conjecture: the adjective is here a secondary predicate, like πυρφόρος above v. 135, and δύστηνος in *Trach.* 936: κἀνταῦθ' ὁ παῖς δύστηνος οὔτ' ὀδυρμάτων ἐλείπετ' οὐδέν: "the boy, like a miserable creature as he was:" (*Construct. Gr. Praecepta*, 51, a).

931—933. οὕτω—γλώσσαις.] The article τᾶς before μανίας is to be explained as in the passages cited above on v. 899. And for this reason, among others, I agree with Emper, that the sentence ends after, not before, κεῖνος; which is emphatically placed last, to mark the parallel between this case and that of Antigone. *She* too had exhibited her madness in violent words: above v. 597: λόγου τ' ἄνοια καὶ φρενῶν Ἐρινύς; and when the parallel comes, the emphasis naturally falls on κεῖνος. I also agree with Emper that the repetition of μανίαις is intolerable, and I would gladly adopt his emendation ἐπέγνω δ' ἀνίαις, if I could believe that Sophocles would make an anapaest of the last word. It appears to me that the proper word for the context is δύαις, and that ἐπέγνω δὲ δύαις was first corrupted by the omission of δὲ before δύ-, and afterwards by the insertion into the text of the marginal gloss ἀνίαις, which was corrupted into μανίαις, in consequence of the copyist's eye having rested on the word μανίας in the previous line (see above on v. 606). That δύαις is the word, which Sophocles would have used here with the strictest propriety, is easily shown. Δύη means the pain or suffering which results from constraint, and is, therefore, a word of cognate signification with ἀνάγκη, δύστηνος (στενός, στεινός), *necessitas*, &c. The *Etym. M.* derives it from δέω, "to bind;" and though Blomfield (*Gl. Prom.* 186) says "*prave*," I have no doubt that the Grammarian is right: (compare the analogies of δύω, &c., *New Cratylus*, p. 188). Now Æschylus employs the word in a sense and application very similar to that before us. *Prom.* 179: πικραῖς δύαισιν οὐδὲν ἐπιχαλᾷς, where the Chorus is addressing the fettered Titan. Again, Prometheus says of himself, (*ibid.* 511): μυρίαις δὲ πημοναῖς δύαις τε καμφθεὶς ὧδε δέσμα φυγγάνω· τέχνη δ' ἀνάγκης ἀσθενεστέρα μακρῷ. And again (*ibid.* 523): τόνδε γὰρ σώζων ἐγὼ δεσμοὺς ἀεικεῖς καὶ δύας ἐκφυγγάνω. As Lycurgus ζεύχθη ἐν δεσμῷ, what would be more in accordance with this phraseology than the mention of the δύαι, which taught him his error? And if, as I believe (see the note on this passage in the Introduction), the Chorus is here referring to Kreon's impiety, he is afterwards made to confess δειλαίᾳ συγκέκραμαι δύᾳ (v. 1276). It is probable that ἐπέγνω, as well as ψαύων, should be considered as governing the accusative τὸν θεόν. He recognized the God, and at the same time discovered his error in meddling with him. The Emperor Julian probably had this passage in his mind when he wrote (*Anthol. Pal.* IX. 368):

Τίς; πόθεν εἶς Διόνυσε; μὰ γὰρ τὸν ἀληθέα Βάκχον,
οὔ σ' ἐπιγιγνώσκω· τὸν Διὸς οἶδα μόνον.

That ψαύων, at any rate, is placed in close connexion with its verb, is clear from the very similar passage in Pind. *P.* VIII. 12: τὰν (sc. Ἀσυχίαν) οὐδὲ Πορφυρίων μάθεν παρ' αἶσαν ἐξερεθίζων, which may have been in the recollection of Sophocles, when he wrote this strophe: the construction here, and the use of ἠρέθιζε immediately after, seem to point to this.

935, 6: φιλαύλους—τ' ἠρέθιζε Μούσας.] Cf. Arist. *Nubes* 311:

εὐκελάδων τε χορῶν ἐρεθίσματα
καὶ Μοῦσα βαρύβρομος αὐλῶν.

937. παρὰ δὲ—πελαγέων.] Although παρά, with the genitive, undoubtedly means "from the side of a thing," and not "by its side," it is clear that the meaning here is juxtaposition, and not removal. So also infra v. 1091. The reason for the irregularity appears to be this. When an aspect or direction is considered rather than mere proximity, although the idea of the one nearly anticipates what is presumed in the other, it is allowable to use παρά, with the case denoting removal, instead of the same preposition or ἐν, with the case of close or immediate position. Thus τὸ παρὰ ποδός (vide Pind. *P*. III. 60 : γνόντα τὸ πὰρ ποδός. *P*. X. 62: φροντίδα τὰν πὰρ ποδός) may be equivalent to τὸ ἐν ποσί (vide Pind. *P*. VIII. 32: τὸ ἐν ποσί μοι τράχον ἴτω), or τὸ παρὰ ποδί (cf. *O*. I. 74), or τὸ πρὸ ποδός (*I*. VII. 13). In Homer *Il*. IV. 468: παρ' ἀσπίδος clearly implies that Elephenor was wounded in the left side, which he exposed as he leant forward to drag away the corpse of Echepolus, i. e. παρ' ἀσπίδος, "where the shield had been, but was no longer." The mixture of aspect and position is best seen in the following passage, where the four points of the compass are described (*Œd. Col.* 1245) : ἄται—αἱ μὲν ἀπ' ἀελίου δυσμᾶν (the west), αἱ δ' ἀνατέλλοντος (the east), αἱ δ' ἀνὰ μέσσαν ἀκτῖνα (the south), αἱ δὲ νυχιᾶν ἀπὸ ῥιπᾶν (the north), where in three instances the place from which the mischiefs proceed is defined ; in the other—ἀνὰ μέσσαν ἀκτῖνα—their locality is intimated.

938. ἰδ'—ἄξενος.] The first word is due to a Dresden MS. Böckh has suggested the necessary supplement ἄξενος.

939. ἄγχιστος.] The metre points to some defect in the word ἀγχίπολις, which I consider to have been a marginal synonym (derived perhaps from Æsch. *Sept. c. Theb.* 503) for ἄγχιστος, a word used by Sophocles (*Œd. T.* 929) and Pindar (*P*. IX. 64), with the same application to a deity. Vide supra on v. 174. Dindorf suggests ἀγχουρος, but would prefer to alter the antistrophe. Some read ἀγχίπτολις, but if the word is to be changed, why not adopt an emendation which will square with the antistrophic metre?

942. τυφλωθέν.] See the passages compared with this, by Matthiä *Gr. Gr.* 409. 5, obs. 1.

943. ἀλαστόροισιν.] Welcker properly explains this as referring to the spirits of vengeance, which cried aloud in the sightless eyeballs of the Phineidæ.

943, 944. ἀραχθέν, ἐγχέων ἄτερθε] At one time I was disposed to agree with Böckh and Dindorf in preferring Lachmann's ἀραχθέντων to Hermann's well-known emendation, ἄτερθ' ἐγχέων. On further consideration, I am convinced that the true reading is what I have given,—namely, ἐγχέων ἄτερθε—which comes to the same thing in meaning with Hermann's ἄτερθ' ἐγχέων, and is equally derivable from the Scholiast; but which I do not substitute for ἀραχθέν,— a word which appears to me peculiarly in its place—but for ὑφ' αἱματηραῖς, which I consider to be interpolated. So that my emendation becomes a new correction, by virtue of the new grounds on which it rests, and the different change which it introduces into the text. My reasons are as follows: I feel convinced that in the strophe, as in the antistrophe, there must be a pause between the Ithyphallicus which follows the two trochaic dipodiæ in v. 943, and that which stands by itself in v. 944, before the anacrusis and cretic which preface the final Ithyphallicus of the stanza. The incision, therefore, in ἀραχθέν—των, would be very objectionable. Moreover, I think that the χιασμὸς in τυφλωθέν—δάμαρτος, ἀλαόν—ἀραχθέν, assisted as it is by the pauses of the rhythm, must have proceeded from Sophocles. So far too we have the MSS. with us, and they also give us the word ἐγχέων which follows, and which is recognized by the Scholiast. After this word, the metre found in the antistrophe (and it is the metre which we should infer here) is deformed by a redundancy of syllables. This must have been borrowed from some marginal Scholium on the text. The *Scholia Laurentiana* are as follows: ἀραχθέν· ἀντὶ τοῦ τυφλωθέν. Again: ἀραχθὲν ἐγχέων· ἀραχθὲν αἱματηραῖς χείρεσσιν ὑπ' ἐγχέων καὶ κερκίδων ἀκμαῖς, τούτεστι γυναικείαις. It is obvious that these words are grievously corrupt, and Hermann has attempted the following correction of the whole Scholium; τυφλωθέν· ἀντὶ τοῦ ἀραχθέν, αἱματηραῖς χείρεσσι, καὶ οὐχ ὑπ' ἐγχέων, καὶ κερκίδων ἀκμαῖσι τούτεστι γυναικείοις ὀργάνοις. My view of the remedy is very different. With regard to the former gloss, I think the true reading is ἀραχθέν· ἀντὶ τοῦ τυφθέν. Triclinius paraphrases it ἀραχθὲν καὶ πληγέν, and ἕλκος τυφθέν would readily occur to the Scholiast, if he were acquainted with Homer, as he most probably was: cf. Il. XXIV. 421: σὺν δ' ἕλκεα πάντα μέμυκεν, ὅσσ' ἐτύπη. The second gloss should, I think, be corrected thus: ἀραχθὲν ἐγχέων [ἄτερθεν]· [ἀντὶ τοῦ] αἱματηρῶς [τυφθέν,] [οὐχ] ὑπ' ἐγχέων [ἀλλὰ] χείρεσσι καὶ κερκίδων ἀκμαῖς, τούτεστι γυναικείαις [χερσί.] The adverb αἱματηρῶς, as applied to the explanation of ὀμμάτων κύκλοις ἀραχθέν, would be suggested by a comparison of v. 52 supra: ὄψεις ἀράξας αὐτὸς αὐτουργῷ χερί, with Œd. Col. 552: τὰς αἱματηρὰς ὀμμάτων διαφθοράς. Indeed the epithet seems to have been applicable to minor affections of the eye: see Eurip. Iph. A. 370: τί δεινὰ φυσᾷς αἱματηρὸν ὄμμ' ἔχων, where it refers merely to blood-shot eyes. It is, at any rate, a strange epithet for χείρεσσι in the text; as if the use of a less deadly weapon made the hands emphatically αἱματηραί! The conclusion of the Scholium shows that the χείρεσσι καὶ κερκίδων ἀκμαῖσι of the text were cited together; for the feminine epithet γυναικείαις can only refer to the former word χείρεσσι, and the meaning of the Scholiast must be, that the poet, by adding κερκ. ἀκμ. to the word χείρεσσι, implied that the deed was done by a woman's hand, the shuttle being the woman's tool in those days. I conclude, therefore, that the ὑφ' in the text has come from the ὑπ' ἐγχέων of the Scholiast, and the epithet αἱματηραῖς from the adverb αἱματηρῶς used by him. The secondary cause for the intrusion of the former may have been a familiarity with the phrases ὑπὸ χερσὶ δαμῆναι, ὑπὸ δουρὶ τυπῆναι, and the like (which, however, would be no justification of a similar usage here, where the sense required is that which is expressed by the instrumental dative alone), and the secondary cause for the displacement of ἄτερθε by αἱματηραῖς, may be sought in the resemblance between the adverb and the last three syllables of the adjective. The use of χείρεσσι, without an epithet, by the side of the words which signify the instrument employed, is justified by *Trachin.* 517: τότ' ἦν χερός, ἦν δὲ τόξων πάταγος. Sophocles employs this word to express nakedly feats of strength and violence; see e. g. *El.* 37: δόλοισι κλέψαι χειρὸς ἐνδίκους σφαγάς. *Ajax*, 27: κατηναρισμένας ἐκ χειρός. 115: χρῶ χειρί· φείδου μηδὲν ὧνπερ ἐννοεῖς. As distinguished from the ἔγχος, the proper weapon of a man, even the bow appeared effeminate to the Greeks of the age of Sophocles: οὐ μεταμέλει μοι τούτου ὅ τι ἀποθανοῦμαι, says the Spartan, ἀλλ' ὅτι ὑπὸ γύννιδος τοξότου. Whence their contemptuous use of ἄτρακτος, to signify an arrow. Thucyd. IV. 40. Most readers will recollect that the contempt of the Hoplite Goliath for David is grounded on his being ψιλός. In a precisely similar case of female vengeance, Euripides makes his Chorus address Polymestor thus: ἀπολέμῳ χειρὶ λείψεις βίον (*Hec.* 1034), which is an exact parallel to ἐγχέων ἄτερθε χείρεσσι, κ.τ.λ.

946, 7. μέλεοι μελέαν πάθαν κλαῖον ματρός,] I have restored the old punctuation. All the Editors since Erfurdt have placed the comma after κλαῖον, and have taken the words, ματρὸς ἔχοντες ἀνύμφευτον γονάν, together, as signifying *ex infausto matris connubio nati*. This, no doubt, is allowable, and would not be harsher than the ξύναιμον νεῖκος ἀνδρῶν, above v. 780. But it seems to me, that unless there were some reference here to a similarity between the fate of the *mother* of the Phineidæ and that of Antigone, the whole passage, and especially the end of this antistrophe, would lose its chief point. The fact that the Phineidæ themselves were blinded by their step-mother, and that they bewailed their own wretched lot, in being sprung from a mother unhappy in her marriage, would not sufficiently connect their case with the catastrophe of this drama. The legend referred to is as follows: Phineus, King of Salmydesus in Thrace, had, by his wife Cleopatra, the daughter of Boreas and Orcithyia, who was the daughter of Erechtheus, two sons, called

Plexippus and Pandion. Now Phineus having fallen madly in love with Idæa, a Scythian princess, not only incarcerated his divorced wife Cleopatra in a treasure-chamber or dungeon similar to that in which Antigone was confined, but was induced by the step-mother to put out the eyes of his two sons, who seem to have been described as attempting her rescue (see Diodorus Sic. IV. 43, 44). Consequently, the imprisonment of Cleopatra, rather than the blindness of his sons, was the point of the story as far as Sophocles was interested in it, and this reference, to the μελέα πάθα ματρός, is the natural transition from the mention of the disaster which befel them, to the more direct allusion to a traditionary imprisonment, with which the Athenians were perfectly familiar, because it was connected with their own national mythology.

949. αὔδασ'.] Although I have adopted Dindorf's correction of the inexplicable ἄντασε, I cannot agree with him in thinking that it is necessary to substitute ἀρχαιογόνοιο Ἐρεχθείδα for the plural genitives which appear in the text. With regard to the metre, the substitution of ἄγχιστος for ἀγχίπολις, in the strophe, will set that right; and as Cleopatra was the daughter of the daughter of Erechtheus, I do not see how the poet could speak of her as claiming the seed of an Erectheides. On the contrary, I think the plural both more accurate and more poetical. The verb αὐδάω with this reference is more frequently found in the passive, as in *Phil.* 240: αὐδῶμαι δὲ παῖς Ἀχιλλέως: cf. *Trach.* 1096. So ἥ τινα Λατοίδα κεκλημένον, Pind. P. III. 67.

965. γνώσει—κλύων.] The translation implies, "if you listen, you will know." So *Electr.* 878: ἴσθι τοῦτ' ἐμοῦ κλύουσα. It has not been sufficiently observed, that when κλύω is discriminated from ἀκούω, it presumes the continuous act of listening, whereas ἀκούω signifies to hear and understand, which, as an act of comprehension, is single. Thus we often find κλύω in the present tense by the side of ἀκούω in the imperfect, aorist, or perfect: cf. Æschyl.

Prom. 456: κλύοντες οὐκ ἤκουον. *Choeph.* 5: κλύειν, ἀκοῦσαι. Eurip. *Suppl.* 1061: ὁρμὴν λάβοις ἄν—κλύων, ἀκοῦσαι δ' οὔ σε βούλομαι, πάτερ. Soph. *Phil.* 53 ; ἤν τι καινόν, ὧν πρὶν οὐκ ἀκήκοας, κλύῃς.

985. δυσμόρου.] The compound *dismal-fatal*, in the translation, is borrowed from *Macbeth*, Act II. Sc. 5:

> I'm for the air: this night I'll spend
> Unto a *dismal-fatal* end.

1001—1003. κοὐδὲ μαντικῆς—πάλαι.] That the words τῶν δ' ὑπαὶ γένους are corrupt, seems to me sufficiently obvious; and that the interpretation ὑπὸ τῶν γένους for ὑπὸ τῶν ἐγγενῶν is inadmissible, has been already seen by Wunder and Emper. The change which I have introduced is very slight, and appears to me not only justified, but required by the context. In the first place, as the whole passage is an address in the second person plural from 1000 to 1006, it seems unnatural that a merely demonstrative sentence should be introduced. I think then, that τῶν is a relative explaining the word ἄπρακτος ὑμῖν. Then, it is impossible to take τῶν ὑπαὶ γένους for ὧν τοῦ γένους ὕπο; and something is wanted to give both the word ἄπρακτος, and the verbs which follow, a definitive value. Now with regard to the former, the force of the adjective is suggested by πράσσομαι in *Œd. T.* 124: εἴ τι μὴ ξὺν ἀργύρῳ ἐπράσσετ' ἐνθένδε: and the same supplement is required here; I have therefore introduced ἀργύρου, to be construed like χρυσοῦ in Eurip. *Med.* 963, or θανάτοιο in Pind. *P.* VI. 39 ;—namely, as a genitive of price or value. And I conceive, that although the construction τῶν ὑπ', ἀργύρου, is faultless, the abruptness of the two genitives, the resemblance between ΤΩΝΥΠΑΙΓΕΝΟΥΣ and ΤΩΝΥΠΑΡΓΥΡΟΥ, and the old trick of anticipating,—in this case, the τὸ μαντικὸν γὰρ πᾶν φιλάργυρον γένος of v. 1023 infra—which seems to have beset this copyist, have led to the corruption which has hitherto remained in the text. Cf. also 1045: καὶ ταῦτ' ἄθρησον εἰ κατηργυρωμένος λέγω.

1004, 5. τὸν πρὸς Σάρδεων ἤλεκτρον.] It is clear that Sophocles is here referring to the pale amber-coloured mixture of ⅘ of gold with ⅕ of silver (Plin. *H. N.* XXXIII. 23). There is a climax here, if the emendation which I have just proposed gives the true reading. Kreon says he has been sold for silver: but that if they bid for him gold mixed with silver, or even the pure gold of India, they would not effect their object. That the word ἤλεκτρον originally and properly designates the substance "amber," and not the metallic admixture of gold and silver, has been fully proved by Buttmann, in an elaborate and admirable essay on the subject in the *Mythologus*, Vol. II. pp. 337—363. His dissertation on the etymology of the word is so instructive, that I may take this opportunity of placing it within the reach of the English student (*ibid.* p. 355 sqq.) :

" I hope to have no difficulty in convincing the philologer, that the word ἤλεκτρον, comes from ἕλκειν 'to draw[1].' In an object which so frequently grew warm from contact with the human body, the attractive power would not only of necessity manifest itself on the earliest acquaintance, but would also at once engage especial attention. Accordingly, we not only find this circumstance mentioned by the Grammarians (see the *Etym. M.* quoted in the note below, and Eustath. *ad Dionys. Periegct.* 294: ἐξ οὗ καὶ λάβαι μαχαίραις γίγνονται ἀχύρων ἐφελκυστικαί, ὡς ἡ μαγνῆτις σιδήρου); but it had also attracted the observation of the most ancient philosophers. The passage in Plato's *Timæus* (p. 80 c: καὶ τὰ θαυμαζόμενα ἡλέκτρων περὶ τῆς ἕλξεως καὶ τῶν Ἡρακλείων λίθων, πάντων τούτων ὁλκὴ μὲν οὐκ ἔστιν οὐδενί ποτε,) is especially important, because the phrase τὰ θαυμαζόμενα shows the impression produced by these phenomena on simple men, and because the words ἕλξις

---

[1] " In Nemnich's *Dictionary of Natural History*, s. v. *succinum = electrum*, after a reference to the derivation from *Elector* by Pliny, we find the following quotation: 'in other writers, *quod confrictum, calefactum, ad se trahet paleas aliasque res minutas.*' I know not whence these Latin words are taken, and Nemnich does not appear to have been aware of any corresponding derivation of the word *electrum:* for he adds no remark to the quotation. One would think it referred to the derivation from ἕλκειν here proposed. As, however, I do not find this elsewhere, I conjecture that we have here an incomplete citation, originating with the words in the *Etym. M.*, in which the inadmissible derivation, παρὰ τὸ ἑλεῖν τὰ ἐκτός, is there maintained : τριβόμενον γὰρ ἁρπάζει τὰ πελάζοντα φρύγανα."

and ὁλκή exhibit the verb ἕλκειν as the proper term to denote this effect. We have, besides, a very ancient historical proof of this physical observation, in the notice which Diogenes Laertius (I. 24) has preserved us from Aristotle—namely, that Thales, induced by the magnet and amber, attributed a soul even to inanimate objects.

I recognize, therefore, in ἤλεκτρον, according to the termination, a verbal from ἕλκειν, which, though quite in accordance with analogy, would be more exactly represented by the harsher form ἕλκτρον, 'the drawer,' or 'drawing-stone.' The change of breathing, so far from appearing strange, is shown to be perfectly analogous[a] by a comparison of ἥλιος, ἠέλιος, ἡμέρα, ἦμαρ, and a number of other words, especially in the case of an old word, which must have come immediately from Ionia into Greece, along with the substance. As for the intrusion of the ε, I might, in accordance with the usual procedure in grammars, content myself with remarking, that the harshness produced by the concurrence of many consonants is thus avoided: but it is more satisfactory to appeal to an analogy, more definite and pervading a number of cases. I have already laid this down elsewhere[b]; but I will take this opportunity of confirming my position by further considerations.

[In the present state of comparative Philology, it is unnecessary to repeat this exposition, which occupies the next paragraph in the original essay.]

That this may not be treated as mere speculation, I will point out the same conformation in two other derivatives from ἕλκω. If the Greek word, which signifies a *Furrow*, occurred only in the form ὦλξ, it would have presented itself at once as a derivative from ἕλκω, and we should merely have noticed the mutability of the breathing, as in many other instances. As it is, this appears as a contraction of the forms ὦλαξ, ἄλοξ, which are known to be old accessory forms of the common word αὖλαξ. According to my view, however, ὦλξ, ὦλαξ, ἄλοξ, have all arisen by vowel-changes (*Umlaut*) from the same root ἕλκω, with and without an insertion of vowels[c].

---

[a] "Compare, in addition to the analogies which follow, ἀλκαία, 'a tail,' from the same root, instead of ὀλκαία, which is likewise used."

[b] "*Lexil.* 15, 2. 28, 2. *Gr. Gr.* § 99, 12, 1."

[c] "I have made it probable (*Lexil.* 59, 4) that the form αὖλαξ has arisen from the digamma." [See also *New Cratylus*, p. 130, 344.]

The other word is ἠλακάτη. But in regard to this also, we must, in the first place, examine some ordinary expositions. We frequently find this word used for the *Spindle*, and yet the Lexica and the explanations of the Grammarians, where they speak clearly, suppose the *Distaff*. And thus the word is confused with the word ἄτρακτος, which, so far as I know, is never understood otherwise than of the *Spindle*. In addition to this, we have a poetical use of both words. Namely, ἄτρακτος is very often used to signify an *arrow*; the same is assumed of ἠλακάτη; and thus we explain the Homeric epithet of Artemis, χρυσηλάκατος. It is certain that ἠλακάτη is also used for a *reed* and a *stalk*: see *Hesychius* and *Schneider*. On this is founded a conception, for which, it seems, a good deal may be said; namely, that both words properly signify a reed, then that which was made of reed, namely, the arrow, and the spindle or distaff. From this statement we must nevertheless detach what has no plausibility. It was very natural that the epithet of Artemis, especially in its usual connexion, χρυσηλάκατος κελαδεινή, should be, by preference, understood of the arrows: yet it is remarkable that, with this exception, ἠλακάτη is never used in the more ancient poetry to signify arrows; and it is more than remarkable that *Homer*, who uses the simple word so often and so constantly of *spinning*, should wish us to understand him as speaking of arrows when he uses this compound. We should also well consider *Pindar's* usage, who gives the same epithet to Amphitrite, the Nereids, and Leto. *Pindar* does not belong to the age and to the class of poets, whose expressions are so easily explicable as awkward misconceptions of Homer's words. It is also quite clear, that χρυσηλάκατος was in general an epithet of Goddesses; and supposing it derived from ἠλακάτη, in its ordinary signification, it must have denoted female excellence, pretty much in the same way as σκηπτοῦχος indicates manly worth. That in *Homer*, however, Artemis alone has this epithet, which is common to all Goddesses, (and yet she has it only three times,) is sufficiently explained, as is the same circumstance in regard to several other Homeric epithets, from the structure of the verse, and from the example of old current popular lays, by means of which such adjectives gradually became, even without any intrinsic necessity, *constant epithets*. At all events, the passage in the *Odyssey* δ, 122 foll. appears to me to be no contemptible voucher for this explanation of the epithet χρυσηλάκατος. There we find that Helena came out of her chamber Ἀρτέμιδι χρυσηλακάτῳ εἰκυῖα, and we are immediately told how her female-slaves brought to her her spinning-apparatus, with the express mention that she got it as a present from the Queen of Thebes, namely: Χρυσέην τ' ἠλακάτην τάλαρόν θ' ὑπόκυκλον. On the other hand, there is no trace that ἄτρακτος ever signified the *reed*, and it means an arrow only in certain passages, which are altogether of a poetical, tragical, or lyrical nature*, which are therefore sufficiently accounted for only by an old transition from one object, thin, long, and thicker at both hands, to another of the same kind. Ἠλακάτη, however, is actually used of the reed and the stalk;—this the old Lexicographers state quite definitely;—and indeed of sedge and cornstalks in particular; although they confirm it only with a passage of Æschylus, who used πολυηλάκατος as an epithet of the bank of a river (*Schol. Victor ad Il.* π, 183. *ap. Heyn.* p. 784. *Hesych.* in the second gloss Ἠλακάτη); but it is also found in this sense in *Theophrast. Hist. pl.* 2, 2., where the shafts of the reeds between the knots are called ἠλακάται.

Nevertheless, several doubts arise in my mind about the opinions, founded upon this, that the spinning-apparatus had its name from the reed; and of these doubts the most important is the usage of Homer. In his writings there are two forms ἡ ἠλακάτη and τὰ ἠλάκατα, which we must consider more accurately. The former is clearly described as the *distaff*, *Od.* δ, 135: αὐτὰρ ἐπ' αὐτῷ (namely, the basket,) Ἠλακάτη τετάνυστο ἰοδνεφὲς εἶρος ἔχουσα. *Voss*, however, understands this of a horizontal spindle, which was stretched across the basket. Among the proofs for our view of the case, I will, in the first place, adduce as the most obvious, the transition to a furniture of an altogether different nature; namely, to mast- and sail- work. Here also Pollux and others have mentioned an ἄτρακτος or spindle, and an ἠλακάτη, both being situated upon and above the sail-yard; indeed, we find in an author cited by Athenæus xi. p. 475. A, that it was the part of the mast which overtopped the θωράκιον, εἰς ὕψος ἀνήκουσα καὶ ὀξεῖα γιγνομένη: and so also the Scholiast on Apollonius i. 565, quotes from Eratosthenes: ἠλακάτη δὲ λέγεται τὸ λεπτότατον καὶ ἀκρότατον μέρος τοῦ ἱστοῦ: a description which throughout reminds us of nothing but a perfectly-straight distaff: and this was consequently *laid straight* across the spinning-basket of Helena. If we compare

* [Buttmann forgets Thucyd. iv. 40; and the modern Greek, ἄρακτος, "an arrow." See above on v. 943, 4. p. 210.]

with this the passage of *Plato* in the tenth book of the Republic (p. 616), where he is describing his symbolical spindle of necessity or of the universe, we shall find that he calls this, ἄτρακτος, and distinguishes from it (but as constituent parts of it,) the ἠλακάτη, and the whirl, σφόνδυλος; as follows: ἐκ δὲ τῶν ἄκρων τεταμένον Ἀνάγκης ἄτρακτον—, οὗ τὴν μὲν ἠλακάτην τε καὶ τὸ ἄγκιστρον εἶναι ἐξ ἀδάμαντος, τὸν δὲ σφόνδυλον μικτὸν ἐκ δὲ τούτου καὶ ἄλλων γενῶν: which means, 'the spindle reaching from above; of which the ἠλακάτη together with the hook were made of indestructible metal, but the whirl, of this and other materials mixed.' In what follows, then, he describes the peculiar mechanism of his whirl, which was distinguished from the actual one by this, that the actual one is simple, whereas his consists of eight whirls joined together. The more accurate description of this does not belong to the present question; as, however, he joins all with one another in a direction upwards, (for he says that each whirl has the hollow, in which the following one was inserted, on the upper side); and as he makes the whole of it a sort of spire *about the* ἠλακάτη, we see clearly that this image is taken from the *perpendicular* spindle, the under part of which rested upon a whirl, upon, and, with this whirl, around, one and the same axis or cylinder. The continuation of such cylinders upwards formed, therefore, the distaff: so that in the Scholion on the *Il.* π. 183, it is correctly stated: ἠλακάτην γὰρ καλοῦσιν—τὸ γυναικεῖον ἐργαλεῖον ἐξ οὗ τὸ νῆμα ἕλκουσιν. From this statement, then, is explained the apparent interchange, which actually occurs here and there, of the ἠλακάτη with the spindle, since it is an essential part of that implement, and, as a cylinder combined with the wheels which revolve around it, actually forms a spindle; there is, on the contrary, no passage in which ἄτρακτος occurred in such a manner that it could be taken for the distaff. But each of the two names might, no doubt, stand equally well for the whole spinning-apparatus, since the whole in its leading features represented a spindle. And so, in fact, we have seen that, in the Homeric passage, the ἠλακάτη alone is named; and it is to be taken precisely so in the well-known poem of *Theocritus*, the subject of which it would be wrong to call 'a distaff,' since it is rather a prettily-manufactured spinning-machine, which we could only call 'spindle,' if we wished to denote it by one English word. In Plato, on the contrary, and in Pollux (4. chap. 28), we find ἄτρακτος as a general name for the whole. In other passages we find both words connected as the two leading parts. *Leonid. Tar.* 78 (Anthol. Cephal. 7, 726): καί τε πρὸς ἠλακάτην καὶ τὸν συνέριθον ἄτρακτον Ἥεισεν.

The other Homeric form is τὰ ἠλάκατα. This has been frequently taken for a thing of the same kind as the former. Others, on the contrary, (v. Hesych.) took ἠλακάτη for the distaff, but τὰ ἠλάκατα for the spindle, because, in fact, the latter form is constantly connected with the verb στρωφᾶν, στροφαλίζειν. The philologer feels of himself that this is not tenable, and is at the same time sensible of the correctness of the explanation, which is undoubtedly also the received one at the present day, and which clearly results from the epithet λεπτά.—*Od. ρ*, 97: λέπτ' ἠλάκατα στρωφῶσα—namely, that ἠλάκατα signifies *the threads, that which is spun*, which is certainly *rolled round* the spindle. But the opinion, that ἠλακάτη originally signified the *reed*, is quite irreconcileable with this. For then, for the idea of spinning, ἠλακάτη would necessarily have been the root-word, and τὰ ἠλάκατα would have been derived from it, which every one who has any taste for analogy must feel to be impossible. Rather, it is certain that neither of these two words can be derived from the other, but that these are both to be deduced from one common root. And this, according to the analogy set forth above, is given us by the verb ἕλκω; for the distaff is, as we have seen above, the implement ἐξ οὗ τὸ νῆμα ἕλκουσιν, and the threads are τὰ ἑλκόμενα. It is very usual, however, for natural objects to be named according to their resemblance to the objects of domestic life; and thus it is very natural for the part of a stalk situated between two knots, to be compared, even in very ancient times, with a spindle or cylinder, and called after it[5].

If then we put together all the etymological deductions which we have made up to this point, it would, according to the usual form of the verb ἕλκω and its significations, be perfectly in accordance with the strictest analogy, if a *Furrow* should be called ὄλξ, spun *threads* ἑλκτά, the spindle ἑλκτή, and amber ἕλκτρον: it is certainly no insignificant confirmation of our opinion, that the forms, which have taken their places, furnish again an equally strong analogy among themselves: for instead of ὄλξ we find among other words ὦλαξ: instead of ἑλκτά and ἑλκτή, ἠλάκατα and ἠλακάτη[6], and instead of ἕλκτρον, ἤλεκτρον.

[5] "Compare the similar case in the German *Spule, Federspule*."

[6] "According to another pronunciation, even without change of vowel, ἠλεκάτη: vide Hesych."

I remark, in conclusion, that this naming of amber from the phenomenon of attraction, frequently appears in other languages also. The vulgar French name at the present day, *tire-paille*, Sacy has already compared with the Oriental *Káh-rubá*, which in Persian means literally the *Straw-stealer*. The second part of the name, *ruba* 'robber' *raüber*, agrees, like so many other Persian words, with German roots of similar signification; and hence it is very probable that the name *raf, rav*, which amber bears in the North-german languages, also belongs to the root *raffen, rauben*, 'rob,' with which again we should compare the Oriental notice in Pliny 37, 2, where Niccas relates of amber:—*in Syria quoque fœminas verticillos inde facere et vocare harpaga, quia folia et paleas vestiumque fimbrias trahit.*—For the German *Bernstein*, I know no other derivation than the one most usually received from *beren*, *bernen*, i. e. *brennen* ('to burn'); but I take this opportunity of directing the attention of my readers, as Gesner has done before me, to the correspondence between this name and the later Greek name for the same material,—namely, βερονίκη, βερνίκη, and βήρυλ- λος, which last genuine Greek name of a known jewel, from the similarity of sound as pronounced by the common people, has obtained this additional signification. See Eustath. *ad Hom. Od.* ô, 73, and Salmas. *ad Solin.* p. 1106. It is possible that the name was brought into Greece by the German Franks: but we have still to wish for something more certain'."

1034. σπλάγχνων.] It is perhaps scarcely necessary to mention that the σπλάγχνα, or *viscera majora* (i.e. the heart, the liver, and the lungs), were considered by the Greeks the seat of the affections: cf. *Ajax*, v. 995, Eurip. *Hipp.* 117. The word is probably connected with σπλήν, i.e. σπλήν-χανα. For the use here, see v. 509.

7 " If this is correct, perhaps there is truth in the derivation of the Italian *vernice*, French *vernis*, *Firnis*, from this βερνίκη, and consequently from *Bern- stein*. Adelung has fallen into a ludicrous error, when he supposes that *Firnis* comes from the "Latin" *vernix*; for this new Latin word is much more likely to have been coined from the Franco-Italian." (The evidence supplied by the researches of Mr. Eastlake, (*Materials for a History of Oil Painting*, pp. 230 sqq.) has made it abundantly clear that the modern word *vernice*, "varnish," must be a lineal descendant of the Greek Βερονίκη, as referring either to the famous golden hair of the Egyptian Princess, or to the city *Berenice*, where the amber- coloured nitre was found. If it is true that the name of *Veronica*, the patron saint of painters, is derived from this designation of the substance which they used, we have here a curious example of a return to personification in the use of a word.]

1036, 7. ἀνθ' ὧν ἔχεις—μετοικίσας.] Here again, as it appears to me, the copyist has made his usual confusion between the true reading and something like it in the same page. In the first place, one of the MSS. gives κατοικίσας, and this is better than κατῴκισας, for as the ἔχεις μὲν of v. 1036 answers to the ἔχεις δὲ of v. 1038, the insertion of an independent verb is scarcely allowable. I have no doubt, however, that κατῴκισας is an older reading than κατοικίσας, and that the latter was introduced by some one who perceived the construction, though he could not restore the text. The original copyist, whom we have to thank for so many blunders of the same kind, allowed κατω- to take the place of μετοι-, because he saw it just above in the preceding line. But the context, no less than the offensive jingle between κάτω and κατῴκισας at the ends of two successive lines, requires the substitution which I have made. In fact, the adverb ἀτίμως itself suggests a loss of franchise by *exsilium*—a deprivation of the political rights of the living, effected by this unnatural banishment to the grave, (cf. v. 25: τοῖς ἔνερθεν ἔντιμον νεκροῖς), and the political allusion to the μέτοικος has occurred twice before in this play with the same reference: cf. 828: οὔτ' ἐν τοῖσιν ἔτ' οὔτε τοῖσιν μέτοικος, οὐ ζῶσιν οὐ θανοῦσι. 865: μετοικίας δ' οὖν τῆς ἄνω στερήσεται.

1048—1051. ἐχθραὶ—πόλιν.] Wunder, whose opinion is adopted by Dindorf, and in part by Emper also, maintains that these four lines are a spurious interpolation. I have not seen any sufficient reasons for this view of the case. On the contrary, it appears to me that the oracular obscurity of the passage is quite in keeping with the lines which precede. In any case, Böckh's interpretation is inadmissible, though I am not aware that any of the commentators have remarked, that the most insuperable objection to it is furnished by the poet's use of the epithet ἑστιοῦχος. Böckh thinks that these lines contain a general sentiment: that the prophet is made to state the general consequences of a corpse remaining unburied. "All cities, in which birds and wild beasts carry fragments of corpses to the altars, are roused to animosity,"—consequently, Thebes is so. Now it appears to me impossible to understand the words in this sense, if for no other reason, because the phrase ἑστιοῦχον ἐς πόλιν implies that the bodies in question lay unburied in some foreign land: cf. Æschyl. Pers. 513:

ὅσοι δὲ λοιποὶ κάτυχον σωτηρίας
Θρήκην περάσαντες μόλις πολλῷ πόνῳ
ἥκουσιν ἐκφυγόντες οὐ πολλοί τινες,
ἐφ᾽ ἑστιοῦχον γαῖαν.

So also δόμους ἐφεστίους "native abodes," Sept. c. Theb. 73. Moreover, the compound συνταράσσονται expresses a conjunction of cities in the act of hostility: cf. supra v. 430: σὺν δέ νιν θηρώμεθα. There cannot, I think, be any doubt that the allusion is to the expedition by which the Argives, aided by Theseus, exacted the burial of their dead, and not to the Epigoni, who came ten years afterwards. In other respects, the meaning has been rightly given by Böckh. Ἐχθραί is of course a secondary predicate = ὥστε γενέσθαι ἐχθραί: and καθήγισαν is quite justified by the passages which Böckh has cited: namely, Gorgias, apud Longin. III. 2: γῦπες ἔμψυχοι τάφοι (cf. Hermogenes περὶ ἰδεῶν I. Vol. III. p. 226, ed. Walz); Ennius, apud Priscian. VI. p. 683, Putsch:

Vulturis in sylvis miserum mandebat homonem,
Heu, quam crudeli condebat membra sepulcro.

Strabo XI. p. 517: ζῶντας παραβάλλεσθαι τρεφομένοις κυσὶν ἐπίτηδες πρὸς τοῦτο, οὓς ἐνταφιαστὰς καλοῦσι τῇ πατρῴᾳ γλώττῃ. Soph. Electra 1480: πρόθες τα φεῦσιν, ὧν τόνδ᾽ εἰκός ἐστι τυγχάνειν: to which may be added, Lucretius V. 991:

Viva videns vivo sepeliri corpora busto.

And Mr. Ford, in his *Hand-Book for Travellers in Spain*, p. 567, speaks of the "bleaching bones, left to the national undertaker the vulture." See also, ibid. p. 349.

1053. καρδίας τοξεύματα.] See above, v. 1000, and cf. Æschyl. Eumen. 103: ὅρα δὲ πληγὰς τάσδε καρδίας σέθεν.

1058. τὸν νοῦν—φέρει.] I am disposed to think, with Wunder, that the words τὸν νοῦν τῶν φρενῶν are to be taken together, as in Homer, *Il.* XVIII. 419: τῆς ἐν μὲν ῥόος ἐστὶ μετὰ φρεσίν, ἐν δὲ καὶ αὐδή.

1064. εἰκάθειν.] Elmsley, Wunder, Ellendt, and others would write εἰκαθεῖν. I have given my reasons for a contrary opinion in the *New Cratylus*, p. 470.

1071, 2. συντέμνουσι—βλάβαι,] i.e. συντέμνουσι τὴν ὁδὸν εἰς τοὺς κακόφρονας "overtake them by a short cut:" cf. Æschyl. *Eumen.* 346: μάλα γὰρ οὖν ἁλομένα ἀνέκαθεν βαρυπεσῆ καταφέρω ποδὸς ἀκμὰν σφαλερ᾽ ἀνυδρόμοις κῶλα, δύσφρον᾽ ἄταν (according to the readings of Ahrens, *de dialect. Dor.* p. 546). For the word βλάβαι, here used with distinct reference to its primitive meaning, see *New Cratylus*, p. 549.

1077—1080. ἀξίνας—ἐκλύσομαι.] Hermann, whose opinion is adopted by Dindorf and Wunder, thinks it necessary to suppose a loss of some few verses, describing more accurately the place referred to, and also speaking more distinctly of Antigone, and they accordingly indicate a lacuna between vv. 1078, 79. This may be so. But we must recollect, on the other hand, that the King is represented as speaking in great haste and trepidation; and it may be asked whether the mention of hatchets to cut down timber for the funeral pile, coupled with a reference to the ἐπόψιος τόπος—the high meadow-land where Polyneikes lay, which has been already mentioned (supra v. 409: ἄκρων ἐκ πάγων: cf. infra 1163: πέδιον ἐπ᾽ ἄκρον), and which was probably depicted on the right-hand περίακτος—would not suffice as a hurried description of his first purpose, while the antithesis in v. 1080, might seem to point to an intentional brevity in describing his proposed liberation of Antigone.

1083—1120. *Tragic Dancing-song.* The following scheme represents the metres:

στροφὴ ά.

1. ⏑⏑ ‖ –́⏑⏑ | –́⏑⏑ | –́ ⏒ ‖ –́⏑ | – ⏑ ‖
2. –́⏑ | – ⏑ ‖ –́⏑⏑ | –́ ‖
3. ⏑ ‖ –́⏑ | – ⏑ | –́⏑ | – ‖
4. –́⏑⏑ ‖ –́⏑ | – ⏑ ‖
5. – – ‖ –́⏑ ‖ –́⏑⏑ | –́ ‖
6. – | –́ – | –́ – ‖
7.   –́ – | –́ – ‖
8. ⏑ ‖ –́⏑⏑ | –́ ‖ –́ – ‖
9. –́⏑ ‖ –́⏑⏑ | –́ ‖
10. –́ – ‖ –́ – ‖ –́⏑⏑ | –́ ‖
11. ⏑ ‖ –́⏑ – ⏑ –́⏑ ‖

στροφὴ β΄.

1. ⏒ – ‖ –́⏑ | – – ‖
2. ⏑ ‖ – – ‖ –́⏑⏑ | –́ ‖
3. –́⏑ | – ⏑ | –́⏑ – ‖
4. – – ‖ –́⏑ | – – ‖
5. ⏑⏑ ‖ – – ‖ –́⏑ | – ‖ –́⏑⏑ ‖ ⏑̇⏑⏑ – ‖
6. ⏒ ‖ –́⏑ | – ⏑ ‖ –́⏑⏑ | –́ ‖ –́⏑ | – ‖
7. ⏑ –́ –́ ⏑ ‖
8. –́⏑⏑ ‖ –́⏑ | – ⏑ ‖

The long syllables which appear in this song are to be explained as in the *Fourth Stasimon*, and were perhaps introduced here to accompany the slow solemn steps of the Emmeleia. For the quantity Ἐλευσῖνίας Böckh quotes Hom.

Hymn. ad Cer. 105, 266. Antimachus, *Fragm.* 55. Schellenburg, Eratosth. *Fragm. Merc.* XV. 15. p. 144, Bernh. Antipater Thessal. *Epigr.* 57; and on the antispasts ὑπὲρ κλιτύν, χορεύουσι, he remarks, that the former expresses in a charming manner the act of climbing the hill, while the latter beautifully imitates the lifting of the foot in the dance.

1083. ἄγαλμα.] Cf. above, v. 695, where the prosperity of a father is called an ἄγαλμα εὐκλείας to his children. In the same sense the deified Bacchus is here called the ἄγαλμα of Semele. "Ἄγαλμα," says F. A. Wolf, *ad Hom. Il.* IV. 144, "is a *bijou*, that which rejoices the heart (cf. Ruhnk. *Tim.* s. v.), a work of art in which we take pleasure. Schol. D: καλλώπισμα, πᾶν ἐφ' ᾧ τις ἀγάλλεται καὶ χαίρει, οἱ δὲ μεθ' Ὅμηρον ποιηταὶ ἄγαλμα εἶπον τὸ ξόανον."

1091. ναιετῶν.] Dindorf's conjecture.

1094—1101.] σὲ δ' ὑπὲρ—πέμπει.] The first three lines describe Bacchus as haunting Parnassus; the last three, as frequenting Euboea, to which both Nysa and ἀκτά refer, (above on v. 589). There is the same reference in 1111, 1112.

1105, 6. τὰν ἔκπαγλα τιμᾷς ὑπὲρ πασᾶν πόλεων.] This emendation of Dindorf's appears to me not only ingenious, but convincing.

1113, 1114. ἰὼ πῦρ πνεόντων χοράγ' ἄστρων.] Lobeck has failed to persuade me that we have here no *Theocrasia*, or confusion between the attributes of Bacchus and the Sun-god. He wishes to explain this passage by a reference to the practice of poets, who make nature participate in the emotions caused by the advent of deity (*Aglaophamus*, p. 218). It appears to me, on the contrary, not only that such an explanation would be inapplicable here, but also that the whole of this *Emmeleia*, which speaks in a mystic or Eleusinian strain, clearly identifies the functions of Iacchus with those of Phoebus, as Sun-god and as the deity who presided over healing and moral purity: compare the very similar chorus in the *Œd. Tyr.* v. 151 sqq. and see the passages which I have quoted in the *Theatre of the Greeks*, (ed. 4 or 5), pp. 14, 15. Nay more, I believe that the dithyrambic or circular chorus itself, which was peculiar to Bacchus, was intended to represent the apparent course of the sun: see the author περὶ λυρικῶν, Boissonade, *Anecd. Gr.* IV. p. 458. *Rheinisch. Mus.* 1833, p. 169: κέκληται δὲ ἡ μὲν στροφή, καθά φησι Πτολεμαῖος ἐν τῷ περὶ στατικῆς ποιήσεως, διὰ τοὺς ᾄδοντας κύκλῳ κινεῖσθαι περὶ τὸν βωμόν, σημαίνοντας τὴν τοῦ ἡλίου κίνησιν. Even the epithet πολυώνυμος at the beginning of this ode is a sufficient proof of the *Theocrasia* in it.

1152. ἀνασπαστοῦ πύλης.] The Greek doors opened into the street; therefore, a drawn-back door is a closed door.

1168. θαλλοῖς.] "Of olive." Demosth. *c. Macart.* p. 1074, 22, quoted by Böckh.

1173. παστάδα.] The meaning of this word in reference to its present application is best furnished by Herodotus, who uses it in speaking of the stone chambers in the great Egyptian Labyrinth (II. 148), which he distinguishes from the αὐλαί, the στέγαι, and the οἰκήματα of the same building. We have seen above (on v. 356), that αὐλή was a place which left a free access to the wind; we know that στέγη was a roofed chamber; that οἴκημα was a single detached room; and that παστάς, contracted from παραστάς (there is a similar apocope in compounds with κατά), was an open porch standing out from a wall or from some other building: see the following passages: Xenoph. *Mem.* III. 8, § 9: τοῦ μὲν χειμῶνος ὁ ἥλιος εἰς τὰς παστάδας ὑπολάμπει, τοῦ δὲ θέρους ὑπὲρ ἡμῶν αὐτῶν καὶ τῶν στεγῶν πορευόμενος σκίαν παρέχει, with which compare Pollux, VII. 122: Κρατῖνος δ' ἐν Διονυσαλεξάνδρῳ παραστάδας καὶ πρόθυρα βούλει ποικίλα. παστάδας δὲ Ξενοφῶν, ἃς οἱ νῦν ἐξέδρας (cf. Hermann *Opusc.* V. p. 220). For ἐξέδρα, see Eurip. *Orest.* 1449: ἐκλῇσε δ' ἄλλον ἄλλοσε στέγης, τοὺς μὲν ἐν σταθμοῖσιν ἱππικοῖς, τοὺς δ᾽ ἐν ἐξέδραισι. Herod. II. 169: παστὰς λιθίνη ἠσκημένη στύλοισι καὶ τῇ ἄλλῃ δαπάνῃ, with which compare Hesych. παραστάδες· οἱ πρὸς τοῖς τοίχοις τετραμμένοι κίονες. Plutarch, Brut. c. 55, uses παστάς as a synonym of στοά, and there can be no doubt that it was the same as the Homeric αἴθουσα. The name agrees in signification with *vestibulum* (from *ve-stare*, like *pro-stibulum* from *pro-stare*, Becker, *Gallus*, p. 189 Engl. Tr., for παρα-στάς = *re-stibulum*, just as παρά-φρων = *re-cors*.) It is clear, then, that Herodotus, in speaking of the multitudinous chambers of the Labyrinth, considered some of them as αὐλαί or "thoroughfares," some as στέγαι or "roofed apartments," some as οἰκήματα or "detached rooms," and some as παστάδες or "projections from the main wall." Thus discriminated, παστὰς is properly applied here to a descending σπήλαιον, or rock-grave, built out and completed artificially with a rude portico of unhewn stones. If the excavation, whether natural or artificial, extended itself into a series of compartments, it would be a λαύρειον or λαβύρινθος—one of those σπήλαια καὶ ἐν αὐτοῖς οἰκοδομητοὶ λαβύρινθοι mentioned by Strabo, VIII. pp. 369, 373. That the παστάς, in the case before us, was made up of rough unhewn stones fitted together, is clear from the description of the opening in v. 1182, as ἁρμὸς λιθοσπαδὴς χώματος. And I must remark, that the first word is partly technical; for the φλιή is defined by Hesychius as ἡ παραστὰς τῆς θύρας, and the same lexicographer tells us that the ἁρμοστῆρες were a part of the φλιή: *s.v.* ἁρμοστής·—καὶ λίθοι δύο πρὸς τῷ αὐτῷ τῆς φλιᾶς τιθέμενοι ἁρμοστῆρες λέγονται, where Heinsius proposes πρὸς τῷ οὐδῷ, and Toup (V. p. 448) πρὸς τοίχῳ τῆς φλιᾶς. Comp. Pausanias' use of ἁρμονία, *Bœot.* c. 38, on which see Leake, *Morea* II. p. 379. Specimens of rude door-ways may be seen in Dodwell's *Cyclopian Remains*, pl. 4, 8, 11, 40, &c.

1184. ἡ θεοῖσι κλέπτομαι.] Milton, *Comus:*
    Yet they in pleasing slumber lull'd the sense,
    And in sweet madness robb'd it of itself.

1194, 5. τίνα νοῦν ἔσχες.] Cf. Plato *Resp.* VI. 492, c: τὸ λεγόμενον, τίνα οἴει καρδίαν ἴσχειν; which shows that there was something colloquial in these phrases, as in our "what possessed you to do it?" From the phrase in the text came the later compound νουνεχής.

1199. διπλοῦς κνώδοντας.] The κνώδοντες were properly the cross-bars in swords and hunting-spears; in the *Ajax* 1004: πῶς σ' ἀποσπάσω πικροῦ τοῦδ᾽ αἰόλου κνώδοντος, the epithet αἰόλου points to the hilt, while πικροῦ "piercing" rather belongs to the blade. See Lobeck's note on the passage. And for διπλοῦν in this passage, cf. Eurip. *Hec.* 573: ἀμφίχρυσον φάσγανον κώπης λαβὼν ἐξεῖλκε κολεοῦ.

1213, 14. ἐς πόλιν γόους οὐκ ἀξιώσειν.] Sc. στένειν. For the phraseology of the Translation, see Shakspere, *Sonnet* LXXI. 13:

Lest the wise world should *look into your moan*,
And mock you with me after I am gone.

1227, sqq. *Second Kommos.* The metre of this lamentation, like that of many others in the Greek Tragedies, is chiefly dochmiac.

στροφὴ ά.

1. ∪ - ‖
2. ∪ ⏑́ ⏑́ ∪ - ‖ ∪ ⏑́ ⏑́ ∪ ⏓ ‖
3. ∪ ⏑́ ∪ ⏑́ ∪ ∪ - ‖
4. ⏑́ ∪ - ‖ ⏑́ ∪ - ‖
5. ∪ ⏑́ ⏑́ ∪ - ‖ ∪ ⏑́ ⏑́ ∪ - ‖
6. ⏑́ ∪ ∪ ‖ ⏑́ ∪ - ‖ ∪ ⏑́ ⏑́ ∪ - ‖
7. ∪ ⏑́ ⏑́ ∪ - ‖ ∪ ⏑́ ⏑́ ∪ - ‖
8. - ⏑́ | ⏑́ - ‖
9. ∪ ⏑́ ∪ ⏑́ ∪ ∪ - ‖
10. ∪ ⏑́ ⏑́ ∪ - ‖ ∪ ⏑́ ⏑́ ∪ - ‖

228 NOTES. [1227—1241]

1. – – ‖
2. Senarius.
3. ⏑ ⏑́⏑   ⏑́⏑⏑   ⏑⏑ ‖ ⏑ ⏑́⏑ –́ ⏑ – ‖
4. Senarius.
5. ⏑̄ –́ –́ ⏑ – ‖ ⏑ – ⏑ –́ ⏑ – ‖
6. – –́ –́ ⏑ – ‖ ⏑ –́ –́ ⏑ – ‖

στροφὴ β΄.

1. – –́ | –́ – ‖
2. ⏑ –́ –́ ⏑ – ‖ ⏑ –́ –́ ⏑̄ – ‖
3. ⏑ –́ –́ ⏑ – ‖ ⏑ –́ –́ ⏑ – ‖
4. ⏑́⏑ ⏑́⏑ ⏑ ⏑ – ‖
5. – – ‖
6. – –́ –́ ⏑ – ‖ ⏑ –́ –́ ⏑ – ‖

1. ⏑̄ –́ –́ ⏑ – ‖ ⏑ –́ –́ ⏑ – ‖
2. ⏑ –́ –́ ⏑ – ‖ ⏑ –́ –́ ⏑ – ‖
3. ⏑ –́ –́ ⏑ – ‖ ⏑ ⏑́⏑ –́ ⏑ ⏑ ⏑́⏑ ‖
4. ⏑ –́ –́ ⏑ ⏑ ⏑ ¦ ⏑ –́ –́ ⏑ – ‖
5. ⏑ ⏑́ ⏑ ⏑́ ⏑ ⏑ – ‖ ⏑ ⏑́⏑ –́ ⏑ – ‖
6. ⏑ –́ –́ ⏑ – ‖ ⏑ –́ –́ ⏑ – ‖

I think these dirges should be arranged in two pairs of strophes, the former pair containing the King's first lament for Hæmon, the second, his aggravation of grief after he has seen the dead body of his wife, and learned the nature of her death, in v. 1266, sqq.

1241. λακπάτητον.] Hermann and others prefer the Aldine reading, λεωπάτητον. The reading which I have retained appears to me to stand in more emphatic connexion with what has preceded, especially to the μέγα βάρος μ᾽ ἔχων ἔπαισε, which requires some mention of the feet or heels, to show that the heavy tramp of an avenging deity is referred to; cf. below 1316: ἐπὶ κρατί μοι πότμος εἰσήλατο Æsch. Eumen. 343: βαρυπεσῆ καταφέρω ποδὸς ἀκμάν. Pers. 517: ὦ δυσπόνητε δαῖμον ὡς ἄγαν βαρὺς ποδοῖν ἐνήλλου παντὶ Περσικῷ γένει. Agam. 1591: εἰ δέ τοι μόχθων γένοιτο τῶνδ᾽ *ἄκος, δεχοίμεθ᾽ ἄν, δαίμονος χηλῇ βαρείᾳ δυστυχῶς πεπληγμένοι, where I have introduced my own conjecture ἄκος for the ἅλις of the MSS. Cf. Eum. 615: ἔστι τοῦδ᾽ ἄκος. Pers. 623: εἰ γάρ τι κακῶν ἄκος οἶδε πλέον.

1243—1245. Ὦ δέσποθ᾽,—κακά.] Wex has a long note upon this passage, in which he collects other instances of the juxtaposition of ἔχειν and κεκτῆσθαι, *habere et possidere*. The meaning of the passage appears to me to be sufficiently clear from what follows: the construction is, ὡς ἔχων τε καὶ κεκτήμενος, "as one who *both* has and possesses," τὰ μὲν "the one class of things" (ἃ ἔχεις). τάδε κακά i. e. "these sorrows" ἥκεις φέρων πρὸ χειρῶν "you have brought with you in your arms," τὰ δὲ ἐν δόμοις κάκα "but the other class" (ἃ κέκτησαι), "namely, the store of evils laid up for you at home," ἔοικας καὶ τάχ᾽ ὄψεσθαι ἥκειν "you seem to have come with a prospect of speedily seeing." The phrase ἔχειν τε καὶ κεκτῆσθαι, is the counterpart of our "to have and to hold;" the one verb expresses possession, and the other ownership. This, as Müller rightly shews, (*History of Literature of Greece*, II. p. 97 of my translation), is the meaning of the κτῆμα ἐς ἀεὶ of Thucyd. I. 22: "it does not mean an everlasting memorial or monument. Thucydides opposes his work, which people were to keep by them and read over and over again, to a composition which was designed to gratify an audience on one occasion only." The word κτῆμα expresses that previous existence and readiness for use which is also conveyed by the adjective ἕτοιμος, and the verb ὑπάρχω, as opposed to γίγνομαι: cf. Aristot. *Eth. Nic.* IX. 9, § 5: ἡ δὲ ἐνέργεια δῆλον ὅτι γίγνεται καὶ οὐχ ὑπάρχει ὥσπερ κτῆμά τι.

1255. τί φῄς—νέῳ.] The vulg. τί φῄς, ὦ παῖ; τίνα

λέγεις μοι νέον λόγον; labours under a double interpolation. It is impossible that the allocution ὦ παῖ should refer to the slave who is addressed here, and it would be quite out of place to transfer the address from him to the corpse of Haemon, as Emper does, by reading: τί φῄς; ὦ παῖ, τίνα λέγει σοι νέον, κ.τ.λ. It is obvious to me that the words ὦ παῖ, which fit neither the metre nor the sense, cannot have proceeded from Sophocles here. Again, the word λόγον at the end of the line interrupts the construction, and is a grievous tautology after the occurrence of the same word at the end of the last line but one, from which the copyist borrowed it with his usual carelessness. The insertion of ὦ παῖ is due to the corresponding line of the strophe, which was probably written in the margin by a Scholiast, who wished to explain the construction of the repeated adjective νέος. If Sophocles, as I believe, wrote here:

τί φῄς; τίνα λέγεις νέον μοι νέῳ;

a commentator might very well quote

ἰὼ παῖ νέος νέῳ ξὺν μόρῳ,

as a parallel passage.

1266—8. ἡ δ᾽ ὀξύθηκτος—κωκύσασα.] As ὀξύθηκτος is not a proper epithet for a person, as λύει would not be the right voice, when her *own* eyes were spoken of as affected by her *own* action (cf. infra 1280), unless τὰ αὑτῆς were added, as in *Trachin.* 926; as the question of *how* she killed herself is answered afterwards (1281 sqq.); and as the *anacoluthon* in κωκύσασα would be intolerable here; I have accepted Hermann's suggestion, that for πέριξ we should read πτέρυξ, but I have placed the lacuna after βλέφαρα, and not, with him, at the end of the first line. The supplement, which I have inserted, is placed here merely *exempli gratiá*, until something better shall be suggested. It rests upon the words of the Scholium: ὡς ἱερεῖον παρὰ τὸν βωμὸν ἐσφάγη παρὰ τὸν βωμὸν προπετής, made up with the help of *Trach.* 906: βρυχᾶτο μὲν βωμοῖσι προσπίπτουσα; and I think that the repetition of βωμοῖσι, in the same place as βωμία in the last line but one, gave occasion for the omission, just as, conversely, interpolations have been made by this copyist, from a similar wandering of the eye. With regard to ἐκεῖ, I have added this, because I think it clear that the body is seen *within* the proscenium, and that the *Exangelus* though he stands by the side of *Ekkyklema*, is not within it, but has come forward to the stage with the sacrificial knife in his hand, just as Orestes, in the *Choephorae*, brings forth the fatal robe. This is also shown by his use of τοῦδε (v. 1270) in speaking of Haemon.

1275, 6. δείλαιος ἐγώ, φεῦ, φεῦ.] As I think it quite impossible to make these words, without the addition of φεῦ φεῦ in the antistrophe, correspond to the ὕπατος ἴτω ἴτω which appears there, I have not scrupled to add these otherwise useless interjections, in the latter case. If any one prefers to omit them here, and so to avoid adding them in the antistrophe, I can have no objection. With regard to the quantity of the second syllable of δείλαιος, supposing it to be susceptible of variation, which I do not deny, it seems to me inconceivable that Sophocles should not have pronounced in the same way this word, and its emphatic repetition in the following line.

1277. συγκέκραμαι δύᾳ.] "I am mixed up with— entirely encompassed by—an inextricable calamity:" see *Ajax* 895: οἴκτῳ συγκεκραμένην. *Electra* 1485: σὺν κακοῖς μεμιγμένον. St. Paul, *Rom.* VII. 24: τίς με ῥύσεται ἐκ τοῦ σώματος τοῦ θανάτου τούτου; Plotin. IV. 3, 12: Ζεὺς δὲ πατὴρ ἐλεήσας πονουμένας, θνητὰ αὐτῶν τὰ δεσμὰ ποιῶν, κ.τ.λ. And for the sense of δύη, see note on v. 932 supra.

1290. βράχιστα—κακά.] See other instances of this mode of secondary predication, in the note on Pind. *O.* IX. 104.

1291. αἰαῖ αἰαῖ.] As I observe that the interjections recur in corresponding places, I have substituted these cries for the ἴτω, ἴτω. which are more in their place lower down.

1299. ἐρῶμεν.] I prefer Bothe's reading to the vulg. ἐρᾷ μέν, or to the correction ἐρῶ μήν, which is worse still. The compound συγκατηυξάμην shows that the reference is plural.

1305. ὅπα—πάντα γάρ.] The corrections which I have introduced into this line, appear to me more probable than the mere omission of πᾷ καὶ θῶ, which Hermann and others have adopted. It seems to me pretty clear that πρὸς πότερον is a gloss upon ὅπα, that ὅπα θῶ got corrupted into καὶ θῶ, and this into κα or πα ἴδω, which was further suggested by ἰώ, and that πρότερον was omitted after πότερον had got into the text. With regard to the interjection which I have introduced, it is scarcely necessary to repeat the remark, that the interjections in these κομμοί regularly recur in the same metrical situations. For θέω in Sophocles, see note on v. 601 supra.

1306. λέχρια.] This adjective, which is connected with λέχ-ος, λοξός, λικ-ριφίς, λικ-ρός, λίγ-δην, *liquus, obliquus, liegen, legen,* &c., is the opposite to ὀρθός, and refers to lying down, or assuming a bent position, as contrasted with that of a man who is standing: cf. Œd. Col. 196: λέχριός γ' ἐπ' ἄκρου λάου βραχὺς ὀκλάσας. I have therefore ventured to make use of the strong metaphor in *Hamlet,* Act I. Sc. 5:

> The time is *out of joint;*—O cursed spite!
> That ever I was born to *set it right.*

Cf. Eurip. Hec. 1026: ἀλίμενόν τις ὡς ἐς ἄντλον πεσὼν λέχριος ἐκπέσῃ φίλας καρδίας.

INDEX.

[*The Roman numerals indicate the pages of the Introduction, the Arabic figures refer to the verses illustrated in the Notes.*]

A, α.

Æschylus *Supplices* 877, emended, 24—29: *Agam.* 1591, emended, 1241: *Suppl.* 976, explained, xxix.
Archæresia, at what time held? x.
Antigone, when acted. xiii.
Article, force of. 185, 899, et passim.
ἄγαλμα. 1083.
ἄγειν. 4—6.
ἀγείρειν στρατόν. 110.
ἄγραυλος. 354.
ἀγρηνόν. xxxviii.
ἄγχιστος, ἀγχιστεία. 174, 939.
αἱματηρός. 943, 4.
ἀΐσσω. 352.
αἰών. 580.
ἀκάματος. 600—2.
ἀκτή, of Attica and Eubœa. 588.
ἀλαλάξαι. 133.
ἄλημα. 320.
ἀντιχαρεῖσα. 149.
ἀπευθύνω, ἀπορθόω. 627.
ἀράσσω. 943.
ἄρδην. 429.
ἁρμονία. 1173.
ἀστοί. 289.

ἀστυνόμος. 352.
ἄτη and ἄλγος. 4, 617.
ἄτην ἄγειν, εἰς ἄτην ἄγειν. 4—6.
ἄτρακτος. 943, 4. 1004, 5. (p. 215.)
αὐδάω, of parentage. 949.
αὐλή. 354, 1173.
αὔω = αἴρω. 612.

B, β.

βέλη, of frost and snow. 355.

C, κ, χ.

Chorus, its functions in the *Antigone*. xxii.
Costume of Antigone, xxxii, iii. (see frontispiece): of Chorus, xxxiii: of Kreon, xxxiii: of Sentinel, xxxiv: of Hæmon, xxxvi: of Teiresias, xxxix: of Eurydike, xl: of the Messenger, xl.
καί, emphatic. 280.
καλός and μανθάνειν. 711—714.
καλχαίνω, 20.
καναχή. 130.
Καπανεύς. 135.
κάρα, in periphrasis. 1.
κάρα νεῦσαι. 269.
κατέχω. 599.

κῆρυξ. 160.
κλύω, ἀκούω. 965.
κνώζοντες. 1199.
κοινός, of consanguinity. 1.
κομψεύω. 324.
κόσμος, τὰ κοσμούμενα. 668.
κουφόνους. 342.
κράτη, "sceptre." xxxiii.
κτῆμα, κεκτῆσθαι and ἔχειν. 1243—5.
κτήματα. 772.
κωτίλλω. 747.
χ, γ, π, χρ, γρ, πρ, confused. 24.
χαλκόδετος αὐλή. 920.
χάριν. 370.
χείρ, of violent actions. 943, 4.
χορός, χῶρος. xxix.
χρῇ = θέλει. 862.

D, δ.

Dirke. 105.
dismal-fatal. 985.
δαιμόνιος. 372.
δεινός, of threats, 96: of power, 332.
δεξιόσειρος. 140.
δικαίως. 292.
δίκη ἐχθρά. 9 4.
δραχμή. 235.
δύη. 931—3. xxxviii.
δυσάνεμος. 586.
δύσαυλος. 354.
δυσχείρωμα. 124—6.

E, ε, η.

Editions of the *Antigone*. xLiii, sqq.
Ekkyklema. xLi, 1267.
ἔθνος of lower animals. 344.
εἰκάθειν, not εἰκαθεῖν. 1064.

εἴκω. c. gen. 709.
εἰμι, present. 607.
εἵνεκα. 19.
ἐκμανθάνω. 176.
ἐκπέμπω. 19.
ἐκτελεῖν, ἐκτίνειν ἆθλον. 833.
ἐμπαίζω. 782.
ἐμπίπτει Ἔρως. 772.
ἐξαυχῶ. 388.
ἐξέδρα. 1173.
ἐπάγομαι. 360.
ἐπάλληλος. 57, 58.
ἐπαρκέω. 605.
ἐπὶ χθονὸς ἄρχειν. 727.
ἐπιγιγνώσκω. 931—3.
ἐπίστασις. 225.
ἔπος. 20.
ἐρεθίζω. 936. (add Eurip. *Bacch.* 148.)
ἐρέσσω, ἐλίσσω. 158, 231.
Ἐρινύς. 597.
ἕρμαιον. 395.
ἑστιοῦχος. 1048—51.
ἔχειν ἔρωτα. 777.
ἠλακάτη, ἠλάκατα. 1004, 5.
ἤλεκτρον. 1004, 5.
ἠνεμόεις. 352.

F.

Foining, of spears. 146.

G, γ.

Genitive of price or value, 1001—3: for epithet, 114.
γ, π, χ, γρ, πρ, χρ, confused, 24.
γάρ. 178.
γενεά, and γένος. 580.

H.

Herodotus and Sophocles. xvi, 885.

I, ι.

Ismenian hill. xxv, 117.
ἴλλω. 340.
ἵππειον γένος, " mules." 340.

L, λ.

λαβύρινθος, λαύρειον. 1173.
λέσχη. 160.
λέχριος, λοξός. 1306.
λύειν βλέφαρα. 1267.

M, μ.

St. Matth. vi. 13, explained. 17.
Menœceus, Megareus, and Autophonus. xxvii, note.
μκμ. 507.
μετά, and ξύν. 115, 116.

N, ν.

Naval metaphors. 162, 189.
Nominative absolute. 260.
νέος, euphemistic. 242.

O, ο, ω.

ὅπλον, and ῥόπαλον. 115, 116.
ὀργή. 352.
ὀρθός, ὀρθόω. 162.
ὀρθός, εὐθύς. 666.
ὁρμαίνω. 20.
ὅροι, ὁρίζειν νόμους. 450.
ὀχμάζω. 350.
οὐ and μή. 687—689.
ὡς ἄν. 215.

P, π, φ, ψ.

Pericles. xv, 352.
Pindar, P. I. 84, explained, 289 :
P. II. 72, explained, 711—714.
Pleonasm. 2, 3 ; 86, 87.

Prolepsis. 135, 772, 778, 856, 928, et passim.
Protagonist, as messenger. xx.
παγκρατὴς ὕπνος. 600.
πάλαι, of a short interval. 279.
πάμπολις. 607.
παρά. c. gen. 937.
παρώπηχυ. XL.
παραστάτης. 662.
πάρεδρος. 782.
πάροδος. xxviii. sqq.
παστάς. 1173.
πικρός, " piercing." 1199.
πορφύρω. 20.
προθεῖναι, προθέσθαι ἐκκλησίαν. 159.
προστίθημι, of additional obsequies. 21—29.
πτέρυξ. 1267.
φαῦλος. xxxiv.
φεύγω. 263.
φίλος, προσφιλής, 873.
φωνεῖν, 117.
φρόνημα, 176, 352.
φώς, of a warrior. 107.
ψαύω. 834.
ψυχρός, of fear. 88.

R, ρ.

ῥεῦμα, ῥεῖν, of a crowd. 129.
ῥιπή. 137, 937.
ῥόπαλον. 115, 6.

S, σ.

Samian war, date of. xiv.
Sophocles, Œd. C. 1245, sqq. explained, 937 : Œd. T. 147 explained, xxx.
σέβω. 721, 899.
σπλάγχνον. 1034.
στάσιμον. xxix, xxx.

στείχειν. 10.
στέργω. 289.
στυφλός, στυφελίζω, 139.
συγγιγνώσκω. 901.
συγκεκραμένος, μεμιγμένος κακοῖς. 1277.
σώζω, σωτηρία. 186.

T, τ, θ.

Thebais, how it described the battles. xxv, xxvi.
Theocrasia. 1113, 14.
Thucydides, son of Melesias. xv.
Thymele. xxx.
Tritagonist. xx.

τᾶλις. 620.
τείνω, of sound and light. 124, 593.
τὸ μέλλον, adverbial. 357.
τόλμη. 370.
τριπόλιστος = τριπόλητος. 835.
θέω, in Sophocles. 600, 1305.
θησαυρός. 29.

U, V, υ.

Varnish, Veronica. 1004, 5.
ve-cors, ve-stibulum. 1173.
Vulture, "the national undertaker." 1048—51.
ὑπέροπλος. 130.
ὑπίλλω. 507.

THE END.

By the same Author.

I.

THE THEATRE OF THE GREEKS, with a new Introduction and other Alterations. Fifth Edition.

II.

THE NEW CRATYLUS; or, Contributions towards a more accurate Knowledge of the Greek Language. Second Edition, enlarged and improved. (*Preparing for publication*).

III.

ΠΙΝΔΑΡΟΥ ΤΑ ΣΩΖΟΜΕΝΑ. Pindar's Epinician or Triumphal Odes; together with the Fragments of his lost Compositions, revised and explained.

IV.

VARRONIANUS: a Critical and Historical Introduction to the Philological Study of the Latin Language.

V.

CONSTRUCTIONIS GRÆCÆ PRÆCEPTA.

Preparing for Publication.

VI.

A COMPLETE GREEK GRAMMAR.

4, Stationers'-Hall Court, London.

SCHOOL BOOKS

PUBLISHED BY

SIMPKIN, MARSHALL, AND CO.

English.

ADAMS.—History of Great Britain, with Six Engravings. By the Rev. John Adams, A.M. 6th Edition, 12mo. 4s. 6d. bd.

ADAMS' Roman History. 4th Edit. 4s. 6d. bd.

ALDERSON's Orthographical Exercises. Revised by the Rev. T. Smith. 25th genuine Edition, 18mo. 1s. cloth.

ALLISON's (M. A.) First Lessons in English Grammar. 6th Edit. 18mo. 1s. cloth.

ARNOLD's (Rev. T. K.) English Grammar for Classical Schools. 3d Edit. 12mo. 4s. 6d. cl.

ASH's Grammatical Institutes; or, an Easy Introduction to Dr. Lowth's English Grammar. 18mo. 1s. bound.

BALDWIN.—BALDWIN's History of England. New Edition, with Portraits. 12mo. 3s. 6d. roan lettered.

BALDWIN's Outlines of English History. New Edition, with Portraits. 18mo. 1s. half-bd.

BARBAULD's Lessons for Children. With Engravings from Harvey's Designs. 18mo. 2s. 6d. cloth lettered.

BIGLAND on the Study and Use of Ancient and Modern History. 7th Edit. 12mo. 6s. cloth.

BINNS' Exercises in False English. 21st Edit. 12mo. 1s. 6d. bound.

BLAIR's (Rev. D.) School Dictionary; or, Entick's Dictionary abridged. 9th Edition, revised, by A. Jamieson, LL.D. 12mo. 3s. bound.

BOYD's Concise View of Ancient Geography: with Seven illustrative Maps, coloured; and the Names of Persons and Places accented. 2d Edit. Two Parts, 4s. 6d. sewed.

BONNYCASTLE's Introduction to Algebra: with Notes. 18th Edition, corrected, containing a Synopsis on Variable Quantities, by S. Maynard. 12mo. 4s. roan lettered.

THE KEY. 12mo. 4s. 6d. roan.

BONNYCASTLE's Introduction to Mensuration and Practical Geometry: with Notes. 19th Edition, corrected by S. Maynard. 12mo. 4s. 6d. roan lettered.

THE KEY. By S. Maynard. 12mo. 4s. roan.

BONNYCASTLE's Scholar's Guide to Arithmetic: with Notes. 17th Edition, corrected by J. Rowbotham, F.R.A.S. 12mo. 3s. 6d. cl.

THE KEY. 12mo. 4s. 6d. cloth.

BROWNE's Classical Dictionary. 7th Edition, 12mo. 8s. roan lettered.

BROWNE's Union English Dictionary: with the Pronunciation. 4th Edit. 12mo. 10s. 6d. bd.

BRUCE's Introduction to Geography and Astronomy: with the Use of the Globes. 10th Edition; containing an Epitome of Ancient Geography, by the Rev. J. C. Bruce, A.M., and 30 woodcuts. 12mo. 6s. roan lettered.

THE KEY. 12mo. 2s. 6d. cloth lettered.

BULLAR's Questions on the Holy Scriptures. New Edition, 18mo. 2s. 6d. cloth lettered.

BUTLER's Introduction to Arithmetic, for Young Ladies. New Edit. 8vo. 4s. 6d. bd.

BUTLER's Large-Text Geographical Copy Slips. 1s. sewed.

BUTLER's (JOHN OLDING) Questions in Roman History, with Geographical Illustrations and Maps. 12mo. 3s. 6d. roan lettered.

BUTLER's Geography of the Globe. 6th Edit. With Additions by J. Rowbotham, F.R.A.S. 12mo. 4s. 6d. roan lettered.

CARPENTER—CARPENTER's School Speaker, selected from the best Writers. 5th Edition, 12mo. 2s. 6d. bound.

CARR's (T. S.) Manual of Roman Antiquities. 12mo. 6s. 6d. cloth.

CARR's (T. S.) History & Geography of Greece. 12mo. 7s. 6d. boards.

CHILD's Guide to Knowledge: a Collection of Useful Questions and Answers. By a Lady. 12th Edition, 18mo. 3s. half-bound.

COBBIN's (Rev. INGRAM) Grammatical and Pronouncing Spelling-Book, on a new plan; designed to communicate the Rudiments of Grammatical Knowledge, and to prevent and correct bad Pronunciation, while it promotes an acquaintance with Orthography. 11th Edition, with fine Frontispiece. 12mo. 1s. 6d. cloth.

COBBIN's Classical English Vocabulary; with the Etymology and Pronunciation. 3d Edition, 12mo. 3s. roan lettered.

COBBIN's Instructive Reader. Illustrated by Cuts, on an original plan. 5th Edition, corrected. 12mo. 3s. roan lettered.

COOPER's History of England, from the Earliest Period to the Present Time. 23d Edition, improved. 18mo. 2s. 6d. cloth lettered.

CROSSMAN's Introduction to the Knowledge of the Christian Religion: in Two Parts. 18mo. 1s. cloth.

English—continued.

CROXALL's Fables of Æsop and others; with a Print before each Fable. 24th Edition, 12mo. 4s. roan lettered.

DILWORTH.—Dilworth's Young Book-keeper's Assistant. 8vo. 3s. 6d. bound.

ENFIELD.—Enfield's Speaker: Pieces selected from the best English Writers. (Genuine Edition.) 12mo. 3s. 6d. roan lett.

Entick's Spelling Dictionary of the English Language. Square, 2s. 6d. bound.

FOSTER.—Elements of Algebra. By the Rev. W. Foster, M.A. 2d Edit. 12mo. 2s. cl. lett'd.

Foster's (Rev. W.) Examples in Algebra. 2d Edition, 12mo. 2s. cloth lettered; with the Answers, 12mo. 3s. 6d. cloth lettered.

Foster's (Rev. W.) Elements of Arithmetic, comprising Logarithms, and the Computation of Artificers. 12mo. 1s. 6d. cloth lett'd.

Foster's (Rev. W.) Examples in Arithmetic, with Exercises in Mental Arithmetic. 12mo. 1s. 6d. cloth lettered; with the Answers, 12mo. 3s. cloth lettered.

GEOGRAPHY.—Geography and History. Selected by a Lady. 19th Edition, revised. 12mo. 4s. 6d. roan lettered.

Geography for Children: divided into Lessons in Question and Answer. 33d Edition, 12mo. 2s. bound.

Goldsmith's History of England, from Julius Cæsar to the Death of William IV. 12mo. 3s. 6d. roan lettered.

Goldsmith's History of Greece, abridged. 13th Edition, corrected. 12mo. 3s. 6d. roan lettered.

Goldsmith's History of Rome, abridged. 12mo. 3s. 6d. roan lettered.

Goodacre's Arithmetic. 9th Edition, corrected by S. Maynard. 12mo. 4s. roan lett.

The Key, corrected by S. Maynard. 12mo. 6s. roan lettered.

Gasio's Young Ladies' New Guide to Arithmetic. New Edition, revised and corrected by Samuel Maynard. 12mo. 2s. cloth.

Guthrie's Atlas of Modern Geography. With 31 Maps, coloured outlines, and a complete Index. 8vo. 10s. 6d. half-bound.

Guy's English School Grammar. 11th Edition, corrected and improved. 18mo. 1s. 6d. cl.

Guy's (Joseph) Pocket Cyclopædia; an Epitome of Universal Knowledge. 11th Edition, enlarged, and illustrated with Woodcuts. 12mo. 10s. 6d. cloth lettered.

HASSELL.—Hassell's Camera; or, Art of Drawing in Water Colours. 8vo. 5s. cloth.

Hewlett's (Mrs.) New Speaker. 3d Edition, 18mo. 4s. roan lettered.

Hoppus' Measurer, for Timber, Stone, &c. London Edition, greatly improved. Oblong, 4s. roan lettered.

Hoppus' Practical Measuring made Easy, by a new set of Tables, by T. Crosby. Oblong, 3s. roan lettered.

Hutton's Compendious Measurer. 11th Edition, augmented and improved by S. Maynard. 12mo 5s. roan lettered.

Hutton's Practical Arithmetic and Book-keeping. By Dr. Gregory. 19th Edition, corrected, by S. Maynard. 12mo. 3s. cloth.

JOHNSON.—Johnson's Dictionary of the English Language: abridged from Todd's Quarto Edition. By A. Chalmers, F.S.A. 8vo. 12s. cloth.

Johnson's Dictionary of the English Language, abridged from the above. By T. Rees, LL.D. 18mo. 2s. 6d. roan lettered.

Johnson's Dictionary of the English Language, in Miniature, by George Fulton. 18th Edit. 18mo. 2s. roan lettered.

Jones' Sheridan's Pronouncing and Explanatory Dictionary of the English Language. Square 12mo. 3s. 6d. roan lettered.

Jones' New Biographical Dictionary. 8th Edition, 18mo. 6s. roan lettered.

Jones' Science of Book-keeping. 8th Edition, royal 8vo. 12s. cloth; or in Parts, 7s. each, cl.

Jones' Exercises in Book-keeping, by Single Entry, converted periodically into Double Entry. 12mo. 2s. sewed.

Ruled Books adapted to the above System, in Five Parts. 6s. sewed.

Joyce's Scientific Dialogues. New Edition, with Cuts, and other additions, by Dr. Olinthus Gregory. 12mo. 3s. 6d. cloth.

A Companion to the "Scientific Dialogues." 18mo. 2s. 6d. cloth.

KEITH.—Keith's Complete Measurer. New Edition, corrected by S. Maynard. 12mo. 5s. roan lettered.

The Key, by S. Maynard. 12mo. 4s. 6d. bd.

Keith's Complete Practical Arithmetician. 13th Edition, corrected, by S. Maynard. 12mo. 4s. 6d. roan lettered.

The Key, corrected by S. Maynard. 12mo. 6s. roan lettered.

Keith's System of Geography, on an entirely new plan. New Edition, 12mo. 6s. roan lett.

Kelly's (Dr.) Elements of Book-keeping. 11th Edition, 8vo. 7s. bound.

Ruled Books adapted to this Course. The Second Set, 5s.; the Third Set, 12s. 6d. sd.

LAWRENCE.—Stories, presenting a Summary of the History of Greece. By Miss Lawrence. 4th Edit. 18mo. 3s. 6d. cloth.

Lewis' Church Catechism Explained. 24mo. 6d. cloth.

MOLINEUX.—Molineux's Introduction to the Knowledge of the Globes; with a Key. 11th Edition, 12mo. 3s. bound.

English—continued.

MANT's (Mrs.) Parent's Poetical Anthology; a Selection of English Poems. 4th Edition, 12mo. 5s. 6d. roan lettered.

PIKE.—Pike's New English Spelling Book. 13th Edition, corrected. 12mo. 1s.6d. cloth.

ROWBOTHAM.—Rowbotham's (J.) New Derivative and Etymological Dictionary. square, 7s. cloth.

SAUL.—Saul's Tutor and Scholar's Assistant. 13th Edit. corrected. 12mo 2s. cloth.
THE KEY. 12mo. 2s. cloth.

SELTON's (Rev. Mr.) Abridgment of the Holy Scriptures. 18mo. 1s. 6d. cloth lettered.

SIMSON's Elements of Euclid; the first Six Books, with the Eleventh and Twelfth. Corrected by S. Maynard. 18mo 5s. roan lett.

SIMSON's Elements of Euclid, with Notes, by Robertson. 25th Edition, revised by S. Maynard. 8vo. 9s. bound.

SIMSON's Elements of Euclid in Symbols, by Blakelock, the first Six, and the Eleventh and Twelfth Books. New Edition. 18mo. 6s. cloth.

SMART's Walker's Critical Pronouncing Dictionary of the English Language. 8vo. 15s. cloth lettered.

SMART's Walker's Pronouncing Dictionary of the English Language Epitomized. 12mo. 7s. 6d. cloth.

TOOKE.—Tooke's Pantheon; or, Mythology of the Greeks and Romans. 36th Edit. with 28 Plates by Moses. 12mo. 6s. roan lettered.

TURNER's Introduction to the Arts and Sciences. Improved by Robert Mudie. 18mo. 4s. roan.

VINES.—Vines' Key to Keith's Treatise on the Globes. 4th Edition, 12mo. 4s. cloth.

WAKEFIELD.—A Family Tour through the British Empire. By Priscilla Wakefield; with Map. 15th Edition, 12mo. 6s. hf-bd.

WAKEFIELD's (P.) Juvenile Travellers: a Tour through Europe, with Map. 18th Edition, 12mo. 6s. half-bound.

WALKER's Universal Atlas, 28 Maps, coloured outlines. 8vo. 10s. 6d. half-bd.

WALKER's English Themes and Essays. 10th Edition, 12mo. 4s. roan lettered.

WALKER's Critical Pronouncing Dictionary, and Expositor of the English Language. 33d Edition (Cadell's), 8vo. 9s. cloth.

WALKINGAME's Tutor's Assistant, by Fraser. 78th Edition, 12mo. 2s. bound.
THE KEY. 12mo. 3s. cloth.

WATTS' Short View of the whole Scripture History, carefully revised. 12mo. 3s. 6d. roan.

WHITE's (Rev. John) Tutor's Expeditious Assistant, founded on a New Discovery. 3d Edition, 12mo. 2s. bound.

WATSON's Tutor's Assistant; with a full Introduction to Practical Mensuration. 4th Edit. 12mo. 2s. 6d. roan.
THE KEY. 12mo. 1s. sewed.

WATSON's Easy and Comprehensive Introduction to Algebra. 2d Edit. enlarged, 12mo. 3s. roan lettered.

WHITE's Elucidation of the Tutor's Expeditious Assistant. 2d Edit. 12mo. 4s. 6d. bound.

WHITE's Practical System of Mental Arithmetic. 3d Edition, 12mo. 3s. 6d. bound.

Books for the Higher Forms.

ADAM.—Adam's Roman Antiquities. 12th Edition, enlarged, by Dr. Major. 8vo. 10s. 6d. boards.

BINGLEY.—Useful Knowledge. By the Rev. W. Bingley. With Plates and 150 Woodcuts. 6th Edition, enlarged, and altered to the existing state of science, by D. Cooper. 2 vols. 12mo. 16s. cloth lettered.

BONNYCASTLE's Introduction to Astronomy. With 17 Plates. 9th Edition, corrected and enlarged, by J. R. Young, Professor. 12mo. 9s. cloth.

BONNYCASTLE's Treatise on Algebra. 2d Edit. revised and improved, 2 vols. 8vo. 25s. bds.

BOSWORTH's Compendious Grammar of the Primitive English or Anglo-Saxon Language. 8vo. 5s. cloth.

CRABB.—Crabb's English Synonymes Explained. 7th Edition, much improved, 8vo. 15s. cloth lettered.

CROMBIE's (Rev. Dr.) Etymology and Syntax. 5th Edition, 8vo. 7s. 6d. cloth lettered.

COMSTOCK's (Dr.) System of Natural Philosophy. Revised by G. Lees, A.M. 24mo. 4s. 6d. roan lettered.

DONALDSON.—Theatre of the Greeks. 5th Edition, by John William Donaldson, B.A. 8vo. 15s. cloth lettered.

GIBBON.—Gibbon's Decline and Fall of the Roman Empire. 8 vols. 8vo. (best Edition), £3, cloth lettered.—Also, an Edition in 1 vol 8vo. 18s. cloth lettered.

HUTTON.—Course of Mathematics. By Dr. Hutton. Edited by Dr. Gregory. 12th Edition, with Additions by Professor Davies. 2 vols. 8vo. 12s. each, cloth lettered; 13s. bd.
Solutions of the principal Questions in ditto. By T. S. Davies. 8vo. 24s. cloth lettered.

HUTTON's Mathematical Tables. 8th Edition, with Additions, by Dr. Gregory. Royal 8vo. 18s. boards.

English—continued.

HOMER's Iliad, translated into English Prose. 4th Edition, revised, 8vo. 16s. boards.

HOMER's Odyssey, translated into English Prose. 8vo. 16s. boards.

HUME and SMOLLETT's History of England, to the Death of George II. New Edition, (Cadell's), 10 vols. 8vo. £4, cloth lettered.

LANDMANN.—LANDMANN's Universal Gazetteer; founded on the Works of Brookes and Walker. 8vo. 14s. cloth lettered.

LEMPRIERE's Classical Dictionary of proper Names occurring in the Ancient Classics. By Anthon and Barker. 4th Edit adapted to the present state of Classical Literature. 8vo. 16s. 6d. roan lettered.

MOSHEIM.—Institutes of Ecclesiastical History, Ancient and Modern. By J. L. Von Mosheim, D.D., with Additional Notes by J. Murdock, D.D. New Edition, edited, with Additions, by H. Soames, M.A. 4 vols. 8vo. £2. 8s. cloth lettered.

POTTER.—POTTER's Antiquities of Greece. New Edition, with Life of the Author, and an Appendix, 2 vols. 8vo. 22s. boards.

ROLLIN.—ROLLIN's Ancient History. New Edition, 6 vols. 8vo. £2. 2s. cloth lettered.

ROBERTSON's Historical Works, complete. By Dugald Stewart, F.R.S. New Edition, 8 vols. 8vo. £3. 4s. cloth.
Ditto, 1 volume, medium 8vo. 18s. cloth. (Genuine Editions.)

RUSSELL's Modern Europe, to the Death of William IV. 4 vols. 8vo. £2. 12s. cloth.

SMART.—SMART's Walker's Critical Pronouncing English Dictionary. 8vo. 15s. cloth lettered.

TYTLER.—TYTLER's Elements of General History; with a Continuation to the Death of William IV. 8vo. 14s. cloth lettered.
Ditto, New Edition, 24mo. 4s. cloth lettered.

WAKEFIELD.—Introduction to Botany. By Priscilla Wakefield. With Engravings. 11th Edition, 12mo. coloured, 8s. cloth.

WHEATLY's (Rev. Charles) Rational Illustration of the Book of Common Prayer. New Edition, 8vo. 8s. cloth.

French, Italian, German, Dutch, Spanish, and Portuguese.

ALLISON.—Child's French Friend. By Miss M. A. Allison. A New Edit. 18mo. 2s. cl. lett.

ALLISON's La Petite Française: a Companion to the "Child's French Friend." New Edit. 18mo. 2s. cloth lettered.

ALLEN's French Delectus. 12mo. 2s. cloth.

BARETTI.—BARETTI's English and Italian Dictionary; with an Italian and English Grammar. 9th Edition, corrected by C. Thomson. 2 vols. 8vo. 26s. boards.

BEAUMONT's Magasin des Enfants. 12mo. 5s. roan lettered.

BERQUIN's Pièces Choisies de l'Ami des Enfants. Dixième Edition. 12mo. 4s. 6d. roan lett.

BOTTARELLI's Exercises upon the Italian Language. 11th Edition, 12mo. 3s. 6d. cloth.
THE KEY, by P. R. Rota. New Edition, 12mo. 2s. 6d. cloth.

BOTTARELLI and POLIDORI's Italian, English, and French Dictionary. 3 vols. square, 24s. bound.

BOUILLY's Contes à ma Fille. 12mo. 6s. roan.

BOUILLY's Conseils à ma Fille. 12mo. 6s. roan.

BOYER and DELETANVILLE's French and English Dictionary. By D. Boileau and A. Picquot. New Edit. 8vo. 12s. bound, lett'd.

BRUNO's Italian Grammar. 3d Edition, royal 18mo. 7s. boards.
THE KEY. Royal 18mo. 2s. sewed.

BRUNO's Studio Italiano: Poesie di più celebri Autori. Royal 18mo. 6s. boards.

CHAMBAUD.—CHAMBAUD's Fables Choisies. Par A. Picquot. Royal 18mo. 2s. cloth lett.

CHAMBAUD's Fables Choisies, à l'usage des Enfans. Par G. Wells, A.M. 18mo. 2s. cloth lettered.

CHAMBAUD's Grammar of the French Tongue. 21st Edition, by M. Des Carrières. Royal 12mo. 5s. 6d. bound.

COTTIN.—Elisabetta; ossia, gli Esiliati nella Siberia. Tradotta dal Francese di Madama Cottin da M. Santagnello. 18mo. 4s. cloth.

COTTIN.—Elisabeth; ou, les Exilés de Siberie. Par Madame Cottin. With a Map, and numerous Notes, by J. Cherpilloud. 12mo. 3s. roan.

CRABB's Elements of German and English Conversation. 8th Edition, with Corrections, by A. Bernays, Ph.D. 12mo 3s. 6d. cloth lettered.

CRABB's Extracts from the best German Authors. 7th Edition, revised, by the Rev. J. G. Tiarks. 12mo. 6s. cloth.

DEFFERRARI.—DEFFERRARI's Selections of Classic Italian Poetry. 2 vols. 12mo. 8s. boards.

French, Italian, German, &c.—continued.

De Fivas' Introduction à la Langue Française. 3d Edition, 12mo. 2s. 6d. roan lettered.

De Fivas' New Grammar of French Grammar. 4th Edition, 12mo. 3s. 6d. roan lett.

The Key. 12mo. 3s. 6d. roan lettered.

De Fivas' Beautés des Ecrivains Français Modernes. Nouvelle Edition, avec des Notes. 18mo. 4s. roan lettered.

De Fivas' Modern Guide to French Conversation. 18mo. 3s. 6d. half-bound.

De Lara's Key to the Portuguese Language. 18mo. 3s. bound.

Des Carrieres' New Set of French Idiomatical Phrases and Familiar Dialogues. 12th Edition, square 16mo. 3s. 6d. cloth.

Des Carrieres' Abrégé de l'Histoire de France. Nouvelle Edition, par Tarver. 12mo. 7s. roan lettered.

Douville's Speaking French Grammar. 5th Edition, corrected. Crown 8vo. 7s. 6d. bds.

The Key. 5th Edition, cr. 8vo. 3s. 6d. bds.

Dufief's Nature Displayed, in her Mode of Teaching Languages to Man. Adapted to the French. 19th Edition, 2 vols. royal 12mo. 16s. boards.

Duverger.—Recueil des plus belles Scènes de Molière, avec retranchemens. Cinquième Edition. 12mo. 6s. bound.

Duverger's Idioma, Genius, and Phraseology of the French and English Languages. 6th Edition, 12mo. 4s. 6d. cloth.

FLORIAN.—Fables de Florian. With a short Introduction to French Poetry. By Lewis Jackson. New Edition, revised. 12mo. 3s. 6d. roan lettered.

Florian.—Gonzalve de Cordoue. Corrigé de C. Hamilton. 12mo. 6s. bound.

Floresta Espanola, o Colleccion de Piezas Escogidas de la Literatura Espanola. 12mo. 6s. 6d. boards.

GOLDONI.—Goldoni, Commedie Scelte. 4th Edition. With Notes, by Gombert. 12mo. 6s. bound.

Graglia's Pocket Dictionary of the Italian and English Languages. New Edition. 18mo. 6s. roan lettered.

Grandineau's Conversations Familières. 5th Edition, 12mo. 3s. cloth lettered.

Gros' New Elements of Conversation, French and English. 8th Edition, 12mo. 2s. 6d. cl.

JORDAN.—Jordan's Art of German Writing, in a Set of Easy Copies. New Edit. Oblong, 1s. 6d. sewed.

Juione's General Table of the French Verbs, regular and irregular. On Sheet, 3s. col'd.

LA FONTAINE.—Fables de La Fontaine, avec des Notices sur sa Vie, celles d'Esope et de Phèdre, et des Notes. Par M. de Lévizac. Septième Edition, entièrement revue et enrichie de nouvelles Notes, par N. Lambert. 12mo. 6s. roan lettered.

Lawrence's Contes Choisis des Veillées du Chateau, de Madame de Genlis. 12mo. 6s. roan lettered.

Lawrence's Contes Choisis. Abridged Edition, for Schools. 12mo. 2s. 6d. cloth.

Le Nouveau Testament de Notre Seigneur Jésus-Christ. Large print, 12mo. 4s. roan.

Le Breton's French Scholar's First Book. 8th Edition, 12mo. 3s. bound.

Levizac's Dictionnaire Universel des Synonymes de la Langue Française. Corrigé par P. N. Rabaudy. 12mo. 6s. 6d. bound.

Levizac's Dictionary of the French and English Languages. Revised and amended by N. Lambert. 12th Edition, 12mo. 9s. roan.

La Liturgie; ou, Formulaire des Prières Publiques, selon l'usage de l'Eglise Anglicane. (Wanostrocht's.) Royal 32mo. 4s. roan lett.

Liturgia; ovvero Formola delle Preghiere Pubbliche, secondo l'uso della Chiesa Anglicana. Da Rolandi. Royal 32mo. 6s. 6d. bd.

MARTINELLI.—Martinelli's Italian and French, and French and Italian Dictionary, in Two Parts. Abridged from Alberti's. Revised by M. Santagnello. 5th Edition, 2 vols. 10s. sewed; and in 1 vol. roan lettered, 10s. 6d.

Manuel Epistolaire:—The Young Ladies' Assistant in Writing French Letters. 8th Edition, 12mo. 6s. roan lettered.

Key to "Manuel Epistolaire." Par Madame de Froux. 12mo 3s. 6d. bound.

NOEHDEN.—Noehden's Grammar of the German Language. 9th Edition, revised by the Rev. C. H. F. Bialloblotzky, Ph. D. 12mo. 7s. 6d. roan lettered.

Noehden's Elements of German Grammar; intended for Beginners. 5th Edition, with Appendix and Vocabulary. 12mo. 3s. cloth.

Noehden's Exercises for Writing German, according to the Rules of Grammar. 7th Edition, corrected by the Rev. C. H. F. Bialloblotzky, Ph. D. 12mo. 6s. boards; 6s. 6d. roan lettered.

The Key. By J. R. Schultz. 4th Edition, with Explanatory Notes. 12mo. 3s. 6d. bds.

Neuman and Baretti's Dictionary of the Spanish and English Languages. New Edition, enlarged by the addition of many Thousand Words. By M. Seoane, M.D. 2 vols. 8vo. 32s. boards.

Neuman and Baretti's Spanish and English Dictionary, abridged from the last improved Octavo Edition. 18mo. 8s. roan lettered.

Nugent's French and English Dictionary, in Two Parts. 25th Edition, revised by J. C. Tarver, A.M. Square 12mo. 7s. 6d. roan.

Ditto, Pocket Edition, 25th Edition, Pearl type, 5s. 6d. roan lettered.

PERRIN.—Perrin's Fables Amusantes. 24me Edition, revue et corrigée par C. Gros. 12mo. 2s. 6d. cloth.

French, Italian, German, &c.—continued.

PERRIN's New and Easy Method of Learning the Spelling and Pronunciation of the French Language. 27th Edition, revised by Gros. 12mo. 2s. cloth.

PERRIN's Elements of French Conversation. Revised by C. Gros. 30th Edition, 12mo. 1s. 6d. cloth.

PORNY's Syllabaire François. 22d Edition, with improvements, by A. Picquot. 12mo. 2s. cloth.

PORNY's Practical French Grammar. 14th Edition, 12mo. 4s. bound.

PORNY's Grammatical French and English Exercises. 14th Edit. 12mo. 2s. 6d. bound.

RABENHORST. — RABENHORST's Pocket German and English Dictionary, in 2 Parts. By G. H. Noehden, LL.D. 6th Edition, improved by D. Boileau. 18mo. 7s. roan.

ROLANDI, Teatro Italiano Moderno. 2 vols. 12mo. 8s. boards.

ROLANDI, Raccolta di Lettere Scelte, agli Studiosi della Lingua Italiana. 12mo. 6s. 6d. bd.

ROWBOTHAM's Practical Grammar of the French Language. 12mo. 5s. 6d. roan lettered.

SANTAGNELLO. — SANTAGNELLO's Complete Grammar of the Italian Language. 4th Edit. revised. 12mo. 7s. 6d. roan lett'd.

SAULEZ's Theory and Practice, preceded by appropriate Rules for Speaking and Writing French. 5th Edition, 12mo. 2s. 6d. bound.

SCHMIDT's Synoptical Table of the German Grammar 8vo. 3s. 6d. cloth case.

SEVIGNÉ et DE MAINTENON.—Lettres Choisies. Par M. De Lévizac. 6me Edition. 12mo. 5s. bound.

SOAVE's Novelle Morale. New Edition. With a Vocabulary. 12mo. 4s. roan lettered.

TELEMAQUE.—Les Aventures de Télémaque, par Fénélon. Nouvelle Edition, corrigée par C. Gros. 12mo. 4s. roan lettered.

VENERONI.—VENERONI's Italian Grammar. Accented throughout. 20th Edition, corrected by P. L. Rosteri. 12mo. 6s. roan lettered.

VOLTAIRE's Histoire de Charles XII Nouvelle Edition, par M. Catty. 12mo. 4s. roan lett.

VOLTAIRE's Henriade, Poëme. Avec Notes. Revue par J. C. Tarver. 18mo. 3s. 6d. roan.

VIEYRA's Portuguese and English Dictionary, in Two Parts. With the Portuguese Words accented. New Edition, considerably improved, by A. J. Da Cunha. 2 vols. 8vo. 36s. boards.

Ditto abridged, by J. D. Do Canto. 18mo. 10s. 6d. roan lettered.

WANOSTROCHT.—Children's French Spelling Book, being an Introduction to the "Recueil." By S. Wanostrocht. 9th Edit. 12mo. 2s. bound.

WANOSTROCHT's (Dr.) Recueil Choisi de Traits Historiques et des Contes Moraux. 12mo. 3s. roan lettered.

WANOSTROCHT's (N.) Sequel to the "Recueil Choisi." 12mo. 4s. bound.

WANOSTROCHT's (N.) Numa Pompilius. Par Florian. Septième Edition. 12mo. 4s. roan lettered.

WANOSTROCHT's (Dr.) Grammar of the French Language. 20th Edition, revised by J. C. Tarver. 12mo. 4s. roan lettered.

KEY to the Exercises in the above. By L. T. VENTOUILLAC. 12mo. 3s. bound.

WANOSTROCHT.—Les Aventures de Télémaque. Par M. Fénélon. Nouvelle Edition, revue et corrigée par V. Wanostrocht. 12mo. 4s. 6d. roan lettered.

WANOSTROCHT's (N.) Voyage du Jeune Anacharsis en Grèce. Dixième Edition. 12mo. 6s. roan lettered.

WANOSTROCHT's (N.) Abrégé de l'Histoire de Gil Blas de Santillane de M. Le Sage. 6me Edition. 12mo. 5s. roan lettered.

WANOSTROCHT. — Histoire de l'Empire de Russie sous Pierre-le-Grand, par Voltaire. Par N. Wanostrocht. 12mo. 5s. roan lettered.

WANOSTROCHT's (S.) Easy and Familiar Dialogues in French and English. 9th Edition, corrected by D. Boileau. 12mo. 2s. bound.

WENDEBORN's Practical German Grammar. By D. Boileau. 10th Edition, enlarged. 12mo. 6s. roan lettered.

WILCKE's Method of acquiring a correct French and Italian Pronunciation. 2d Edition, 12mo. 2s. bound.

WILLIAMS' Modern German and English Dialogues and Elementary Phrases. 7th enlarged Edition, 12mo. 4s. cloth.

ZOTTI. — ZOTTI's Grammaire Italienne et Française; Corrigée, et Augmentée, par P. Z. E. Veroni. 12mo. 8s. roan lettered.

THE KEY. By G. Comelati. 12mo. 3s. bound.

ZOTTI's Nouveau Vocabulaire Français, Anglais, et Italien Cinquième Edition, corrigée par P. Veroni. 12mo. 4s. bound.

ZOTTI's Opere Scelte dell' Abate P. Metastasio. Quinta Edizione. Revista da G. Comelati. 2 vols. 12mo. 12s. sewed.

ZOTTI's Gerusalemme Liberata di Torqu. Tasso. Sesta Edizione. 2 vols. 12mo. 12s. sewed.

ZOTTI's General Table of the Italian Verbs, Regular and Irregular. New Edition, by C. Bruno. On a sheet, 3s. coloured.

Latin, Greek, and Hebrew.

ADAMS.—Lectiones Selectæ. Select Latin Lessons in Morality, History, and Biography. By the Rev. J. Adams. 14th Edit. 18mo. 1s. cloth.

ARNOLD's (Rev. T. K.) Henry's First Latin Book. 5th Edition, 12mo. 3s. cloth.

ARNOLD's (Rev. T. K.) Historiæ Antiquæ Epitome. By Jacobs and Doering. 2d Edition, 12mo. 4s. cloth.

AINSWORTH's Latin Dictionary, abridged by T. Morell, D.D., and improved by J. Carey, LL.D. 8vo. 12s. bound and lettered.

ALLEN's Collectanea Latina; or, Easy Construing Lessons. New Edition, with Notes, 12mo. 3s. bound.

BALLANTYNE.—BALLANTYNE's Introduction to Latin Reading. 6th Edition, 12mo. 3s. 6d. cloth.

BEARD's (Rev. J. R.) Latin Made Easy; comprising a Grammar, Exercise-Book, and Vocabulary, 12mo. 4s. 6d. cloth.

BOSWORTH's Rudiments of Greek Grammar, as used in the College of Eton. 4th Edition, 12mo. 4s. cloth lettered.

BOSWORTH's Introduction to Latin Construing; with Questions. 5th Edition, 12mo. 2s. 6d. cloth lettered.

BOSWORTH's Latin Construing: Progressive Lessons from Classical Authors. 4th Edit. 12mo. 2s. 6d. cloth lettered.

BLAND's Elements of Latin Hexameters and Pentameters. 17th Edition, 12mo. 3s. cloth.
THE KEY. New Edition, 12mo. 5s. cloth.

CAREY.—Latin Versification Simplified. By Dr. John Carey. 3d Edition, 12mo. 3s. cloth.
THE KEY. 12mo. 2s. 6d. cloth lettered.
*** This book is recommended by the Rev. T. K. Arnold, as an Introduction to his Latin Verse Composition.

CARR's Dictionary of Latin Homonymes. 12mo. 3s. cloth.

CARR's (T. S.) Manual of Classical Mythology; with a Lexicon-Index, 12mo. 6s. 6d. cloth.

CARR's Classical Pronunciation of Proper Names; with an Appendix of Scripture Proper Names. 12mo. 5s. cloth.

CATECHISMUS; sive Prima Institutio Disciplinæque Pietatis Christianæ, Latine explicata. Authore Alexandro Nowello, 18mo. 3s. bound.

CÆSARIS quæ Extant, Interpretatione et Notis illustravit Johannes Goduinus, in usum Delphini. 8vo. 12s. bound.

CICERONIS Selectæ Orationes, Interpretatione et Notis in usum Delphini. Accuravit J. Carey, LL.D. 8vo. 10s. 6d. bound.

CICERONIS de Oratore Libri Tres.; ex Editione Ernesti, cum Notis Variorum, A. J. Greenwood, D.D. Editio Nova, 8vo. 12s. boards.

CLARKE's Introduction to the Making of Latin. 37th Edit. corrected, 12mo. 3s. 6d. bd.

CLAVIS HOMERICA, Greek and Latin. New Edition, by Duncan. 8vo. 10s. bound.

CORDERII Colloquia Selecta. Revised by S. Loggon. 22d Edition, 12mo. 2s. bound.

CROMBIE's (Rev. Dr.) Gymnasium, sive Symbola Critica. 6th Edition, enlarged, 2 vols. 8vo. 21s. cloth.

CROMBIE's Clavis Gymnasii. 8vo. 6s. cloth.

CROMBIE's Gymnasium Abridged. 3d Edition, 12mo. 6s. cloth.

COWIE's Questions on Crombie's Gymnasium, adapted to the abridged edition. 12mo. 2s. 6d. cloth.

DALZEL.—DALZEL's Collectanea Græca Majora; ad usum Academicæ Juventutis accommodata. 3 vols. 8vo. Tomus I. 10s. 6d.; Tomus II. 12s.; Tomus III. 15s. 6d. bound.

DALZEL's Analecta Græca Minora; with a Lexicon in Greek, English, and Latin. By J. Bailey, A.M. Crown 8vo. 6s. bound.

DAWSON's Lexicon to the New Testament. Translated into English, by W. C. Taylor, LL.D. New Edition, 8vo. 10s. bound.

DONNEGAN's (Dr.) New Greek and English Lexicon. New Edition, enlarged and improved, large 8vo. £2. 2s. cloth lettered.
A careful collation of the latest edition of Passow has been made throughout, for the improvement of this edition.

EDWARDS.—EDWARDS' Accented Eton Latin Grammar. 20th Edition, carefully revised and corrected, 12mo. 3s. 6d. cloth.

EDWARDS' Eton Latin Accidence: with the Stress and Quantities. 9th Edition, 12mo. 1s. cloth lettered.

EDWARDS' Latin Delectus; or First Lessons in Construing. 8th Edit. 12mo. 2s. 6d. cloth.
THE KEY. 12mo. 4s. cloth.

EDWARDS' Sententiæ Selectæ. 12mo. 2s. 6d.
THE KEY. 12mo. 4s. cloth.

EDWARDS' Exempla Græca Minora. 12mo. 2s. 6d. cloth.

EDWARDS' Greek Delectus: First Lessons in Greek Construing. 4th Edition, 12mo. 3s. 6d. cloth lettered.
THE KEY. 12mo. 4s. 6d. cloth.

EURIPIDES.—The Medea, Phœnissæ, Hecuba, and Orestes; Porson's Text, with a literal Translation into English Prose, and an Index to the Medea. By T. W. C. Edwards, M.A. 8vo. 20s. cloth.
*** Either Play may be had separately, 5s. sd.
Also by T. W. C. Edwards, and on the same plan, 8vo. 5s. each, sewed,
The Prometheus Chained of Æschylus, Blomfield's Text—The Antigone of Sophocles, Brunck's Text—The Philoctetes of Sophocles, Brunck's Text—The Alcestis of Euripides, Monk's Text.

ELLIS' Collection of English Exercises, from the Writings of Cicero, for Boys to re-translate into Latin. Revised by the Rev. T. K. Arnold, M.A. 19th Edition, 12mo. 3s. 6d. roan lettered.

Key to the Second and Third Parts of the above. 12mo. 3s. cloth.

ENTICK's English-Latin and Latin-English Dictionary. Revised by the Rev. M. G. Sarjant, B.A. New Edition, with improvements, by John Carey, LL.D. Square, 9s. roan lettered.

ENTICK's Tyronis Thesaurus; or, Latin-English Dictionary. 5s. 6d. roan lettered.

SCHOOL BOOKS PUBLISHED BY SIMPKIN, MARSHALL, & CO.

Latin, Greek, and Hebrew—*continued.*

EUTROPII Historiæ Romanæ Breviarum. Studio R. J. Neilson, A.M. Edinburgh. 18mo. 2s. cl.

GROTIUS.—Grotius de Veritate Religionis Christianæ; with English Notes. (Valpy's.) New Edition, 12mo. 6s. bound.

GRÆCÆ SENTENTIÆ, selected from the Greek Writers and the New Testament. 12mo. 3s. 6d. bound.

HODGKIN.—Sketch of the Greek Accidence. By John Hodgkin. 2d Edition, 8vo. 2s. 6d. sewed; 3s. bound.

HOMERI Odyssea, Greek, with Latin Translation on the same page. By S. Clarke. 2 vols. 8vo. 20s. bound.

HOMERI Ilias, Greek, with Latin Translation on the same page. By S. Clarke. 2 vols. 8vo. 18s. bound.

HOMER'S Iliad (Greek), from the Text of Heyne; with English Notes. By the Rev. W. Trollope, A.M. 2d Edition, 8vo. 18s. bds.

HOOK's Key to the Greek Testament. 12mo. 3s. 6d. cloth.

HORATII Flacci Eclogæ, cum Scholiis Veteribus. Notis illustravit Baxteri, Gesneri, et Zeunii. 8vo. 15s. boards.

HORATII Flacci Opera, cum Selectis Scholiis, et Observationibus Baxteri, Gesneri, et Zeunii. Charterhouse Edition, 8vo. 10s. 6d.

HORATII Flacci Opera: with Annotations in English. To which is added, the Delphin Ordo. By the Rev. H. Pemble. 8vo. 11s. boards, 12s. bound.

HORATII Flacci Opera Omnia, ex Recensione F. G. Doering: with Notes. By Charles Anthon, LL.D. 8th Edit. 12mo. 7s. 6d. cl.

HUNTINGFORD's Introduction to the Writing of Greek; in Two Parts. 15th Edition, 12mo. 3s. cloth.

HARMONICAL Greek Grammar. By a Member of Trinity College, Cambridge. 2d Edition, 12mo. 4s. cloth lettered.

HARMONICAL Latin Grammar. 2d Edition, 12mo. 2s. 6d. cloth lettered.

JACOBS.—Jacobs' Latin Reader, Part I. 9th Edition, 12mo. 2s. 6d. cloth lettered. Ditto, Part II. 6th Edition, 12mo. 3s. cloth.

JOHNSON's Eton Greek Epigrams. 12mo. 3s. 6d. bound.

JUVENAL and PERSIUS (The Satires of), from the Texts of Ruperti and Orellius: with English Notes. By C. W. Stocker, D.D. 2d Edition, 8vo. 14s. boards.

LEICESTER Latin Grammar. By Cyrus R. Edmonds, and James F. Hollings. 12mo. 2s. cloth.

LITURGIA (Harwood's).—Liber Precum Communium, in Ecclesia Anglicana Receptus. Editio Octavo, royal 32mo. 4s. roan lettered.

LIVY (Drakenborch's), with Crevier's Notes. 3 vols. 8vo. 31s. 6d. cloth.

LIVY, the Twenty-first Book; the Text, with English Notes. By Cyrus R. Edmonds and James F. Hollings. 12mo. 3s. cloth.

LIVII Patavini Historiarum ab Urbe conditâ Libri Quinque priores. Ad fidem optimorum exemplarium recensuit. Gul. M. Gunn. 12mo. 4s. 6d. roan lettered.

LONDON Vocabulary, English and Latin. By J. Greenwood. 18mo. 1s. 6d. cloth.

MAIR.—Mair's Introduction to Latin Syntax. New Edit. much improved, 12mo. 3s. bound.

MALTBY's New and complete Greek Gradus. 2d Edition, 8vo. 21s. cloth.

MAVOR's Eton Latin Grammar: with explanatory Notes. 15th Edition, by Dr. Carey. 12mo. 2s. 6d. bound.

NOVUM TESTAMENTUM Domini Nostri Jesu Christi. Interprete Theodoro Beza. 12mo. 3s. 6d. roan lettered.

NOVUM TESTAMENTUM Græce. Accurante G. Duncan. 12mo. 4s. 6d. bound.

OVID.—Ovidii Nasonis Metamorphoseon (Decerpta ex). Studio J. Dymock. Editio Nova, 18mo. 2s. 6d. cloth.

PARKHURST.—Parkhurst's Hebrew and English Lexicon, without Points. 8th Edition, corrected, royal 8vo. 21s. cloth.

PARKHURST's Greek and English Lexicon to the New Testament; to which is prefixed, a plain and easy Greek Grammar. New Edition. By H. J. Rose, B.D. and Dr. Major. 8vo. 24s. cloth lettered.

SALLUST.—Sallustii Bellum Catilinarium et Jugurthinum: with Explanatory Notes. By J. Mair, M.A. 10th Edit. 12mo. 4s. bd.

SALLUSTII Opera Omnia quæ Extant, in usum Delphini. 8vo. 6s. bound.

SCHREVELII Lexicon Manuale, Græco-Latinum et Latinum-Græcum. 8vo. 12s. bound.

SCHREVELIUS' Greek and English Lexicon (Valpy's): with many New Words. Edited by Dr. Major. 6th Edition, 8vo. 15s. cloth.

SELECTÆ e Profanis Scriptoribus Historiæ. Editio nova, 12mo. 3s. 6d. cloth.

SELECTÆ e Veteri Testamento et Apocryphis Libris Historiæ. Editio nova, 12mo. 2s. bd.

TAYLER.—Rudiments of the Eton Greek Grammar, literally translated into English: with Notes. By the Rev. H. J. Tayler. 12mo. 4s. cloth lettered.

VIRGIL.—Virgil's Bucolics; Heyne's Text, with a Literal Translation into English Prose. By T. W. C. Edwards, M.A. Imperial 8vo. 8s. cloth.

VIRGILII Maronis Opera, ad usum Delphini. Studio et Opera J. Carey, LL.D. 8vo. 11s.

VIRGILII Maronis Opera. Curâ J. Dymock, LL.D. Editio Nova, 18mo. 3s. 6d. cloth.

VIRGILII Maronis Opera, ad usum Delphini. Studio et curâ G. Duncan, Edinburgh. 8vo. 10s. bound and lettered.

XENOPHON.—Xenophontis Cyri Expeditio, Greek and Latin. By T. Hutchinson, A.M. 8vo. 9s. boards.

YEATES.—Yeates' Hebrew Grammar. A New Edition. [*In the press.*